PRAISE FOR *THE GAMBLER*

"Mr. Rempel paints a picture of a man who lived to do deals. . . . [Kerkorian was] a billionaire so shy that he rarely spoke in public, so secretive that when he applied for a credit card in 1996, at age 79, he was rejected for lack of a personal credit history. . . . Entertaining."
—*Wall Street Journal*

"Gripping and fast-moving. . . . The reporting and the level of detail are astounding. . . . A riveting picture of a figure the world does not know very well, but should."
—*Washington Post*

"A fast-moving, dramatic narrative of [Kerkorian's] larger-than-life business career."
—*Washington Times*

"Rempel assembles a dizzying amount of information about the deals that made [Kerkorian] one of the richest men in America. . . . Now in this most exhaustive biography, he remains as he was in life, a man of great wealth, power, honor, and mystery."
—New York Journal of Books

"*The Gambler* is an excellent tour de force biography of a true rags-to-riches impresario. . . . A class act of a biography!"
—*Seattle Book Review*

"I recommend that every Armenian buy a copy of Kirk's biography and suggest it to their non-Armenian neighbors, friends and colleagues. Kerkorian's incredible accomplishments bestow a great honor upon Armenians worldwide!" —*California Courier*

"The book provides a remarkably detailed and fascinating look at the career of an idiosyncratic tycoon." —*Booklist*

"Chockablock with dialogue and intimate detail assembled by deep research.... All sorts of celebrities—in business, sports, and elsewhere—glide through the text.... [*The Gambler*] is the compelling story of a Horatio Alger." —*Kirkus Reviews*

"An engrossing story of a self-made man." —*Publishers Weekly*

"Informative and entertaining... Rempel's *The Gambler* does justice to Kerkorian's life and legacy."
—CDC Gaming Reports, Inc.

"With *The Gambler*, Rempel has done Las Vegas and a generation of business entrepreneurs a great service, adding rich detail to the business titan's deals and controversies. Kerkorian's life is a reminder of how far Americans can go." — KNPR

THE GAMBLER

THE
GAMBLER

HOW PENNILESS DROPOUT
KIRK KERKORIAN BECAME
THE GREATEST DEAL MAKER
IN CAPITALIST HISTORY

WILLIAM C. REMPEL

DEY ST.
An Imprint of WILLIAM MORROW

HarperCollins books may be purchased for educational, business, or sales promotional use. For information, please e-mail the Special Markets Department at SPsales@harpercollins.com.

A hardcover edition of this book was published in 2018 by Dey Street Books, an imprint of William Morrow Publishers.

FIRST DEY STREET BOOKS PAPERBACK EDITION PUBLISHED 2018.

Designed by Suet Chong

Library of Congress Cataloging-in-Publication Data has been applied for.

ISBN 978-0-06-245678-6

HB 08.30.2023

For my wife, Barbara Hyde Pierce.

When she gambled on a writer,

I hit the jackpot.

CONTENTS

III
THE MAKING OF A LEGEND

A NOTE TO READERS

There is an inspiring life story in the ninety-eight years that belonged to Kirk Kerkorian, a boy who ran barefoot in the rich dirt of California's San Joaquin Valley before family financial chaos made him a city boy fighting for his place on the dirty sidewalks of Los Angeles. He was a tough guy who wept at funerals, a humble man privately proud of his accomplishments, a business genius who ignored his MBA advisers, a daring aviator and movie mogul, a gambler at the casinos and on Wall Street who played the odds in both houses with uncanny skill. But I was already sold on this project the moment I discovered that he started with nothing and inherited nothing, yet he parlayed that nothing into billions of dollars.

I never planned to write a biography of Kirk Kerkorian. We had never met. When I started, I knew no one among his advisers and friends. He was little more than a familiar name on the pages of the *Los Angeles Times,* my professional home for more than thirty-six years. Shortly after Kirk died I received a call from HarperCollins editor Julia Cheiffetz. She didn't know Kirk, either, but she had just read his obituary in the *New York Times.* She, too, wanted to know more. This book is a tribute to her foresight, curiosity, and instinct for a good tale.

We both underestimated the challenge. Kirk was also a very private man. He rarely did press interviews, never gave speeches, and treasured his privacy above all else. Many of his business aides and associates still believe that his privacy should be protected even beyond the grave. Consider my first contact with Kirk's chief legal adviser, Patty Glaser. She responded by phone to my request for an introductory interview, catching me driving up Vermont Avenue on a sunny day near Griffith Park. I said "Hello" and she got straight to the point, "No one is going to help you. No one from his inner circle will be available. We will not cooperate."

I regret that adamant decision. Fortunately, there would be major exceptions to the official stonewall. Fortunately, too, Kirk's extraordinarily thin public record of interviews and personal insights would be offset by equally extraordinary discoveries. A collection of oral histories filed away in the Special Collections library at the University of Nevada Las Vegas was a gold mine—gaming pioneers, early Kerkorian partners, and then a ninety-minute tape of Kirk himself telling stories about the early days of Vegas and his personal adventures.

An excellent documentary for PBS called *Flying the Secret Sky* included excerpts from an on-camera interview with Kirk talking about his experiences with the Royal Air Force Ferry Command during World War II. Producer William VanDerKloot generously shared a full transcript of Kirk's interview.

One other notable gem made available to the author was a wonderful family video with relatives and boyhood friends talking about growing up with Kirk. It was professionally produced and edited but had never been released to the public.

Kirk's thirty-day wife, the former professional tennis star Lisa Bonder, was among those who declined to be interviewed for this book. She canceled our only scheduled interview saying that she'd decided to tell her own story, "to tell it myself," presumably in her own words and in her own book or article.

However, details of Kirk's fraught relationship with Lisa can be found in the underground vaults of the Los Angeles Superior Court. That's where I read through reams of Kirk's and Lisa's sworn statements, correspondence, and deposition transcripts—all part of case archives filling tens of thousands of pages. Their court battles spanned more than a decade and covered issues ranging from paternity and child support disputes to breeches of contract and invasion of privacy allegations. Tens of millions of dollars went to attorneys' fees. Media coverage was sometimes sensational.

Unless otherwise noted, this narrative relies on that voluminous archival record and those factually undisputed details submitted in court filings by the estranged couple, as well as numerous expert witnesses and the sworn declarations of friends and family.

Thanking the long list of individuals who helped tell the story of Kirk Kerkorian for this book cannot include everyone. And a number of Kirk's "inner circle" asked to remain anonymous. But very special thanks go to:

* TERRY CHRISTENSEN, one of Southern California's top lawyers and for decades Kirk's closest confidant. He hired a private eye to help investigate false paternity claims against Kirk and ended up indicted on federal wiretap charges.
* ALEX YEMENIDJIAN, who headed MGM studios when Kirk sold it for the last time. The former accountant, who became one of Kirk's top negotiators, also ran the MGM Grand and was, some said, the son Kirk never had.
* DON KING, the boxing promoter and a good friend of Kirk's. They worked together to get a multifight deal at Kirk's MGM Grand Garden for King's client Iron Mike Tyson.
* HARUT SASSOUNIAN, publisher of the *California Courier*, an English-language Armenian weekly based in Glendale, California, was also president of the United Armenian Fund and the driving force behind Kirk's Armenian charity efforts.
* MICHAEL MILKEN, the billionaire philanthropist and investment banker who helped finance many of Kirk's casino

and movie studio deals. Kirk often encouraged Mike to write a book about some of the many deals they did together.

* RON FALAHI, Kirk's fitness guru, flight steward, and personal assistant spanning thirty-three years. The gentle muscleman and his warmhearted wife, the late Wendy Falahi, were among Kirk's most loyal aides. Kirk encouraged Ron to write a book about their adventures.

* UNA DAVIS, who remained a loyal friend and advocate through Kirk's serial romantic adventures spanning fifteen years. And she was his wife on the day he died.

* JERRY PERENCHIO, the Hollywood deal maker and former CEO of Univision, was a close friend of Kirk's for decades. He broke his own anti-interview pledge to pay tribute to Kirk's life and legacy shortly before he followed his friend in death.

* Former U.S. senator BOB DOLE (R-Kansas), who, along with his wife, Elizabeth Dole, befriended Kirk and supported many Armenian causes. Kirk became a major supporter of the American Red Cross when Elizabeth Dole was its president.

* JACK HOLDER, a Pearl Harbor survivor and former U.S. Navy flight engineer who worked for Kirk at Los Angeles Air Service after the war. They were lifelong friends.

* DARRYL GOLDMAN, tennis coach to the stars. He was a regular at Kirk's weekend games called "the grudge match" played on Kirk's private courts. He coached the billionaire to national ranking on the seniors' tennis circuit when Kirk was in his mideighties.

* MANNY (MIKE) AGASSI, one of Kirk's oldest pals in Las Vegas. He was one of Kirk's earliest tennis teachers. Mike is more widely known as the father of U.S. tennis legend Andre Kirk Agassi.

* GENE KILROY, a straight-talking former marketing executive and boxing aficionado, seemed to know just about everyone in

Las Vegas, and opened many doors for the author. Gene once worked for Kirk and was for many years the business manager of boxing great Muhammad Ali. He was also one of Kirk's inner circle of Vegas friends, a pal of sister Rose and a familiar figure to most of the extended Kerkorian family and staff.

* BOBBY MORRIS, the former musical director at the International Hotel whose band backed up Elvis at the pop star's Las Vegas comeback in Kirk's first hotel.

* DANIEL M. WADE, a former co-CEO and chief operating officer of MGM Mirage. He explained why Kirk's people were so loyal: "He always took the risks. He never took the credit." The devout Mormon says he still prays for Kirk every night.

This book is nonfiction. All direct quotes and descriptive scenes are based on the recollections of eyewitnesses or on previously published accounts. Many books, news accounts, and magazine articles informed this story, but one book in particular requires special mention—*Kerkorian: An American Success Story* by Dial Torgerson. It was published in 1974 and is, to my knowledge, the only other Kerkorian biography ever attempted. It was a tremendous resource for details about Kirk's youth, his war experience, and early business history. Dial had the good fortune to receive considerable assistance from Kirk himself, opening doors to his family and friends who shared great insights, many of which have been gratefully resurrected in this version. Most of Dial's sources would precede Kirk in death.

Dial was my colleague at the *Los Angeles Times,* a senior foreign correspondent during my tenure at the paper. He was killed in 1983 doing the job of reporting in a Central American war zone. He was an admired and heroic figure to many of us at *The Times* long before we lost him. Press critics in high and low places sometimes fail to appreciate the daring and dedication of real men and women in the serious business of protecting our right to know.

So, thanks to Dial. Thanks to William VanDerKloot, producer of *Flying the Secret Sky*. Thanks, also, to every source who shared an insight, whether for attribution or not.

And especially thanks to Barbara Hyde Pierce, my wife and two-time Emmy Award–winning television news producer, whose research skills, editing finesse, and story advice are all part of every page that follows.

Bill Rempel
Los Angeles
July 2017

INTRODUCING KIRK KERKORIAN

"Life is a big craps game."
—KIRK KERKORIAN

It's a spring night in Las Vegas, 1972. An elegantly attired Cary Grant shares an outdoor podium with movie bombshell Raquel Welch. They are about to signal an explosion of fireworks, a gaudy spectacle to mark another milestone in the gambling mecca's colorful history. Already the black desert sky is alive with dancing klieg lights, the surrounding boulevards ablaze with neon and jammed with limousine traffic. The biggest hotel in the world is about to break ground, and the elites of Hollywood and the gaming world have thronged to the intersection of Flamingo Road and the Strip to salute its daring entrepreneur.

But where is he?

The actors scan the crowd. The man of the hour is one of Cary Grant's best friends, a publicity-shy financier who never met a million dollars he wasn't willing to risk on a roll of the dice, a scrappy former boxer who never backed away from a fight, an eighth-grade dropout who was now schooling the entire U.S. business community.

Somewhere out in the shadows among fellow movie moguls and casino tycoons was the fifty-five-year-old son of Armenian immigrants living the American dream, the Mean-Street-to-Main-Street success story, a thrill-seeking gambler with a knack for blockbuster investments.[1]

"Kirk, are you out there?" Grant's famous English accent drifts across the crowd. Heads turn. Where's Kirk? No one responds.

The film idol knows that his friend isn't likely to be coaxed into the spotlight. He knows that Kirk Kerkorian—the head of MGM Studios and the man behind the massive, soon-to-rise MGM Grand Hotel—is out in that throng purposely keeping a low profile, likely nursing a scotch, and pretending to be the most average Joe in Nevada.

Kirk was uncomfortable in crowds and dreaded the attention of strangers.

Raquel Welch moves to center stage, stepping up to a plunger device—something like a cartoon dynamite igniter. With dramatic flair—and a provocatively exaggerated pose—she plunges the plunger handles. The move sets off an eruption of whistling rockets, flashing starbursts, and a thundering avalanche of sparks.[2] Leo the MGM Lion lights up the sky, roaring in pyrotechnic glory.

Kirk no doubt welcomed the noisy diversion. He had dodged another public appearance. And his lifelong aversion to the trappings of celebrity would make him what he remains years after his death: one of the least known of America's richest men.

He seemed to burst out of nowhere onto the American business scene in the late 1960s, a small businessman with a gambling habit and a junior high school education who struck it rich at the mature age of fifty. He was a heroic wartime aviator who ferried factory-fresh bombers and fighter planes for the Royal Air

Force over the treacherous North Atlantic in an era before navigational aids. He nursed a small charter air service through cycles of hard times after the war, until selling his company for a windfall fortune.

But the gambler decided to bet it all on some kind of capitalist trifecta. Suddenly, he was on business news pages across the country risking huge sums in a puzzling range of eclectic markets. He called it "the leisure industry."

On the West Coast he moved to control America's oldest commercial airline. In New York and Hollywood he waged a takeover battle for the faltering but fabled MGM Studios. In Las Vegas he built the world's biggest hotel—despite a secret campaign to stop him by rival Howard Hughes, the country's richest man. At the same time, Kirk snatched Bugsy Siegel's Flamingo casino out from under decades of mob control. He made Elvis Presley a Vegas icon.

Overnight he was a major player in the movie, resorts, and gaming industries. Friends would call him a "deal junkie,"[3] addicted to financial thrills—whether at a craps table or at the negotiating table. Two more times he would build the world's biggest hotel. In business, as in gambling, Kirk believed there was no point in placing small bets.

In later years he would shake up the automobile industry with separate takeover bids for each of the Big Three carmakers.

There were no tycoons in Kirk's family tree. His immigrant father, an illiterate farmer and fruit peddler, was in constant financial trouble. Kirk learned English and how to brawl growing up in Los Angeles. Eviction was a recurring family predicament. He said he studied in the school of hard knocks.[4] It turned out to be an advanced course in survival and the value of trust, loyalty, and hard work.[5]

He avoided press interviews most of his life, making him appear reclusive. He hated being compared to the hermitlike Howard Hughes, whom he otherwise admired. Kirk had a thriving social life with celebrity friends and business associates—among them Frank

Sinatra, Dean Martin, and Tony Curtis. He was often noted in news and gossip columns attending charity and other public events. He double-dated with Cary Grant, and their families vacationed together.

Fellow casino owner Donald Trump called Kirk "the king" and told friends: "I love that guy."[6] Kirk was, however, Trump's polar opposite in style and temperament. Kirk was soft-spoken and understated with a paralyzing fear of public speaking. He wished, he said, that he "could talk like Trump."[7] Kirk also wanted his name on nothing—not on buildings, not on street signs, not even on his personal parking spot at MGM Studios. And Kirk never defaulted on a loan and always regarded his handshake as a binding contract.

Kirk traveled without an entourage. He carried his own bags and drove his own car, typically a Ford Taurus or Jeep Cherokee. He jogged the streets of Beverly Hills and walked to lunches without a bodyguard. He refused comps, personally paying for meals and rooms even at his own hotels. Once after a business trip to New York, Kirk was halfway to La Guardia Airport when he ordered his driver back into the city. He had forgotten to tip the maids at The Pierre hotel.[8]

He gave away millions to charity and to people in need on the strict condition that his gifts were kept secret. When his donations grew into the tens of millions, he formed a charitable foundation. It gave away more than a billion dollars, much of it to his ancestral homeland after a deadly earthquake. In Armenia, Kirk Kerkorian is regarded as one of the saints, but at his insistence there are no monuments to his lavish generosity.

The master deal maker would finally meet his match in his mid-eighties. A charming former tennis pro would trick him into believing he was the father of her baby, force him into a courtroom, and strip him of his most cherished asset—his privacy.

"Never look back," Kirk liked to counsel.[9] But in the end, he reflected on what mattered most in his life. It was neither his successes nor his disappointments. It was the thrill of the risk.

"Life is a big craps game," he told the *Los Angeles Times*. "I've got to tell you, it's all been fun."[10]

What follows is an account of that great craps game, the life of Kirk Kerkorian.

I

THE
MAKING
OF
A MAN

"NECESSITY IS THE MOTHER
OF TAKING CHANCES."

—MARK TWAIN

1

GAMBLING
ON THE WIND

EARLY JUNE 1944
RIDING THE HURRICANE EXPRESS

Skies over the North Atlantic were mostly clear when the unarmed twin-engine DH-98 Mosquito climbed out of Goose Bay, another factory-fresh fighter-bomber on its way to help the British repel Hitler's war machine.[1] The pilot, an American civilian employed by the Royal Air Force Ferry Command, banked out over the Labrador Sea and powered his agile aircraft toward a rendezvous with "the hurricane express"—a fierce but friendly tailwind blasting out of Canada at nearly seventy-five miles per hour. RAF meteorologists called it "the Iceland Wave." By whatever name, the rushing wind stream promised a faster-than-normal ocean crossing, possibly even another world record, since the captain was taking a rather daring direct route to Prestwick.[2]

Under normal circumstances, the Mosquito's limited range made such a plan suicidal. A straight line to the coast of Scotland was about twenty-two hundred miles—nearly a thousand miles beyond the plane's maximum fuel range. Even with a temporarily installed two-hundred-gallon gas tank lashed to the floor of its empty bomb bay, this fighter-bomber would need a hefty tailwind to avoid ditching hundreds of miles short of land.

Young Captain Kirk Kerkorian was feeling lucky. A month earlier he rode that same air current and shattered the existing nine-hour speed record for an Atlantic crossing by nearly two hours. It was exhilarating, the way winning big at poker was exhilarating. He liked it—the thrill of victory, the rush of adrenaline, the payoff. For a quiet, seemingly mild-mannered guy, Kirk was surprisingly comfortable with risk. At least that's what his poker face suggested.

His first claim to a speed record was very brief, however. Another Mosquito pilot departing Goose Bay at the same time had used slightly different altitudes and course variations that got him to Scotland twenty-three minutes ahead of Kirk. To RAF Wing Commander John D. Wooldridge[3] went the honors and the headlines for crossing in six hours and forty-six minutes.

Now, back for his second consecutive Mosquito ferry run, Kirk found the supercharged wind stream still roaring eastward. And despite Ferry Command admonitions against pursuit of speed records,[4] he knew conditions were right to try again. Besides, it was the eve of his twenty-seventh birthday. What a great present to give himself.

His new calculations for the direct route to Prestwick were promising. If the tailwinds held up, he figured, he would have plenty of fuel left over when he reached the Scottish coast. It was a gamble—but a sound bet, based on math and experience. Kirk put his chips on the shortcut. The gambler went all in.

Ferry Command pilots were a competitive bunch, none more so than Kerkor (Kirk) Kerkorian, youngest son of an immigrant fruit peddler from Los Angeles. His skills as a flier had already overcome substantial educational shortcomings. He was an eighth-grade dropout. He used fake high school documents to get into an elite RAF training class in Montreal. Once admitted, he was a standout among the international aviators in his class.

During his first few months ferrying planes across the Atlantic, Kirk assumed the commander's seat in a variety of makes and models—from the Lockheed Hudson that everyone trained on to the newer Martin Marauder B-26 and the Mitchell B-25 from North American Aviation.

Kirk's first takeoff on a transatlantic flight came with his first serious scare. It originated at Dorval Field in Montreal. He was already rolling down the runway when he realized that his twin-engine Hudson didn't feel right. Of course, it had a spare gas tank in its belly that wasn't there on routine training flights. But Kirk also hadn't set his flaps for the extra weight. At rotation speed when he expected to take flight, his tail still didn't have lift enough to get off the ground. He reached for his trim tab, adjusting quickly as the Hudson lumbered toward grass at the end of the runway. Liftoff came much later than it should have—but not too late. The Hudson[5] soared off safely toward the Canadian coast, and Kirk would never make that mistake with his flap settings ever again. The most effective education of a rookie Ferry Command captain—unforgiving real-life experience—had begun.

For this latest ferry transit, Kirk's Toronto-made de Havilland 98 Mosquito would require all the skill and experience he could cram into its snug little cockpit. The "Mossie," as the Brits called it, was the newest set of wings in the British air fleet. It had earned mixed reviews. The plane was notoriously delicate in bad weather and suffered the highest per capita crash rate among the various planes flown by the Ferry Command. Any measurable ice buildup on its high-speed, high-performance wings risked catastrophic stalls. Pilots, in moments of dark humor, groused that it couldn't handle ice enough to chill a decent martini, shaken or stirred.

Some veteran Ferry Command pilots turned down or otherwise avoided assignments to fly the Mosquito. Not Kirk. He loved it—the speed, maneuverability, its climb rate. He considered it the hottest plane in the fleet.

And it was by far the fastest plane in the European theater, capable of speeds approaching four hundred miles per hour. No Luftwaffe aircraft could catch it. And it could intercept the fastest German buzz bombs—the V-1 rockets just starting to rain down on London. It could fly at high altitudes, beyond the reach of antiaircraft guns, up to twenty thousand feet. And it could be mass-produced without depleting already short supplies of metals. Like a canoe, the airplane was built primarily of wood, its fuselage constructed with a double-birch plywood skin over a balsa and spruce frame.

To fliers like Kirk it was "the Wooden Wonder." He never bothered to do the math that also made it the most dangerous plane in the ferry fleet. During one spate of winter months, only one out of four Mosquitos made it. A crew had better odds playing Russian roulette.

More than two hours into his second spring gamble with a direct run to Prestwick, Kirk's confidence had been rewarded. Good weather and a hearty tailwind had him and his navigator crewmate on track for a sub-seven-hour crossing. They figured to land before dark, avoiding a more hazardous nighttime approach in a plane with few navigational aids.

The view outside was nothing but sky and an endless white-capped sea, not much to talk about. There were occasional course adjustments and then the navigator's midcourse notice of the "equal time point"—more commonly known outside aviation as the point of no return. It wasn't far beyond that critical marker when the navigator first detected the waning booster wind. The Canadian kid, at least five years Kirk's junior, repeated a series of locational fixes before confirming his ominous discovery: the hurricane express had stopped.

Kirk reacted immediately, throttling back the engines and adjusting the Mosquito's prop pitch for maximum fuel efficiency. There would be no speed record this day. The new priority was reaching dry land before the gas tanks went dry. The plane slowed to what seemed like a crawl. Hours ticked by. Kirk switched to reserve fuel supplies. Their forecast arrival time came and went. They were still hundreds of miles out, over water so cold they wouldn't last twenty minutes if they had to bail out now. Daylight was fading fast and a low, thick overcast spread below them.

Finally, they were in radio range of Prestwick. But the news was dismal. The overcast was deep and the ceiling dangerously low. It was unlikely to lift anytime soon. From the air above that thick gray blanket of clouds, land and sea were indistinguishable. There was no way to glimpse the Firth of Clyde, spot the coastal towns, or locate a welcoming runway. In darkness and fog, attempting to land was a fool's wager. But the fuel gauge was pinned at empty. The Mosquito's engines could stop at any moment.

Kirk kicked open the jettison hatch on the cockpit floor. Bailing out was a terrible choice . . . but his only choice.

2

THE KID
FROM WEEDPATCH

It was nearly noon, a midweek workday in the fall of 1939. The two-man crew from the Andrews Heating Company was taking a break from installing ventilating gas wall heaters. Crew chief Ted O'Flaherty, a twenty-five-year-old navy veteran from Louisiana with an obsession for flying, liked to use his lunch hour to squeeze in flight lessons or a few practice takeoffs and landings at the old Western Air Express field in the San Gabriel Valley.[1]

His twenty-two-year-old assistant, Kirk Kerkorian, always seemed uninterested, hanging back, watching from the ground as he ate his sandwiches brought from home. But after months of gentle prodding and cajoling, Kirk had finally agreed to ride along. He would even pay half of the plane rental—a dollar for a quick sample flight.

Ted was feeling downright evangelical. He loved sharing the wonders of flying. He also liked to preach the promise of aviation's future. Rapidly developing commercial airlines, some pioneering

transcontinental service, were eager for qualified pilots—a career offering more adventure and much better pay than the forty-five cents
an hour Kirk took home. And it didn't involve wrangling 270-pound
wall furnaces.

The Andrews Heating truck pulled through the airfield gates and
stopped across the tarmac from two bright yellow Piper J-3 Cubs.
The boxy, single-wing plane was the Model T of the sky. Ted's flight
instructor, Dick Lentine, was waiting. Ted paid him the dollar,
signed the form on his clipboard, and motioned for Kirk to climb
into the back of the two-seater. Ted took the controls. Lentine spun
the single nose-mounted propeller as Kirk tried to work his first seat
belt. The motor fired up, and the little yellow plane kicked up a spray
of sand and grit wheeling around toward the runway.

Weight distribution was of no consideration on this flight. Kirk
weighed barely half as much as the wall furnaces he installed. For
a scrawny kid, he had turned out to be much stronger than Ted expected. Wiry . . . determined . . . hardworking. And he didn't talk
too much, either. Ted liked him.

It was a clear day and Ted wasn't going to waste a precious minute. He turned into the wind, found the center of the runway, and
accelerated hard.

In the back, Kirk's senses were instantly assaulted by the deafen-
ing scream and forceful lurch of the Piper's fifty-horsepower engine.
He had barely gathered a breath before they reached speeds matched
only by childhood memories on the back roads of Bakersfield in his
father's snazzy Stutz Bearcat.

But if Kirk was unnerved by the noise, the power, the speed,
or—seconds later—the altitude, he didn't show it. His big grin said
it all. Kirk was smitten. It was love at first takeoff—a passionate
until-death-do-us-part kind of love. Suddenly, his entire future was
banking sharply in a new direction.

Until that takeoff over the rooftops of Alhambra, Kirk had been
focused on quite a different career path—professional boxing. Moving heavy wall heaters served as an extension of weight training in a

gym. His big dream had been getting his name on the marquee of a title bout: "Rifle Right Kerkorian," fighting for a world championship in the ultimate international arena—New York City's Madison Square Garden.

It was an especially audacious ambition even though Kirk had been very successful as an amateur welterweight. His own trainer, who agreed that Kirk had the heart of a champion, warned him not to go pro. His lean and slender frame wasn't built for the pounding of a professional fight. Kirk bristled at the notion that he might be too fragile. But his older brother had been forced from the ring with cognitive issues and slurred speech. The damage was blamed on a string of poundings Nish absorbed in more than a hundred bouts from San Francisco to San Diego.

Flying may have rescued Kirk from a similar fate.

Born Kerkor Kerkorian in Fresno, California, on June 6, 1917, he was the youngest of four children in a close-knit Armenian immigrant family. His grandfather Kasper was the trailblazer, moving halfway around the globe in his midsixties, an age when most farmers are slowing down, not starting over. That was in 1890. A collapsing Ottoman Empire was devolving into violence and especially harsh treatment for Armenian Christians. Life in the agricultural heartland of the American West sounded like a better option.

Kasper's youngest son, Ahron, followed him through New York's immigrant portal at Ellis Island more than a decade later. The teenager reached California penniless but full of grand plans and big ambitions, expecting to become a millionaire. He was a natural-born entrepreneur. He finagled the use of a horse-drawn wagon to launch his first business—fruit distribution. Ahron bought citrus from rural ranches and hauled it to towns for sale up and down the San Joaquin Valley.

He called himself Harry, but his swarthy good looks and a ferocious mustache prompted customers and friends to call him

"Pancho"—as in Pancho Villa, the legendary Mexican bandit-revolutionary. Fruit-hauling profits soon allowed him to bring over the girlfriend he left behind in Armenia. Ahron and Lily became a family of five with Art, Rose, and Nish. And by the time Kerkor joined the clan, Ahron had already made and lost a few small fortunes.

Remarkably, Ahron achieved impressive business successes despite the fact he could neither read nor write. He was illiterate in English *and* Armenian. His handshake was his contract, but when he had to sign a formal document, his signature was an "X." But he was a whiz at numbers . . . and a fearless opportunist.

During World War I, Ahron started buying up vineyards to take advantage of surging civilian and military demand for raisins. The lowly sun-dried grape became a wartime staple—inexpensive, easily shipped and stored, and resistant to spoilage. The best raisins came from the green seedless Thompson grapes grown throughout the valley.

By Armistice Day, Ahron was the raisin baron of the San Joaquin. His holdings, about a thousand acres on ten ranches, had a gross value of nearly a million dollars. Most, however, were heavily leveraged with mortgage or crop loans. Behind the scenes, he was juggling debt to stave off financial ruin. Still, by all appearances, the dashing Ahron in his jaunty Stutz Bearcat convertible seemed the picture of immigrant success.

Eventually, Ahron's numbers wizardry and debt juggling weren't enough. Market fluctuations played havoc with his cash flow. His debt load became unbearable as the national economy soured. And piece by piece his million-dollar property portfolio was picked apart by creditors. The recession of 1921–22 finally wiped him out.

Ahron still hoped to hang on to the prized family farm, a 120-acre spread known as the Captain Fuller Ranch in a place south of Bakersfield called Weedpatch. Here, a Kerkorian family farm empire could rise again. Ahron had borrowed heavily to develop a vineyard on the land, but he really hoped to strike oil. He knew it was there—black gold, Texas tea. Every morning the ranch pump house delivered petroleum-perfumed water that made its first few gallons undrinkable and unsuitable even for washing. Oil engineers from San Francisco tried to discourage Ahron's dream. There was no oil under his land, they assured him. Ahron borrowed more money for a watermelon crop.

Finally, a rising tower of debt threatened to collapse on the Kerkorian family farm. Ahron put his "X" on an official title transfer document trying to shift ownership of the Captain Fuller Ranch to four-year-old Kerkor. County officials and lien holders ignored the ploy. Creditors filed suit, going so far as to name the boy as an accomplice of his father's attempted fraud.

Two constables showed up one day while Ahron was eighty miles away on business in Los Angeles. The ranch and its crops had been attached for nonpayment of a loan and the officers were there to supervise an unannounced creditors' auction—beginning with fifteen tons of harvested watermelons. Lily sent her boys running to a neighbor's house to call Ahron at his hotel in the city.

The auction had ended but buyers still mingled waiting for trucks to haul away their watermelons when in the distance a dust plume rose above a dirt road. It was headed toward the ranch house. As it neared, the source of that brown cloud became clear: it was Ahron's speeding Stutz Bearcat.

At the house Ahron braked to a stop and dispatched eldest son Art to saddle his horse. The father rushed inside and emerged moments later, a Colt revolver tucked in his belt. He mounted up and rode slowly but directly toward the small gathering of auction customers. Before anyone could react, he drew his gun on the armed constables. They froze. Some in the group immediately took off running. Ahron marched the others at gunpoint toward his property line marked by an irrigation canal. He ordered them to swim for the other side.

Ahron's cold fury was as obvious as the muzzle of his Colt, but one of the businessmen in the group railed against the inconvenience and indignity of splashing across a fifteen-foot canal. He was threatening severe legal consequences when Ahron reached down from the saddle to grab a long-handled hoe. Suddenly, he was "Pancho Villa" Kerkorian, flailing the hoe wildly, nearly severing the recalcitrant man's ear. Everyone promptly plunged into the water. Ahron was later arrested for assault. It was not, however, the last ride of Pancho Villa Kerkorian.

Standard Oil Company sent a collector from San Francisco to serve a writ of attachment on the farm for an unpaid loan.[2] Ahron didn't much like creditors in the first place, but he also harbored suspicions that the big oil boys hadn't been honest with him about the drilling potential on his land. Something snapped when William Breitinger showed up on Ahron's property with that unwelcome writ. He ordered the man off his land. To emphasize the point, Ahron fired up his old 1916 Lincoln and started chasing Mr. Breitinger around the ranch. And when the car bogged down in a sandy patch, Pancho Villa jumped out, grabbed a grape stake, and chased the bill collector on foot.

The oil company's representative filed a criminal complaint alleging assault with a deadly weapon. This time friends had to post bond to get Ahron out of jail. About a year later Ahron returned to Bakersfield from his new home in Los Angeles and pleaded guilty to the lesser charge of simple assault. A ninety-day jail sentence was suspended. He was fined $50. The previous assault charge was later dropped.

The Kerkorian family's financial collapse and forced relocation to Los Angeles would be among the earliest and most unsettling memories of young Kerkor's life. It also ushered in prolonged periods of economic uncertainty that would extend more than a decade—deep into the Great Depression. Missed rent payments and evictions, sometimes as often as every three months, repeatedly uprooted the family and made the boy a new kid in a new neighborhood over and over again.

There were lessons to be learned from adapting and readapting to sudden changes, unfamiliar surroundings, and frequent disappointments. The bond growing from shared struggles and distress—"us against the world"—fostered fierce family loyalty and underscored the value of friendships over possessions.

But all the moves were also chances for Kerkor to reinvent himself. A first step was to Americanize his name. In the big city, Kerkor became Kirk. And the farm boy who arrived in Southern California speaking only Armenian had to learn English on the streets of Los Angeles.

By age nine Kirk was hawking the *Evening Express* on street corners, making about fifty cents a day and turning over pocketfuls of pennies to help support his family. His earliest experience with gambling was pitching pennies and bottle caps with fellow newsies.

Ahron tried to stay in the farm business as a produce broker. For a time he had his own fruit stand near what is now Universal Studios at the intersection of Ventura and Lankershim Boulevards. With another Armenian neighbor he started a produce-hauling business, trucking fruit to the city from the San Joaquin Valley over the Tehachapi Mountains. Kirk's older siblings, sometimes including sister Rose, drove the notoriously steep and winding Ridge Route over the mountains. The family enterprise ended after one summer growing season. The trucks were repossessed.

In his teen years Kirk came to regard his father as a heroic figure. Ahron was the man who had sailed to America in steerage, landed in California without a dime, built that million-dollar agriculture empire and then lost it all—but who never stopped working hard and dreaming big. And he managed all the ups and downs despite the handicap of illiteracy, with what Kirk always regarded as "two strikes against him."[3]

With perhaps a mix of pride and chagrin, he would later describe his father as "a big, rough man who didn't take anything from anybody." But Kirk and his father shared an important gambler's trait—a degree of comfort with risk.

One of Ahron's biggest scores came when he cornered the watermelon market in the Imperial Valley east of San Diego. Summer in that desertlike area had been uncommonly cool and overcast. Watermelon farmers accustomed to sunny days with temperatures well over one hundred degrees feared cucumber-sized crops and financial ruin. Many opted to cut their losses by suspending irrigation and saving on water costs.

Ahron saw opportunity. He scraped together every dollar from his fruit stand business and drove more than two hundred miles to El Centro. He had enough cash to get an audience with just about every farmer in the region. Few could resist. Ahron found as many takers as he had cash for buyouts.

As gambles go, it wasn't like Ahron was shooting craps or wagering on pure chance. He was betting on the weather, something familiar to the farmer from Weedpatch. His was a big risk, but a smart bet. When the sun finally came out in the Imperial Valley, Ahron ended up with truckloads of big, ripe melons in the midst of a region-wide watermelon shortage. His watermelon jackpot was an $18,000 profit, a twenty-first century equivalent of about $250,000.

Flush with cash, the family moved into a bigger house in a better neighborhood just west of the University of Southern California. Ahron bought a new car, invested in new business opportunities, and saw his small fortune once again ebb steadily away. Frequent family moves resumed all too soon.

Kirk discovered early in those vagabond years that every new neighborhood and every new schoolyard was likely to be his own personal testing ground. His shy nature and slender build made him an easy target for bullies. But he was also scrappy and determined never to back down, even when the odds—and the sizes of his tormentors—were against him. Kirk became something of a legend among pals after a beating he suffered one afternoon on his way home from school.

"This kid beat him up, really beat him up good," recalled Leo

Langlois, a friend who was there. "The next day, Kirk waited for this kid and fought him again. And the other kid beat him up again."

They did this for three or four days in a row. What Kirk noticed, even in defeat, was that each time they fought, the bully was a little less aggressive. What the bully noticed, even in triumph, was that Kirk was getting to be a serious nuisance. For Kirk, the contest was a matter of honor. For the bully, it was increasingly a chore. He was losing heart. Finally, Kirk was the last boy standing. The bully "kind'a gave up," by Leo's account. The fights stopped. "And they wound up being best of buddies."

As Kirk entered his teen years, his closest friends tended to be the sons of working-class immigrants of limited means. They called themselves "the League of Nations" for the diversity of their family origins—French, Swedish, Mexican, Armenian . . . and more. Their idea of mischief was slipping into entertainment venues, like movie houses or the car races at Ascot Speedway, without paying for admission. When Kirk's sister, Rose, dropped out of school to dance in a vaudeville revue downtown, she offered her brother's band of friends complimentary tickets. They declined the freebies.

One night while waiting in the wings to go onstage, Rose gasped when she caught sight of Kirk and pal Norman Hungerford (the Swede) crawling across the backstage. They slipped down into the orchestra pit, jostling musicians, before disappearing into the dark rows of seats. When she confronted him after the show, he shrugged and said, "It was more fun to sneak in." Something about a little danger clearly appealed to the prankster side of this otherwise mild-mannered kid.

Public school held little interest for Kirk, and in all the family moves he was falling behind other boys his age academically. He was a bright enough student, but he was bored by the repetition of math. One of his worst subjects: geography. To Kirk the world was pretty small. He never traveled outside the two-hundred-mile stretch of California separating his Los Angeles home from his Fresno birthplace.

His education ran into fresh difficulties when he entered Foshay Junior High School, just west of the Memorial Coliseum. Kirk's growth spurts were adding to his length but not his heft. The campus bully was bigger—and better connected. His father was a gym teacher. Once again Kirk didn't back down. A series of challenges and long-forgotten provocations led to an alley off campus. Minutes into the fray Kirk's fist smashed the bully's Adam's apple. The brawl stopped as the coach's son grabbed his throat, gasping for air and making desperate gurgling sounds.

Kirk was promptly transferred to Jacob Riis School for Boys in South Los Angeles. It was only five miles away, but for the students sent to Riis it may as well have been South San Quentin. Discipline was corporal. The all-male faculty was armed with swinging two-inch, rivet-studded leather belts. And fights were more common than ever. Nonetheless, pal Norman missed his friend so much back at Foshay that he provoked scuffles of his own in order to be reunited with Kirk at Riis.

After another year Norman moved on to high school. The closest Kirk got was some vocational training—an auto shop class at Metropolitan High School. It was enough for him to pick up some valuable mechanical skills, but it turned out to be the end of his formal education—the equivalent of eight grades.

Kirk entered the Southern California job market as a middle-school dropout at the worst possible time—the depths of the Great Depression. It was the early 1930s. He had to settle for a series of odd jobs, caddying at the old Sunset Fields Golf Course on Crenshaw Boulevard, selling orange crates for curbside benches at the Pasadena Rose Parade, anything to bring home a few cents a day. Everyone in the family had to contribute. Art worked with Ahron in the produce brokering business. Rose danced. And Nish parlayed his schoolyard brawling into a hard-earned meal ticket as a boxer known on fight cards up and down the state as "the Armenian Assassin."

Kirk dreamed of his own prizefighter's moniker—but he was still too young, too small . . . and too nice.

In the fall of 1934, Kirk and Norman, both seventeen, were among the nation's 11.3 million people looking for work—part of the official 21.6 percent unemployed that had prompted creation in 1933 of a New Deal program called the Civilian Conservation Corps (CCC). The goal was government-funded public works employment in national parks and forests for young men that would ease demand for the limited number of private sector jobs. The pay was $30 a month, more money than Kirk or Norman had ever made. One problem: the boys weren't yet eighteen, the minimum age. Of course, getting into places where they didn't belong had become something of a sport for these charter members of the League of Nations club. This time they begged their parents to lie a little . . . to swear that they were each a year older. It worked. The pair reported for duty at Fort MacArthur, a harbor area military reservation, where they donned World War I–era uniforms and got their assignment—the California Sierras.

After an all-night train ride to Sequoia National Park, they went immediately to work. It was especially demanding high-altitude work—digging, chopping, and clearing paths on terrain like the 14,505-foot face of Mount Whitney and in the nearly inaccessible wilderness area of Mineral King.

From day one there was an obvious difference between the limited stamina of city boys like Kirk and Norman and the superior endurance of farm-raised youths. Familiar faces from the Los Angeles train started disappearing as the workload and demanding schedule drove many to sneak off down the mountain to thumb rides home.

Privately, Norman asked Kirk if they should bail out, too. Kirk shook his head.

"Let's stay. We can do it."

At first, "the farm boys pretty near killed us . . . we couldn't keep up," recalled Norman. "But we worked hard and we got tough." The boys had signed on for six months, promising to work into April 1935. Winter turned out to be especially rugged. Kirk was snowed in for a time at an outpost camp in the high country. But their work so impressed CCC management that both were invited to stay on in the spring. It was good money and good experience, they agreed, but Kirk and his friend wanted their freedom back. And they wanted off the mountain.

K irk probably didn't realize how much he had changed until he got home. He was as lean as ever, but more muscular. Rock hard where he had once been soft. Also, he was near his full height, right at the edge of five foot eleven, and a lot more confident. He and Norman lined up outside MGM Studios in Culver City along with dozens of other would-be day laborers late one afternoon and got the once-over from a job foreman looking for strong bodies—men who could move boulders on a movie set. They got the call. The boys spent a night shift pushing and shoving rocks around a big tank used for filming underwater scenes. They made $2.60 each, personal bests for a single day's work.

With regular work still hard to come by throughout the mid-1930s, Kirk turned entrepreneurial. He bought equipment for steam-cleaning car engines and rented space at a gas station as his operations center. Used car dealers became Kirk's primary customers. He made enough money to start buying and trading old clunkers. He'd get them running with his auto shop skills, swap out bald tires for other used tires with a few more treads, and then wash, polish, and steam clean. Presto—he could clear a $15 profit.

One of those who had noticed Kirk's physical transformation after his CCC stint was Nish. His older brother's own fighting days were over by the mid-1930s. After more than a hundred bouts, Nish had slowed down considerably. He stumbled easily. His equilibrium was off and his speech slurred. The Armenian Assassin hadn't brought in any fight payouts for more than two years when he offered to teach an eager Kirk what he'd learned. Nish became Kirk's backyard trainer.

By late 1937, Kirk, now twenty years old, was learning footwork, defensive strategies, and counterpunching. He still didn't pack a lot of weight in the ring, but he had other advantages—long arms, quickness, and an easy, graceful style. Kirk's debut was a preliminary bout at the Hawthorne Arena a few miles south of Los Angeles. He won on points. But the fight that got the most attention came out of town a short time later—in Bakersfield, not far from Weedpatch.

The Bakersfield Arena, in a converted barn on Twenty-Second Street, held up to twelve hundred spectators and was a popular venue for top California amateurs. Kirk must have hit town looking particularly young and inexperienced. Promoter Steve Strelich took Nish aside to warn him that Kirk's opponent that night would be a seasoned amateur, undefeated in his first four fights.

Kirk entered the ring for his four-round preliminary bout wearing hand-me-down gear from his older brother and a practiced air of confidence. But moments later, watching his opponent warm up and shadowbox in the far corner of the ring, Kirk's expression darkened.

"Nish, I can't do it. I can't fight the guy."

"Why not?"

"Look at him! He's no good. You can see that, can't you? I might hurt him."

If Nish had any doubts about his little brother's confidence, they disappeared in those moments before the prefight introductions. His advice was simple: "Look, Kirk, just go in and put him out quick—and he won't get hurt much."

The bell rang.

Kirk circled his foe at the center of the ring, moved in close, and kept him busy deflecting a left jab . . . jab . . . jab . . . jab. The kid never saw the right hand that staggered him, an uppercut to the side of his face. Kirk saw his eyes go dead. Seconds into the first round the bout was over and Kirk had his first knockout—and a feeling he would never forget.

"There's nothing like it," he would say. "The most beautiful feeling in the world is when you know it's the other guy that's going down."[4]

For making the drive over the Tehachapi Range that evening and spending a few seconds in the ring, Kirk pocketed $4 in amateur expenses. He also went home with a cherished keepsake, his new fighter's nickname—"Rifle Right" Kerkorian.

Early success brought Kirk to the attention of George Blake, a prominent fight referee and manager from Westlake Park (what is now the MacArthur Park area of Los Angeles). He had a private training facility. Nish took his brother in to spar and work out under Blake's supervision. Kirk was invited to join Blake's stable of potential professionals.

Through the year and into mid-1939, Kirk won thirty-three of thirty-seven fights and was never knocked out. His only losses were decisions. But he was frustrated by Blake's refusal to let him go pro. In response, Kirk sometimes took on bigger opponents to prove he could stand a pounding.

At another fight in Bakersfield against the bigger Johnny Mendoza, who outweighed Kirk by fifteen pounds, press accounts[5] described how Kerkorian "uncorked a stunning salvo of right crosses and uppercuts to the chin" to turn Mendoza's jitterbug style "to a slow waltz." Kirk went on to win the Pacific Coast amateur welterweight championship.

Still, Blake worried that Kirk wasn't putting on enough weight. He seemed to consider the youngest Kerkorian too fragile. Sure, he had the grit and drive of a champion, he had classic boxing skills, he had endurance, and he always got up on those rare occasions when he was knocked down. But he also needed to be able to take heavy body blows and shake them off. That required more physical heft. Blake feared that Kirk could get seriously hurt and end up physically impaired like his brother.

The issue remained unresolved that day when Kirk touched down after his first plane ride with Ted O'Flaherty. Within weeks of that fifteen-minute flight over Alhambra, Kirk was back in a Bakersfield ring to win a decision over Buddy Souza of Fresno. The victory preserved Kirk's Pacific Coast amateur welterweight title. It also marked Rifle Right's last big fight.[6]

Kirk's new love was flying—and she was a demanding mistress. He needed more money to pay for $3-an-hour flight lessons. So he took an extra job at a bowling alley bar as a bouncer. He saved fifty cents a lesson by declining the parachute rental during practice loops and rolls. Kirk also looked for flight academies that might admit a middle-school dropout but was repeatedly disappointed. Many even required some college.

Along with O'Flaherty, Kirk enrolled in night school classes to study the same math that once bored him as a schoolboy. He had to solve the mysteries of a compass and protractor. He had plenty of motivation now. Math was essential to all aspects of aviation. From navigating to tracking fuel consumption, a pilot's computations were serious matters . . . life or death matters. And Kirk now had one overriding goal in life: a pilot's license.

Sometime around the spring of 1940, a newspaper advertisement caught Kirk's attention. The famous American aviatrix Florence "Pancho" Barnes had opened a flight school at her dairy farm in the Mojave Desert—the Happy Bottom Ranch and Riding Club. Pancho was a Hollywood stunt pilot and the reigning "fastest woman" in the sky after topping Amelia Earhart's speed record a decade earlier.[7]

Kirk hitched a ride more than eighty-five miles to the Mojave and made Pancho a proposition. He was short on education and money for flight lessons, but he was willing to work hard. If that meant getting up at dawn to milk cows, slop hogs, and muck out the barn, Kirk was ready to start immediately.

Pancho Barnes seemed very impressed with the young man's initiative and obvious ambition. She also may have found it especially hard to turn away such a polite, good-looking young man so eager to fly that he would shovel manure every day. In any case, she winked away her own requirement of a high school diploma and Kirk became one of fifteen young men entering her next flight academy class later that year.

The timing was a happy coincidence for both of them. It turned out that Pancho, like Kirk, was in financial difficulties. The farm wasn't self-sufficient. Fortunately for the Happy Bottom's bottom line, there were other would-be young aviators with cash to pay for flight training. And extra farmhands like Kirk helped keep dairy costs down.

After morning chores, ground school was a short drive to Antelope Valley Junior College. Flight instruction was in the afternoon. And evenings were story times. Pancho regaled her cadets with tales of barnstorming, air derbies, and stunt flying—spiced with accounts of Hollywood parties and her work for filmmaker Howard Hughes. On the weekends, Kirk hitched a ride back to Los Angeles to see his family and talk planes with O'Flaherty. His friend drove him back to the Happy Bottom on Sunday nights.

For entertainment they sometimes stopped in to the newest nightspot in Hollywood, a dance club called the Palladium on Sunset Boulevard. That's where Kirk met a dark-haired beauty with a cinematic smile from Nebraska. She was a dental assistant named Hilda Schmidt. Everyone called her Peggy. She lived in Lincoln Heights, one of Kirk's old neighborhoods on the east side of town. She had a warm but quiet demeanor and, like Kirk, a sense of style in her dress. Peggy was an instant hit with the Kerkorian clan. Most important, sister Rose approved: "She was so pretty . . . a really good lady." But the couple's romance still had to fit in between Kirk's flight lessons and extended stays at the Happy Bottom.

Kirk came out of Pancho's flight academy barely six months after plunging into intense pilot training and physically rigorous farm chores. Kirk's sister, for one, was confident of his new aviation skills but highly skeptical that he'd learned much about dairy operations. "Kirk don't know how to milk a cow!" she insisted. But he turned out to be a top student where it counted most. When he left the academy, Kirk had already qualified for a commercial pilot's license. And he already had a job offer.

Nearly two years of war in Europe had created a huge demand for trained pilots. And despite official U.S. neutrality, the American military was rapidly preparing for what seemed its inevitable future role in the fighting. Kirk was needed immediately by a civilian defense contractor in the Salinas Valley to teach aviation cadets for the U.S. Army Air Force. In the rush to fill that job, no one at the company had bothered to ask about gaps in Kirk's formal education. He could fly. He could teach. He was hired.

He reported to King City, a small farm town with few lodging choices. Flight instructors had to rent rooms in the homes of local residents. Their mission was to fast-track national preparedness for war in the air. Paul Blackman and Kirk were fellow instructors and roommates. They considered it a matter of personal pride to get their cadets through training. "The need was great, the pressure was great, and we did all that we could possibly do," Blackman recalled.

But for Kirk, still wrapped up in the romance of flying, a significant downside to the job was flunking unfit young aviators. He hated that almost as much as he hated making speeches to his students. He avoided the speeches, but his low tolerance for mistakes and recklessness made him a demanding instructor. He often repeated the mantra of Dick Lentine, his first trainer: "There are old pilots and there are bold pilots—but there are no old, bold pilots."

The Japanese attack on Pearl Harbor intensified pressure on pilot training. It also had a sobering effect on Kirk's personal life. He made time for a return to Los Angeles where he proposed to Peggy. They were wed at Trinity Lutheran Church on January 24, 1942. He signed their license with his formal name, "Kerkor." Nish was his best man. The newlyweds returned to the King City area and their first home together in nearby Greenfield.

Kirk was also starting to weigh his career options. Some of his friends and fellow instructors were moving on to fly multiengine transport planes for the government. Canada was looking for American civilians to ferry freshly built warplanes to Great Britain. Kirk also considered enlisting. As a flight instructor and defense contractor, Kirk was exempt from the draft but he was also confined to light planes, basic training aircraft like the PT-17 Stearman. It was a biplane, a favorite of crop dusters, with a cruising speed of ninety-five miles per hour. In an emergency, it could land between the goalposts on a football field. It was, to an ambitious aviator, like riding a bike with training wheels. The single-wing PT-19 Fairchild was only slightly faster. Kirk was eager for bigger challenges. He was also conflicted—drawn to playing a more direct role in the war but comfortable in his new life with Peggy.

He was still in the Salinas Valley in the summer of 1942 when Kirk's pilot-training skills earned him a major promotion—to flight commander for the Morton Air Academy, a defense contractor operating in the Southern California desert. He would be issued an officer's rank in the U.S. Army Air Force Training Command but retain his civilian status. Lieutenant Kirk Kerkorian and his bride reported to Blythe. Compared to the lush vegetable-growing region around King City, Blythe more closely resembled a bleak lunar plain—except where the Colorado River cut a swath of green along the California-Arizona border.

Kirk was troubled to learn that Executive Officer Roger Pryor, a Hollywood actor and bandleader, expected him to address his first class of flight cadets with a brief welcoming speech. He nearly panicked. Surely the actor was better suited for public speaking, he suggested. But Pryor insisted that Kirk had to step up and speak. There is no record of what Kirk had to say, but his remarks reportedly were short of sixty seconds. And the awkward moment would long rank among Kirk's most uncomfortable recollections.

As it turned out, Morton Air Academy was one of the flight schools young Kirk had contacted when first shopping for pilot lessons. He was rejected for lack of a high school diploma. Now, because of proven piloting skills and valuable training experience, he was employed less than three years later by that very same academy . . . and in a senior management capacity.

Kirk was fully qualified by skill and experience for the academy position, but he was sometimes haunted by fear that his academic shortcomings might be found out. He asked a friend of a friend of a Los Angeles school official for a measure of bureaucratic insurance. It arrived in the form of a letter saying, to whom it may concern, Mr. Kerkorian was a graduate of Metropolitan High School in Los Angeles. It went unquestioned into Kirk's permanent record.

His pals in the old League of Nations would have been proud. And though Kirk continued to feel self-conscious about his poor education, in Blythe at that time he mostly felt liberated from the fear that it might come back to haunt him—or even knock him out of the sky.

It wasn't long before Kirk was chafing over his limited role in the war effort. He was twenty-five years old, and the world was blowing up. But he was going to work every morning in far-flung Blythe. It was the cadets he was training who would get to fly the skies over exotic places and perform heroic duty, living lives that Kirk could only dream about. He was tired of being a distant spectator, and he was losing his enthusiasm for teaching instead of doing. He wanted to fly the biggest and fastest planes. He wanted in on the action. He wanted to see the world, but he'd never even been out of California.

As an aviator, he had no shortage of other options. He was offered a captain's commission in the U.S. Army Air Force, but that was more of the same—flight-training work. And joining the military had serious drawbacks. He told Rose that he was reluctant to give up his civilian status.

The army could order him here, there, or anywhere. It didn't appeal to Kirk's independent nature. He wanted to call his own shots.

"I'd like to think for myself," he told his sister. Besides, he had heard the call of the North. The Royal Air Force Ferry Command needed contract pilots to fly new warplanes across the North Atlantic for the astonishing sum of $1,000 a month. Rose knew he was sold even before he added, "And I'll still be a civilian."

Kirk was confident he could qualify. He met all the preliminary requirements: a commercial pilot's license, more than enough recorded flight hours . . . and that high school diploma.

In the spring of 1943 Kirk and Peggy pulled out of Blythe and headed for Montreal's Dorval Field. It was an exciting time for both of them. They moved into a redbrick apartment in the Mount Royal neighborhood. Kirk found the Ferry Command operations an exhilarating beehive of activity and the variety of aircraft awaiting delivery a pilot's dream. He was thrown in with a gifted and colorful assortment of bush pilots, old-time barnstormers, stunt flyers, and commercial airline crews.[8]

Demand for more pilots paralleled a growing war demand for more planes delivered faster. A steady stream of ferry crew casualties also fed demand for fresh recruits. The roster of dead and missing flight crews was well on its way to exceeding five hundred when Kirk came to town.

His class of replacements would fill a gap left by one devastating crash in February of a four-engine B-24 Liberator. It was shuttling several crews back from Scotland when it encountered monster headwinds and ran out of fuel. It was ten miles short of the Gander airfield in easternmost Newfoundland when it crashed. Nineteen fliers died.

Flying the North Atlantic was something very new in those early war years. Commercial airlines didn't do it. It was widely considered unflyable. Only aviation pioneers had dared challenge the treacherous weather and unforgiving terrain. Charles Lindbergh had made his famous flight to Paris only fifteen years before Kirk moved to Montreal. And Lindbergh spent months preparing for his crossing. Once Kirk was cleared for the ferry service, he would be expected to make two crossings every month in all sorts of weather with planes so fresh off the assembly lines that each transatlantic crossing would double as its test flight.

Ground school placed a heavy emphasis on navigation, meteorology, and North Atlantic geography. Then came the Link trainer for simulated crises—like lost engines, those monster headwinds, icing conditions, fog, storms, anything unexpected. Learning on the job over the North Atlantic was inevitable to some extent . . . but it wasn't recommended.

Kirk had to go under a hood and demonstrate that he could fly blind, by instruments only, maintaining a course within five degrees of straight and within an altitude variation of no more than a hundred feet. He had to account for the effects of wind on speed, course, and fuel consumption. And he had to navigate in clouds or by night and without benefit of a radio.

Any graduate of the RAF training program who moved directly into command of an aircraft did so on the basis of performance—after demonstrating skill and accuracy in calculating, navigating, and flying. Out of his class of nearly a hundred, Kirk was one of only three immediately awarded the RAF captain's insignia. He liked the way it looked on his RAF uniform. The civilian pilots all wore RAF uniforms, as Kirk would recall, "in case you were shot down in enemy territory, they wouldn't shoot ya."

Kirk's first flight was the twin-engine Lockheed Hudson he had trained on at Dorval Field. It was pure adventure—once he remembered to trim his flaps for the extra fuel load. He seemed amazed to find himself in such an exotic place. The kid from Weedpatch who'd never been out of California was steering a course through the clouds to Prestwick, Scotland!

It was a long flight, made longer by a series of refueling stops along the way. He chose a route from Montreal to Gander, then to Greenland and Iceland, before a 750-mile final leg over open ocean to Scotland's west coast. His first landing at Greenland's Bluie West One airfield fit in his memory somewhere between a thrill and a chill.

The only approach was up a narrow fjord with the remains of a sunken freighter serving as a directional indicator. Shooting the wave tops between black rock walls, there was no margin for error. But there were seldom any margins for error in the Ferry Command.

One night in a snow squall, Kirk was lifting off out of Gander when he encountered severe turbulence just beyond the end of the runway. The fuel-laden bomber began to sink. It took all his strength and both hands to hold it steady. Snow-flocked trees flashed by perilously close to the ship's belly. He was squinting into the harsh reflection of his headlights in the snow, half-blinded but afraid to let go and reach for the light switch. It may have been a couple of minutes—it seemed like forever—before he could pull up his landing gear and snap off the lights. It was, to that time, his most harrowing moment in the sky. But icing lurked as the biggest villain waiting in the skies.

It seemed that everyone working the North Atlantic routes eventually had his struggles with ice building up on wing and flap surfaces. It could alter aerodynamics enough to turn a beautiful flying machine into something more like a rock. Ice forced Kirk into emergency landings at least twice, once over Quebec[9] and again at Reykjavik after heavy icing on that final leg to Prestwick forced him to turn around.

Icing was a killer that left few clues. It was considered the most likely culprit in dozens of unsolved ferry aircraft disappearances. Incident reports[10] had haunting similarities:

"8 Dec 42: Lost out of Gander . . ."

"6 Dec 43: Lost out of Goose Bay . . ."

"7 Mar 44: Lost out of Reykjavik . . ."

These and others like them accounted for losses without a trace—no debris, no bodies, no flight recordings, no explanations.

And icing wasn't the only killer. Did the crew get lost . . . run out of fuel . . . encounter a violent storm . . . have some sort of mechanical failure? Kirk had "two very dear friends who disappeared completely" on Mosquito deliveries. He tried not to dwell on the risks or his very private concerns that "these were a lot of strange bombers and some weren't reliable."

He would still be shaking his head about those strange planes and strange routes decades later. "It was like a grab bag. Get this airplane or that airplane. Go here; go there. No questions asked, just get it there."[11]

Despite the casualty rate, crew camaraderie was great. Most RAF contract fliers were Americans and Canadians, but there were also Australians, Poles, and Czechs. It was as if Kirk had joined another "League of Nations." The stakes were higher in this neighborhood, but once again Kirk and his daring young pals were sharing risk—more than enough to keep things interesting.

Some days he could hardly believe his good fortune. He was part of an elite unit that was steadily changing the balance of power in the war. He was commanding some of the biggest, hottest, most powerful planes in the air. And day after day he was flying the "unflyable" North Atlantic.[12] Kirk Kerkorian was having the time of his life.

3

BET OF A LIFETIME

EARLY JUNE 1944
LOST SOMEWHERE OVER SCOTLAND

All good cheer and eager anticipation had evaporated from the tense cockpit of Kirk's fighter-bomber. In the eternity of hours since losing the critical boost of that seventy-five-mile-per-hour tailwind, his attention had been fixed on coaxing every extra minute and extra mile out of the precious remains of a dwindling fuel supply.

A chill breeze buffeted the cabin through the open floor hatch. He had ordered his navigator to make the first jump. It was going to be a tight squeeze for each man and his parachute to slip cleanly through that small manhole. Clearly, the DH-98 Mosquito was not designed for easy midair evacuations. But it also wasn't supposed to run out of gas over the North Atlantic.

"No! Please . . ." pleaded the voice next to him.

Kirk turned to notice for the first time that his Canadian navigator was in tears, his wide, wet eyes begging for an alternate command, a better solution.

"We'll die when we hit the water down there," the young man's voice quavered.

The deep inlet water of the Firth of Clyde was notoriously cold. If rescue took longer than fifteen minutes, the navigator was probably right. But the twin engines could choke and quit at any second. Kirk was steering a slow wide circle over thick clouds concealing what he hoped was at least close to the Scottish shore.

"Gee, let's take one pass. Just one," implored the navigator.[1]

A blind descent through overcast with a very low ceiling was hazardous enough. If the engines died within a few hundred feet of ground, a safe parachute jump could be impossible. Still, the fear-stricken navigator was giving his captain permission to take that chance—to roll the dice for both of them.

Kirk took the bet.

In the dull light of dusk, the fighter-bomber nosed over into a gradual descent. Kirk was poised to pull back and climb in an instant if the engines stopped, to recover as much altitude as possible before bailing out. At least they might have a chance to parachute onto some patch of unseen dry land.

The Mosquito slipped into the fluffy overcast, then into an ever tighter and darker cocoon of mist and fog. Kirk watched his instruments, maintaining a shallow angle of descent, feeling his way deeper into dimness, listening for the slightest engine misfire, until suddenly—black water appeared through the bottom of the clouds. The Firth of Clyde! And then, in the near distance, the familiar lights of Prestwick.

Kirk knew his way from there. He soared across the shoreline, trimmed his flaps for landing, and lined up on the centerline of a runway he'd never been happier to see. His touchdown was perfect.

In the cockpit, neither man spoke as the plane rolled down the runway. Kirk realized only then that his legs were shaking so badly that he couldn't work the brake. He couldn't operate the rudder. There was nothing he could do but sit there, waiting for a massive surge of adrenaline to flood through his body. The Mosquito rolled until gravity brought it to a stop in darkness near a grassy field at the end of the runway. There, pilot and navigator remained for about ten minutes.

Kirk finally wheeled the Mosquito toward an area reserved for

Ferry Command arrivals. He was almost parked when his engines sputtered, coughed, and stopped. The gambler with the most confounding poker face in the Ferry Command was ashen.

P restwick was usually a quiet place for pilots killing time awaiting transportation back to Canada. An old hotel run by Miss Gray provided the lodging. Deluxe rooms had mattresses on the floor. In a crunch, overbookings were assigned to more primitive quarters in "the annex"—a converted produce cellar.[2] All-night craps games were common, as was poker. Kirk loved the camaraderie but confessed that it "ended during our poker games."

When he checked in with Ferry Command after his harrowing arrival that night, it was clear that Kirk was in no shape to operate heavy equipment, count cards, or make wagers. His superiors diagnosed him with a case of "flight fatigue" and prescribed a dose of R & R—a few days of rest and relaxation in London.

The Germans had been knocked back on their heels the week before by the massive allied invasion of the Normandy coast on D-Day. Under the circumstances it seemed that the defense of Western democracy could afford to give Kirk a few days off.

He reached London on Friday, June 16, 1944, just in time to join Londoners watching the skies and running for cover at the terrorizing sounds of incoming German V-1 rockets—what the Brits called "doodlebugs" or "buzz bombs." The rocket barrage, as many as a hundred per hour, came at all times of day or night and in weather foul or fair. London had to endure it. But Kirk headed back to Canada for another ferry assignment and, with any luck, a couple of nights with Peggy.

Back in Montreal, Peggy had the wives and girlfriends of Kirk's fellow fliers as companions. It was a lonely existence compounded by constant anxiety. Heart-wrenching news of lost planes and crews doubled as "good news" when she learned it wasn't Kirk. She wanted a baby. They were trying.

Meanwhile, the war was turning for the Allies. The ice-sensitive, limited-range Mosquito fighter-bombers that Kirk and company were flying across the Atlantic turned out to be well worth the extra risk. They were highly effective at intercepting and destroying German rockets. Of the thirty-three warplanes that he ferried over, eight of them were the buzz-bomb-killing Mosquitos that so many ferry pilots preferred to avoid.

Kirk's stint as a contract pilot lasted more than two years, through the end of war in Europe. In that time, he qualified to fly seven different planes and accumulated thousands of hours of flight time, thousands of dollars in savings, and untold tales of adventure on five different continents.

He dropped by the Sphinx on a stop in Cairo, hitched a ride on a camel, and once, on a lark, faked a minor mechanical problem in Morocco so he could drive into nearby Casablanca. He had just seen the movie that would remain among his favorites for a lifetime. He went to town hoping he might find a gin joint like "Rick's Café Americaine."

He pulled off a successful landing in the middle of the night without runway lights at Basra. He found a speck of land in the Atlantic called Ascension, a mountain landing strip in the middle of the ocean so tiny yet so critical to refueling that he called it "a little spooky." And he managed to dodge malaria in the fever capital of West Africa, a place known to his British colleagues as "White Man's Grave."

Crews making plane deliveries to British bases in North Africa used a southern route across the Atlantic through the Gold Coast colonial capital of Accra or nearby Takoradi (in what is now Ghana). Often those trips involved long layovers, especially for returning crews forced to wait for limited westbound shuttles back to Montreal and New York. Downtime was especially well suited for poker. And poker had become Kirk's game—a collateral benefit of his RAF tour.

In Takoradi, the cards came out early and play often ran into the wee hours. Kirk would have been among the diehards playing deep into the night, except for the sunset invasions of mosquitos—the swarming bugs, not the "wooden wonders." In West Africa, arrival of those mosquitos meant the odds of malarial fever had shot up.

No matter how Kirk's luck had been running, when the sun went down, so did he. Before bug bites could start dealing out malaria, he had crawled into the safety of his mosquito net. And he was never stricken.

His buddies figured he was lucky. Maybe so, but Kirk also tried to keep the odds stacked in his favor. While fellow pilots were sometimes unprepared and risked losing fingers and toes to frostbite on those long, cold shuttles back to Canada, Kirk always traveled with extra socks and warm gloves.[3]

Like most of the Ferry Command flight crews, Kirk hated that return trip. The B-24 Liberator was a heavy bomber. It wasn't outfitted for passengers, who typically had to sit for more than twelve hours on the bomb bay floor, an uncomfortable space that was neither pressurized nor heated.

Kirk wasn't sure what was worse—the cold, the butt-numbing accommodations, sucking on oxygen tubes at high altitudes, or the sheer tedium of the marathon flights. But he agreed with the standing joke of fellow pilots that they were paid the big bucks not for taking planes across the Atlantic, but for enduring the rides home.

In October 1944 Kirk and an extralarge contingent of fliers got the chance to ride home aboard the ocean liner RMS *Queen Mary*. They sailed out of Gourock, Scotland, and landed six days later in New York Harbor. It was anything but luxury.[4]

The *Queen Mary*'s decks and passageways were clogged with hospital beds and badly wounded soldiers. This was the war that ferry pilots seldom faced from their cockpits in the clouds. Kirk roamed the grand liner encountering "so many cases of kids hurt, without arms or legs." That crossing and another like it on the SS *Ile de France* left lasting impressions: "It made me feel how lucky I was."

With the war's end in sight by spring of 1945, the aviators of the RAF Ferry Command were increasingly aware that the end was also near for the extraordinary adventure they had all shared—for the most exciting two years that Kirk, for one, could ever have imagined.

Besides providing an enormous boost to the war effort, in particular Britain's domination of the air, another far-reaching contribution by the Ferry Command was the opening of new air routes for commercial aviation. The so-called polar route was tamed, and years ahead of its time, thanks to the pioneering experiences of intrepid wartime aviators—Kirk Kerkorian among them.

In the end, many of the Ferry Command pilots looked for ways to stick together after the war. Some shared dreams of starting their own airline. They would need seed money for such a venture.

Kirk, like several of his buddies, reached into his pocket to ante up a starter fund. The price to get into this game: one thousand dollars each.

4

SCRAPS, CRAPS, AND JOHN WAYNE

A civilian job in postwar Southern California figured to be a letdown for Kirk. What could possibly replace the adrenaline rush of repeated flights into the war zone over a treacherous North Atlantic?

He returned to Los Angeles knowing only that he wanted to fly and that he had to be his own boss. In a matter of days, he set up a pilot training school at Vail Field in Montebello, a small oil town just east of the city. He was a teacher again, specializing in helping licensed pilots obtain instrument ratings as required by commercial airlines.

The booming aviation business needed large numbers of instrument-rated commercial pilots, so Kirk's flight school roster was quickly filled. Within weeks the business was turning a reliable profit. But there was no excitement, no adrenaline rush. The teacher was bored with teaching.

Vail Field already was a busy place. The former home of Western

Air Express in the 1920s, when it flew the U.S. mail between Los Angeles, Las Vegas, and Salt Lake City, was now attracting so many charter plane operators that air traffic was getting congested. Kirk decided to get in on the charter business, too.[1]

Late in the summer of 1945 he stopped in to visit the branch manager of a Bank of America on Whittier Boulevard, not far from the airfield. Kirk convinced Walter Sharp to finance his purchase of a twin-engine Cessna, a surplus U.S. Army Air Force UC-78 five-seater. Besides launching him in the air charter business, the new relationship with a banker was—as Rick says in Kirk's favorite movie of that era—"the beginning of a beautiful friendship."

One of Kirk's first charter customers was a Los Angeles scrap metal entrepreneur with a gambling habit. Jerry Williams operated a recycling yard about five miles from the airport and wanted regular lifts over the mountains to a budding gaming resort in the desert 250 miles east called Las Vegas.

The town of about eighty-five hundred was a collection of saloons and gambling joints before the war, but it was already starting to boom. The two newest and biggest hotel-casino operations in town—the El Rancho and the Last Frontier—had opened just outside city limits on a stretch of Las Vegas Boulevard soon to be known as the Strip. The local action included dancing girls and sexy lounge acts. Liberace was in town trying out his New York nightclub act. But most important: gambling was open and legal.

Craps, poker, blackjack, roulette—it was all there, all day and all night. Williams was a regular, hiring Kirk and his Cessna for weekly flights to the gaming center. Kirk was enthralled by the action. "I was just overwhelmed by the excitement of the little town." The adrenaline rush was back in his life.

Kirk and Williams would become good friends and regular gambling buddies. On one of their Vegas visits they emerged from a casino shortly before dawn after a particularly difficult night at the tables. They had only five dollars between them. Williams figured it was enough to cover breakfast. Kirk figured it was worth one more visit to the craps table. "What good's five dollars going to do?" he lamented, heading back to the gaming floor. When Kirk returned, they went off to breakfast with $700.

Good luck or bad, Williams kept hiring Kirk's charter service, sometimes two or three times a week. He was, said Kirk, "an extremely good businessman. I won't say he was a terrible gambler, because everyone loses. But he did gamble an awful lot."

Another early charter customer was John Wayne. The actor wanted Kirk and his plane to take him around the Arizona desert as he scouted locations for his next movie, *Angel and the Bad-man*. It was to be Wayne's first time in the dual roles of actor and producer.

Their four-day tour of canyons, buttes, and mesas included dodging desert thunderheads across Monument Valley and among the red rock formations outside Sedona. Kirk repeatedly touched down in the dirt of improvised landing strips. Each night they pitched tents and slept on the ground. For Kirk, it was a grand adventure. He was camping with John Wayne!

"He was such a nice man. I wanted to stay in touch with him, but I always was shy about going back and meeting celebrities."

The charter business in those days was very good. Gamblers and couples in a hurry for Nevada's quickie weddings dominated customer traffic. And Las Vegas was poised for the boom. More hotels and casinos were on the drawing boards or under construction. Kirk's operation was too small. He sold off his flight school and planes, paid off his Bank of America loans, and pocketed a healthy profit that he intended to parlay into something bigger.

Kirk still wanted his own airline—his own fleet of planes, his own company. He watched pilots from the Pacific war zone combine forces to launch a cargo service named after their volunteer fighter unit, the Flying Tigers. A similar dream shared by his fellow RAF Ferry Command pilots never got off the ground. But Kirk was still dreaming.

One way to build capital fast was in the surplus military plane market. The versatile twin-engine C-47 "Gooney Bird," better known to civilians as the DC-3, was in especially big demand among new and expanding freight haulers from Alaska to South America. Fleets of planes coated in olive drab paint were parked all over Hawaii, stranded at war's end by a fuel range limiting them to island hopping or a maximum of five hundred miles.

Kirk had a plan. He bought seven of the planes stranded in Hawaii—each worth at least double its purchase price if he could get it to the U.S. mainland. And doubled again for any plane he ferried all the way down to Rio de Janeiro. He was figuring on profits that in 2018 dollars ranged from about $90,000 to $250,000 per plane. Kirk was back in the ferrying business, this time as a broker of scrapped and surplus planes—gambling on the used aircraft market and his own ability to fly just about anything with wings.

Now the only thing he had to do was get those short-range planes from Honolulu to San Francisco—across twenty-four hundred miles of ocean.

5

ON A WING
AND A SPARE TANK

Kirk had paid $12,000 for the first C-47 he intended to fly to the mainland. He had more than one customer already waiting. In fact, he had likely customers lined up from Hollywood to Rio to buy just about all his surplus planes, sight unseen. And this one was a sight, with more than its share of dents and scuffs and that tired military drab paint job. But like the teenager who restored used cars, Kirk figured he could always give it a good steam cleaning and a fresh set of "newer" wheels. Far more critical was expanding the Gooney Bird's fuel range.

All those flights out of Montreal and Goose Bay in short-range Mosquito fighter-bombers had taught Kirk a few tricks . . . and useful precautions. He rigged this first plane with extra fuel tanks that were lashed to racks installed behind the cockpit.

After calculating and recalculating his expected flight time to California, taking into account possible variations in winds forecast over the Pacific, Kirk personally monitored the fuel-loading process as if his life depended on it.

It would be a very long flight, about fifteen hours. A late-night takeoff from Honolulu would put him in the vicinity of Mills Field in San Francisco by sunset the following evening. By Kirk's mathematical reckoning he had fuel enough to circle a fogged-in Frisco for two hours or to easily reach an alternative airport farther inland. He was leaving no chance of repeating that close call over Scotland.

Taking off from Oahu well after midnight, Kirk was accompanied in the cockpit by radioman and navigator Eugene Bergeron. Two pilot friends who would be Kirk's backup crew for future flights were riding along. Eight hours later tedium and stiff muscles were spreading. The steady drone of the twin engines was hypnotic.

Kirk's friends were asleep in back. Bergeron had dozed off in the next seat. The pilot himself was feeling drowsy as well. He flicked the autopilot switch and felt control of the plane slip from his hands. He stretched and shifted into a more comfortable position. At ten thousand feet over the Pacific and another seven hours to the Golden Gate, Kirk was going to sit back and relax. And then, he dozed off, too.

It was the quiet that woke him. Both engines had shut down. The Gooney Bird had become an unintended glider.[1]

Kirk lunged for the autopilot switch, restoring manual control as he struggled to understand what was happening. Was there a fuel leak? There should have been considerably more fuel in that now-empty spare tank. Did he miscalculate?

But first things first—could Kirk save the plane?

He adjusted flaps and trim to slow the plane's descent. They had already dropped nearly a thousand feet. And the weather was deteriorating. They were in and out of rain clouds, buffeted by light to moderate turbulence. Kirk steered away from the worst of it. They descended in eerie silence through eight thousand feet.

A now wide-awake radioman was tapping out a message in Morse code. They were out of range for any voice communication.

And there was no certainty that anyone on land or sea would pick up the coded signal. Still, Bergeron broadcast the plane's global coordinates and repeated his urgent message in dots and dashes:

"Engines out. Going down. Going down."

It was around noon on the California coast when the SOS signal was received at Hamilton Field, an army air base and weather station on San Pablo Bay just east of San Francisco. The weather crew promptly alerted the U.S. Coast Guard and waited, hoping for another message. Nothing.

There was no point in dispatching rescue vessels. The C-47 descending through those rainsqualls with two dead engines was about seven hundred miles away. It could take days for ships from the coast to reach a crash site that far out.

By early afternoon radio news bulletins were on the air broadcasting details of the SOS as it had been reported to the Coast Guard. The plane and its captain were identified. Some of those news flashes were airing 350 miles farther south in Los Angeles where Kirk's friends and family were among the shocked listeners.

"Aviators facing death in the sea . . . a mayday signal . . . then silence."

At the Kerkorian family home, Kirk's brother Nish heard it first. He told his wife, Flo, but kept the news secret from parents Ahron and Lily. When sister Rose walked into the tense household, she demanded that Nish tell her what was wrong. He finally took her aside.

"Kirk's plane went into the drink," he said.

Rose was puzzled. She wasn't sure what he meant. But the couple's grave expressions gave it away. Rose felt cold all over.

Ahron sensed the dread as well and insisted on answers. Nish explained the situation. The old man collapsed into a chair and fainted. He had to be revived but only to wait. All agreed to keep the reports secret from Kirk's mother, Lily.

Ted O'Flaherty, the friend and former furnace installer who introduced Kirk to flying, was at Los Angeles Airport when a fellow pilot asked, "Have you heard what happened to Kerkorian?" He rushed to his car radio to listen for news updates.

And gambling buddy Jerry Williams drove out to the Kerkorian home to wait with Kirk's family. As the afternoon dragged on, the wait on the ground seemed more and more desperate.

B ack in the C-47 Kirk had been racing time and gravity with a methodical air that masked the urgency. He had switched over to another spare fuel tank and was following procedures to reduce air in the fuel lines. Switching tanks in flight with engines running was routine. But having a tank run dry, it was almost certain that air had been pumped into the fuel lines along with the last drops of gas. An air lock could prevent or catastrophically delay a restart.

Even without the risk of air locks, a quick engine restart was no sure thing—especially under the pressure of time and an impeding belly landing in the Pacific.

They were descending through four thousand feet when Kirk launched the restart process. He didn't hesitate. He was out of time and options. Bergeron was already bracing himself in anticipation of a hard landing, but he was reassured by Kirk's outward confidence.

The restart involved several steps—pushing one lever, then another, flicking an overhead switch once . . . twice . . . three times, and then punching and holding a red starter button. It might take multiple tries. But when Kirk kept pressure on that red button, the response was immediate: a shudder, smoke billowing from the first engine, and a roar.[2]

Moments later, with the second engine also back online and relief sweeping the cockpit, Kirk brought the plane up to its former cruising altitude. Now he faced the troubling mystery: Why did the spare tank run out of fuel so much sooner than expected?

Back on autopilot, Kirk stepped away from the controls to inspect his rack of spare tanks for the first time since he supervised loading and fueling on the ground. With the plane now flying level, he saw the problem almost immediately. During fueling, while parked on the tarmac, the C-47 fuselage had rested at a pronounced downward slant toward the tail. The spare tanks were tilted so that fuel would overflow their open caps before full capacity was reached. Unfortunately, that meant all the spare tanks were a few inches short of filled to the brim.

A quick inventory revised Kirk's estimate of onboard fuel. It was substantially less than he expected. Bergeron watched him pencil out fresh calculations, the twenty-nine-year-old pilot's intent expression giving away nothing. The radioman couldn't tell if the captain's numbers were reassuring or alarming. He still wasn't sure as Kirk calmly delivered his verdict.

"We gotta lose weight," Kirk said, directing Bergeron to open the cargo door and start tossing out everything—"everything that's not bolted down"—everything, except that yellow rubber life raft. Bergeron rushed from the cockpit.

Kirk eased up on the power and set his controls for maximum fuel economy. By his math, there was no spare fuel. Reaching San Francisco was in doubt. He was focused on how to squeeze every minute of flight time out of what was left in his tanks. Of course, there was also what Kirk called his "back door" or Plan B—the yellow dinghy.

In the back of the plane, Bergeron and the passengers were finding lots of loose items to pitch out the cargo door. Wrenches and tool kits, suitcases, fire gear, empty gas tanks, and dismantled racks—all of it hurled out into the slipstream. Some of the jetsam rattled against the plane as it spilled out.

Up front, Kirk was startled by a sudden lurch. Something heavy—maybe a rack or an empty gas tank—had smashed into the plane's vertical stabilizer. The tail fin was still intact. He figured it must have been slightly bent. Again Kirk adjusted the C-47 trim, holding the plane just above its minimum speed to maintain level flight.

Making matters worse, in the scramble to avoid storms and restart the engines, they had strayed about a hundred miles off course. The uncertainty only grew. Time and progress crawled by, giving Kirk time to ponder his situation. It was all too familiar—Scotland all over again.

With the sun setting behind them, they were flying into an on-rushing black sky. No signs of city lights loomed on the horizon, and they were still beyond radio range of San Francisco's airport tower. Bergeron, who had never thought to update his Morse code distress message, kept trying to make voice contact.

They were a couple of hours off the coast when radio static gave way to the sound of a voice at air traffic control in San Francisco. Kirk calmly reported low fuel and requested priority landing upon arrival. The tower dispatched a pair of Coast Guard planes to escort them in.

At the Kerkorian house in Los Angeles, the lights were on. It was dinnertime but no one was hungry. Lily had finally forced her family to explain, "What's going on here?" She was remarkably sanguine. Kirk's mother seemed to be the only one in the room with confidence that her son would survive.

Jerry Williams was still at the house, too. He offered to make some calls, hoping for news following an afternoon without an iota of information. He finally reached the San Francisco airport tower. Kirk's gambling companion had the happy privilege of telling his family that their boy was not in the drink. Kirk had radioed in. He was still flying.

Shortly before eight o'clock that night all inbound flights to San Francisco's Mills Field were diverted into holding patterns. All runways were cleared. Fire and rescue trucks rolled into position. Kirk was coming in out of the west. His Coast Guard escorts were missing, having been unable to find the C-47 in the darkness offshore.

When his plane appeared to traffic controllers, it was coming in low over the coastal hills. It banked hard over the Bay into its final approach and moments later touched down to the sweet squeal of rubber on runway—more than sixteen hours out of Honolulu.

Press accounts recorded the arrival in headlines: "4 Pacific Fliers Beat Death in Race to Mills." Witnesses described Kirk's prized surplus plane as a "crippled . . . beat up DC-3." To a reporter from the *San Mateo Times* Kirk acknowledged: "I thought we'd have to ditch."[3]

Before heading off to answer inquiries from aviation safety regulators, he shrugged off questions about high drama over the high seas. There was no going back, he explained with typical understatement, "so (we) just kept going, expecting to exhaust our fuel supply at any moment."

Kirk went on to deliver most of his surplus acquisitions personally—and without drama. His partnership with a Brazilian flier in Rio added to his international reputation as an aircraft trader. That is, until Kirk flew down to visit his money. Most of it had disappeared without proper accounting.

It was a hard lesson to learn about sloppy accounting and partnerships with strangers—and the drawbacks of conducting business by the seat of his pants. There wasn't enough cash left over in Brazil to fight about. Kirk walked out. "Take it and shove it," he said and returned to California where he went into business with his best friend—his sister, Rose Pechuls. She had recently divorced, ending a marriage in which her husband chafed at feeling inadequate compared to Rose's high regard for her brother Kirk.

When a small charter airline at Los Angeles Municipal Airport went on the market in 1947, Kirk and Rose bought it—a three-plane fleet with a DC-3, a twin-engine Cessna, and a single-engine Beechcraft. Kirk put up most of the $60,000 purchase price after borrowing $15,000 from the Montebello branch of Bank of America. Rose invested an additional $5,000 and managed the office.

They filed for a business license with the City of Los Angeles, calling themselves "Kirk Kerkorian and Rose Pechuls doing business as Los Angeles Air Service." The airline flew charters all over the West, but much of the business was to Las Vegas. To avoid another Rio fiasco, he also hired an accountant.

Kirk's new bookkeeper, Arnold McGraw, would introduce him to the tax benefits of lease deals and depreciation and capital gain profits. Both his used plane brokerage and his charter service were making money. He wasn't rich, but the entire Kerkorian clan was sharing in his growing financial security.

For a time Kirk kept track of the C-47 that started him in the used plane business, the "crippled . . . beat up DC-3" that barely got him to San Francisco. He sold it to Howard Hughes's aide Glenn Odekirk, who fixed the dents and its bent vertical stabilizer and had it completely refurbished by the Hughes Aircraft Company. Once outfitted as a luxury private plane, it flew Hollywood celebrities around the country, including Tyrone Power and Cesar Romero.

Before turning over the plane to Odekirk, however, Kirk had retrieved the yellow life raft—for old times' sake. It was uncharacteristic of a man who was seldom sentimental about possessions, things, any kind of stuff. But the yellow raft had once represented something more than a rubber flotation device when the stoic Kirk was wrestling with dark fears of ditching in the Pacific. It was hope, potential salvation.

When beach weather returned to Southern California the next summer in 1947, Kirk took the raft to Santa Monica Bay for a day in the water. It inflated moments after he activated the compressed gas canister. But then, with a great hiss, it just as quickly deflated. The rubber was old and cracked. The yellow raft could not have saved him and his crew.

Once again, Kirk had to accept the fact: sometimes he was lucky.

6

BUGSY SIEGEL'S LAST FLIGHT

JUNE 1947
ABOARD THE BAMBOO BOMBER

The mobster didn't talk much. He just needed a quick lift to Las Vegas and back. He had a meeting. Kirk at the flight controls wasn't big on small talk. And he knew better than to ask any questions. Mr. Siegel was a familiar customer.[1]

Benjamin "Bugsy" Siegel was the closest thing to royalty in postwar Las Vegas, a giant among the new breed of out-of-state gambling racketeers flocking to the sanctuary of legal gaming in Nevada. He had gangster cachet for his links to Al Capone's gambling operations. He had Hollywood good looks, was generous with his cash, and despite his notorious reputation—or, perhaps, because of it—he was usually surrounded by an entourage of celebrities. He was also a regular passenger of the Los Angeles Air Service flights, shuttling between his girlfriend's home in Beverly Hills and his lavish casino project on the Strip.

On this summer night he had dropped into the LAAS offices

just before closing and without a reservation. The last-minute timing was unusual.

Kirk could have delegated the late charter to another pilot. He had only recently brought in extra hands to ease his own workload. Business was very good. He was starting to run junkets for the New Frontier casino, opening a whole new revenue stream. Besides, he was tired of trying to do it all—from flying passengers to handling their baggage, from collecting fares to collecting cabin trash. Throw in some travel to buy or sell a plane and Kirk was away from home a lot and seeing less and less of wife Peggy. They still had no children. It was a disappointment to both of them.[2]

One of his first hires had been Barney Aguer, a pipe-smoking pilot friend from their prewar days as flight instructors at King City and Blythe. Barney offered to flip a coin, to let luck pick the pilot. But Kirk insisted that he would take the flight himself.

All they knew was that Bugsy—"Mr. Siegel" to his face—had a meeting. Whatever it was couldn't be handled on a telephone call. Besides, Kirk was trying to sell Mr. Siegel one of his planes.

Weeks earlier Kirk had been gambling at Siegel's fancy new casino when his friend Jerry Williams introduced him to the owner. There was a bit of small talk about airplanes and Bugsy said he was in the market to buy one. Kirk immediately drove him to the airfield to inspect the twin-engine Beechcraft he was using that day.

"I like it. I'm going to buy it," he told Kirk.

But this was unrelated. The unplanned evening charter would have to use a different plane—Kirk's personal favorite. He called the Cessna Bobcat his "Bamboo Bomber." It was neither a bomber nor was there so much as a splinter of bamboo anywhere in the airframe. Its lightweight wings, however, were constructed with plywood ribs and laminated spruce spar beams. It was fast and could make the 250-mile flight in ninety minutes or less. It was perfect for the occasion.

The five-seat bamboo bomber took off that night with just one passenger and a minor mystery: What was so urgent about getting to Las Vegas and back that night? Of course, Kirk wasn't about to ask any questions.

What everyone in Las Vegas knew already was that Bugsy was the money and the brains and the class behind the Flamingo, the newest, most exciting hotel and casino development in town. It was an opulent third addition to the Strip and a striking departure from the traditional Old West style common around old Las Vegas.

The Flamingo began as the brainchild of Hollywood nightclub impresario Billy Wilkerson, whose stylish venues included Café Trocadero and Ciro's on Sunset Strip. He was also founder and publisher of the *Hollywood Reporter*. But wartime material shortages and high costs jeopardized his Vegas plans until Siegel stepped in with financing provided by East Coast gambling racketeers, including Charles "Lucky" Luciano and Meyer Lansky. The investors had already tested the new Vegas market by turning a quick profit buying and selling the downtown El Cortez Hotel-Casino.

Wilkerson retained a nominal share of the ownership, but Bugsy took over the project late in 1945. Right away he gave it the name it would take into history, inspired by his girlfriend, Virginia Hill. She was a redhead with long legs nicknamed "the Flamingo."

The project, however, was no love affair. Delays and cost overruns led to rumors of investor unhappiness. The big grand opening celebration on the day after Christmas in 1946 was rushed. The hotel construction wasn't finished. Guests had to be put up at other hotels. Bugsy's best friend in the Hollywood crowd, actor George Raft, ended up at the New Frontier. His celebrity opening acts stayed at the El Rancho Vegas. It turned out to be a publicity bust.

By all accounts, headliner Jimmy Durante was a big hit with the crowd that showed up. Opening night also included Xavier Cugat and his band and singer-actor-comedienne Rose Marie, whose gangster father once ran with Al Capone. But when the casino lost $300,000 over the next two weeks, Bugsy pulled the plug—shutting it down until the hotel portion was ready for guests.

What was supposed to be the country's "first million-dollar casino" had already cost the gangster investors at least five times that amount. And now it was closed. Bugsy scrambled to borrow money from friends, including Raft. Two months later, on March 1, 1947, he reopened a completed hotel-casino with a new name for luck—the Fabulous Flamingo.

It appeared to outsiders that the Flamingo was soon doing decent business. And appearances were correct. By May, the casino was showing a $300,000 profit. Behind the scenes, however, Bugsy was dealing with impatient investors and ominous suspicions. There were suggestions that some of the cost overruns were skim that went directly into Bugsy's pocket—or into a Swiss bank account. He flew to Cuba for a face-to-face with Luciano and Lansky to straighten things out. It didn't go well. Bottom line: they wanted their money back . . . now.

Bugsy was a naturally paranoid person in the best of times. His fourth-floor suite at the Fabulous Flamingo had bulletproof windows, steel plates in the walls, and secret ladders leading to secret escape tunnels.

But if Bugsy was under pressure that night or felt vulnerable, he wasn't showing it. Kirk remembered nothing unusual or otherwise remarkable about his passenger's demeanor.

Alamo Field south of town (the future McCarran International Airport) was little more than a patch of sand off the Las Vegas–Los Angeles Highway in 1947, but at night its runway lights blazed against the black desert landscape. A limousine was waiting for Kirk's passenger. Bugsy didn't expect to be gone long. He asked Kirk to stay with the plane, and then he walked to the car and disappeared into the night.

There would be no time to hit the casinos on this trip, no time for Kirk to meet with friends. The field was so far out of town that he couldn't even see the distant neon.

Kirk was gambling pretty heavily in those days. He loved it.

Some might have called him obsessed with it. When he wasn't at the craps table, he liked to play the dollar slot machines. He sometimes hired a caddy, of sorts, to tote his heavy bag of silver dollars while making the rounds of casino floors looking for the hot slots.[3]

He would eventually have lines of credit at all the top casinos—Benny Binion's Las Vegas Club and later the Horseshoe, Beldon Katleman's El Rancho, Bill Miller's New Frontier—and more. His reputation as a player was spreading. Kirk didn't have the financial resources to be "a whale," one of those superrich high rollers, but he had enough that he could also afford to lose. And he relished taking big gambles, reined in only by the house limit.

Binion, a recent immigrant from Texas, didn't have much use for any man who never rolled the dice. He considered Kirk a real man, "a brave man." And Kirk always paid his gambling debts. "He'd get down ten, fifteen thousand and say, 'gimme a few days,' and he'd go off and sell a plane in South America," recalled a Binion casino executive. "He always settled his markers."[4]

But Kirk still had a lot to learn about gambling. Too often he stayed at the tables chasing bets—riding winning streaks into the ground or turning small losses into big ones. He was still the kind of gambler that made casinos rich. That's why Bugsy knew about Kirk even before they were formally introduced. And the gangster's favorable impression of the gambler probably benefited Kirk's brother one night at the casino when Nish brashly greeted Mr. Siegel with a hearty and cringe-inducing "Hey, Bugsy—how are ya?" Anyone but Kirk's punch-drunk brother might have left with a bloodied nose.

Outside of aviation and the casino worlds, one of Kirk's best friends was a cop—a Clark County deputy sheriff. They met during a brawl outside the El Rancho. James "Bad Boy Jimmy" Williams had been engaged in heated conversation with a tall, blond plainclothes deputy when their dispute turned physical.

Kirk was part of the crowd that had gathered around the fringe of the tussle. Bad Boy Jimmy was clearly losing but refusing to surrender. Rifle Right Kerkorian was impressed with the young deputy's cool, methodical fighting style. He had a boxer's stance, a boxer's eye for opportunity, and his quick fists landed like hammers.

"Who's the big blond kid?" Kirk asked casino manager Katleman next to him.

"That's Ralph Lamb," he said. "I'll introduce ya."

It would mark the beginning of Kirk's longest-running Vegas friendship, with one of the most colorful characters in a city of colorful characters. Years later, Lamb would end up the chief law enforcement officer in town with a reputation for fighting the mob. He was also among the last of the cowboy lawmen in the modern West.

Once, when Kirk and Lamb were horseback riding well outside city limits, Kirk was stricken with appendicitis. Doubled over in pain, he could barely stay in the saddle. Ralph strapped Kirk to his horse, grabbed the reins, and rode hard back to civilization for just-in-time medical attention.

Kirk always told friends, "Ralph saved my life."[5]

Lamb also helped Kirk land his plane from time to time. Back before Interstate 15 cut through Las Vegas, a large empty lot behind the Stardust Hotel became Kirk's makeshift landing strip on various nighttime visits. Lamb would prepare for Kirk's inbound plane by starting a small bonfire at one end of the sandy landing area and then drive his sheriff's squad car to the other end—turning on his flashing emergency lights and illuminating the landing surface with the beam of his spotlight.[6]

That June night in 1947, Bugsy and the limo showed up back at the airfield no more than thirty minutes after they left. Kirk was puzzled that a customer would fly three hours round-trip for a half-hour meeting in a car, but mostly he was glad to have the business. Barney Aguer greeted him with questions first thing the next day. "How'd it go? What happened?"

Kirk could only shrug. "The strangest thing . . . but it was nothing."

Two days after the trip, a special EXTRA edition of the *Los*

Angeles Herald-Express carried the banner headline "'BUGSY' SIE-GEL MURDERED" and said he had been "Rubbed Out in Beverly Hills in Hail of Bullets." Page one photos of the crime scene showed Bugsy's sheet-covered corpse in the living room where he had died reading a copy of the *Los Angeles Times*.[7]

The shooting occurred at 810 N. Linden Drive, the mansion residence of girlfriend Virginia "the Flamingo" Hill. It was one of the swankest of Beverly Hills neighborhoods, just off Sunset Boulevard.

In a lengthy news story and related features that jumped to various inside pages, this paragraph may have stood out back at the office of Los Angeles Air Service:

"Siegel, co-owner of the fabulous $5 million Flamingo gambling casino in Las Vegas, flew in from the Nevada resort town yesterday, and went directly to the home of Miss Hill, who had left on a trip to Paris."

The gangland-style assassination was never solved. And Kirk never solved the mystery behind his last flight with Bugsy.

7

ART OF
THE JUNK DEAL

EARLY 1950
BURBANK, CALIFORNIA

Kirk was especially proud of the latest piece of aviation junk he had picked up in Louisiana. It cost a mere $70,000. He talked like someone who might have found a Picasso at the dump.

It was the gleaming silver aluminum four-engine DC-4 Skymaster parked out in the Southern California sun just outside the new offices of Los Angeles Air Service. The company had moved to the Lockheed Air Terminal in Burbank and made the San Fernando Valley its new home.

LAAS accountant Arnold McGraw was curious to see what such a bargain looked like up close. He knew it was a beauty on the ledger page, an accountant's dream. Any airworthy Skymaster was easily worth twice what the boss paid for it.

Kirk had negotiated the deal with an export outfit in New Orleans, a company that delivered Mississippi Valley dairy and beef cattle to Guatemala. That's about all McGraw knew about its history. On this particular afternoon, he was extending his lunch break to inspect the new prize.

A ladder leaning against the fuselage led to an open door. He scampered up eager for his first look. The full import of the plane's prior service hit the accountant the instant he stepped into the dark cargo hold. He choked, fighting his gag reflex, and steadied himself against the edge of the doorframe. The Skymaster atmosphere was thick with an overpowering odor—extreme barnyard—no doubt intensified by a couple of days fermenting in the sun.

In the bowels of the airship, structural damage was dangerously widespread. The old bell frames, the metal ribs of the fuselage, were so badly rusted from sloshing cattle urine that the plane was unsafe for man or beast. Much of the aluminum skin lining the belly of the plane would have to be ripped out and replaced due to more corrosion from animal waste.

Kirk knew what he was buying. He had factored in repair and retrofitting costs to make it a passenger plane. The boys at nearby Flying Tiger would do the work, making the former cargo plane airworthy and aromatic for a fraction of the cost required for a new DC-4. And Walter Sharp at the Montebello branch of Bank of America agreed to finance the $100,000 acquisition and rehabilitation costs. The amount would also cover the purchase of used passenger cabin seats.

Kirk helped fly his rust-infested gem home from Louisiana. McGraw had to wonder: How did the boss endure the intensity of that choking stench for more than seven hours in transit? Maybe his days mucking out the barn at the Happy Bottom Ranch helped him cope. More likely the foul atmosphere was simply offset in Kirk's head by the sweet scent of success.

In the end, Kirk's Skymaster emerged from rehab a bright, shining beauty—the new queen of his fleet. It even smelled new. He christened it the *Californian* and started service between Burbank and Newark, with stops in Amarillo and Cleveland. And with the launch of transcontinental service, Kirk's little airline finally joined the big leagues of aviation.[1]

Life in the nonscheduled airline business remained filled with uncertainties, many from federal regulations intended to protect competing commercial carriers. The Civil Aeronautics Board (CAB), which once encouraged expansion of charter services, came under increasing pressure to crack down on their intrusions into profitable commercial routes.

Kirk figured that his run of good luck wasn't going to last indefinitely. He started cashing in some of his chips. Over the next year and a half he sold off some of his biggest planes—including the *Californian*.

His $100,000 cattle scow went to Northeast Airlines for the remarkable price of $340,000—and that was without the used passenger seats. The inveterate scrap dealer sold those separately. That transaction produced a milestone for the thirty-five-year-old entrepreneur. For the first time, Kirk's annual income broke $100,000. He also learned a lesson: pilots don't make big money, businessmen do.

With proceeds from his downsizing moves, Kirk was able to pay off his bank loans, buy out sister Rose's interest, and reorganize the company. Business operations were split into two ventures—the charter service and his used plane trade. The trimmed-down airline could go dormant periodically, subject to the economy's ebb and flow or the shifting burdens of CAB regulation. But his used plane brokering and bartering business never closed, keeping Kirk especially happy and financially sound.

"We must've traded sixty planes" in those days, he once estimated. But few trades gave him greater satisfaction than two deals he brokered in Europe to put together one working Lockheed Constellation from a pair of cannibalized "Connies."

In January 1951 one of the sleek four-engine planes operated by British Overseas Airway Corporation (BOAC) was being ferried without passengers from London to Bristol. The Constellation, with its distinctive triple tail—three vertical stabilizers like the sails of a clipper ship—was a favorite of long-haul commercial carriers. The plane already held the U.S. transcontinental speed record.

Howard Hughes had met secretly with Lockheed officials just before the war advocating for performance specifications that would revolutionize commercial air travel. He pressed for greater speed, greater range, and higher altitudes. Barely thirty-five years after Wilbur and Orville Wright stunned the world by staying airborne fifty-nine seconds, Hughes was demanding planes that could fly nonstop across the continent. The result was the Constellation.

Even before the new design went into production, Hughes ordered the first forty models for his own airline, Transcontinental and Western (later, TWA). That big purchase order was scratched by Lockheed's abrupt shift to prewar military production. Postwar the plane maker couldn't produce the popular Connie fast enough to catch up with demand. BOAC, Air France, and TWA got some of the earliest deliveries.

Coming into Bristol on a cold and blustery day that January, the BOAC Constellation, christened the *Baltimore*, landed hard on an icy runway. It bounced once, twice, and then lost the centerline, veering off the runway toward a fuel storage building containing fifty-five thousand gallons of aviation petrol. It could have been a disaster for the crew. Instead, it was a photo op.

Newspapers around the world carried a remarkable AP photo that weekend showing the BOAC Constellation perched on the roof of a single-story brick building—looking much like an airplane model mounted on a brick stand.[2] Structurally, it looked largely undamaged. Kirk had the same impression. But BOAC insurance adjusters declared the $750,000 plane a total loss.

Given the high demand for Constellations in the open market, Kirk figured a repaired plane could be worth more than $1.5 million. He dispatched his own inspection team to Bristol for an assessment.

They found that the right wing (not visible in the press photo) had been destroyed, but the damaged nose section was repairable. Kirk offered underwriters $150,000 for the plane's remains. They grabbed the deal.

Kirk insisted on one condition—four, actually: that the insurers throw in four zero-time engines to replace those on the crashed Constellation. (A zero-time engine is a new or refurbished engine that has never been operated in flight.) It was a classic Kerkorian deal. He immediately leased those engines to TWA, pretty much covering his initial expenses.

The Connie's broken body was lashed to the deck of a cargo ship, the largest plane at that time ever transported by sea, and delivered to Newark for storage. Kirk figured that over time he could scrap other Constellations for parts. It was a smart bet.

That same year, an Air France Constellation of the same model and vintage made a hard landing in Toulouse. Insurance carriers declared it a total loss. But left intact was a right wing and an undamaged nose section, precisely what Kirk needed.

He bought the French parts for $122,000 and shipped them to Newark, where Lockheed raised a makeshift airplane factory for the meticulous reassembly project. The aircraft maker took the lead to ensure that the re-created Connie met the highest factory standards. It was completed in a few months in a tented dockside compound that came to be called "Splinterville."

His good-as-new plane cost Kirk about $300,000. He hung on it a price tag of $1.6 million. His first sales call was to Howard Hughes. He left a message with Glenn Odekirk—the Hughes aide who bought that C-47 from Hawaii, the one with the yellow rubber raft and barely enough gas. The next night Hughes called back personally. They talked planes and flying. They talked price. Hughes was easygoing, friendly, but a hard sell. They agreed to meet in Las Vegas at the new Thunderbird Hotel, at the casino bar.

Though they had never met, Kirk knew Hughes by reputation, as did most of America. Hughes was a famed aviator, test pilot, and aircraft designer with many speed records and daring flights to his credit. He'd had his own ticker-tape parade through Manhattan. He owned an airline (TWA) and a movie studio (RKO) and was worth millions of dollars.

Kirk had noticed Hughes coming and going from the Las Vegas airport with a mixture of respect and hero worship. Hughes always seemed to be flying interesting planes—a B-17 or B-26, not a work-horse like the DC-3.

On one occasion, Kirk watched Hughes climb down from the cockpit of a B-26 with a newspaper under his arm looking like a swashbuckling flyer right out of Hollywood's Central Casting cata-log. "He was one helluva pilot . . . a real pilot's pilot," he recalled.

When Kirk first met Hughes, it was at the Thunderbird's ca-sino bar to discuss his Connie sale. The famous aviator, twelve years older than Kirk, was gracious and down-to-earth. Again, they talked about planes and flying . . . then about Las Vegas. But when conversation turned to business, Hughes seemed argumentative. He didn't like the price, but he also didn't like a litany of other things—including the size of the airliner's lavatories.

Kirk was always flexible about price, but he was surprised and put off by the nitpicking, especially over the design of in-flight toilets. And though Hughes was always very polite, his stubborn pettiness made Kirk wonder if he might have somehow personally offended the multimillionaire.

After three or four more meetings without agreement, Kirk gave up. He would instead lease the reassembled plane to a Burbank-based neighbor—California Hawaiian Airlines, a charter company serving San Francisco and Honolulu. When that operator ran into financial troubles a couple of years later, Kirk recovered the Connie and sold it to El Al Israel Airlines for $750,000.

His net profit from separate lease deals, both for the plane and its engines, plus the El Al sale, came to $600,000.

Kirk was making a reputation as one of the top aviation brokers in the country. He had a small business on the verge of moving from modest annual revenues into the million-dollar club. He had impeccable credit at traditional banks and at the finest gambling houses in Las Vegas. Life was good.

Then his wife, Peggy, filed for divorce.

Friends and family speculated about Kirk's many business absences, about too many gambling trips to Las Vegas, about the couple's disappointment over having no children, about the possible smothering effect of Kirk's close-knit, old-country family.

Kirk never wanted to talk about it.

Peggy's divorce filing listed the grounds as "extreme cruelty and grievous mental suffering." It was standard boilerplate language used throughout California in the era before no-fault divorces. No further details were provided in those documents, but Kirk had a temper that friends said could flare up in harsh—even mean—verbal assaults.

After an evening together that raised Kirk's hopes for reconciliation, Peggy declined. "I can't. You'll only hurt me again," she told him.[3]

Divorce proceedings continued. A property settlement simply noted their "unhappy differences." She got the couple's two-year-old Ford and all household furniture in the Inglewood residence they rented near the newly dedicated Los Angeles International Airport. Kirk agreed to provide $50,000 in spousal support spread out over seven years.

Their nine-and-a-half-year marriage officially ended on September 27, 1951. Kirk slipped into depression. He stopped working, stopped talking to his family, and holed up alone in a Hollywood apartment. During that same period, he tried to shake his dark mood with electroshock therapy. He later told friends that it worked but the effects didn't last very long.[4]

What finally shook him out of his depressed state was his friend

Jerry Williams banging on his door. *Get out of this lonely apartment,* Williams said. *Move in with your parents. Get back with people who love you.* It proved to be just the tonic. Soon Kirk was also back brokering used plane deals.

He was still lucky, too. He had one legendary streak while shooting craps at the Golden Nugget Casino. Management finally asked him—politely, as the story goes—to please take his hot hand to another casino.[5]

The remarkable thing about Kirk the gambler was that no one could ever tell from his demeanor whether he was winning or losing, whether the stakes were small or staggering. He always appeared relaxed, like one of the coolest crooners of his day. "He was the Perry Como of the craps table," a casino exec told the *Los Angeles Times.*[6]

That same demeanor, the best poker face in the RAF Ferry Command, was also making Kirk an inscrutable force in business. He was developing a reputation as a highly effective negotiator. But his reaction to Peggy's rejection revealed that at least in matters of love and romance, Kirk had a vulnerable side, as well.

8

GAMBLING
ON GAMBLING

MID-1950s
LAS VEGAS, NEVADA

A decade after the war, hotel and casino development in Las Vegas was still booming. Old Route 91, the Los Angeles–Las Vegas Highway, was now called the Strip, where sprawling new resorts replaced barren sandlots. Seven busy casinos lit up black desert nights, and twice as many more were already in development. As University of Nevada gaming historian David G. Schwartz described those heady days: "It looked like opening a successful Las Vegas casino was as easy as tripping and hitting the ground."[1]

Everyone wanted in on the action—from Midwest mobsters to investment managers at the Teamsters Union pension fund, from real estate developers to car dealers, from actors like the Marx Brothers and Pat O'Brien to an aviator like Kirk Kerkorian.

As a gambler himself, Kirk knew better than most the fundamentals of a casino business model: customers come in all day and night to throw money at the owners. And they love doing it . . . win or lose. Kirk consistently lost more than he won and yet he called his visits to Vegas "the best times" of his life. "I was just overwhelmed by the excitement of the town."[2]

He accumulated many friends among casino owners and managers, some of them clients of his Los Angeles Air Service. One of those was Marion Hicks, an energetic L.A. real estate developer who built the El Cortez Hotel in downtown Las Vegas and then the Thunderbird on the Strip. During his many commutes with Kirk, Hicks had opportunities to share some of his hard-earned wisdom. He was uniquely qualified to answer that enduring question: What could possibly go wrong?

Hicks had been on a roll with his early Vegas investments. After selling the El Cortez to Bugsy Siegel and Meyer Lansky for a quick six-figure profit, Hicks and his partner, Clifford "Big Juice" Jones, built the handsome Thunderbird. Their opening-night gala attracted a big crowd, but then things went terribly wrong. The craps table absorbed a $160,000 run of extraordinary good luck—at the casino's expense. The house could barely scrape together $40,000.

Banks in the 1940s and 1950s did not make loans to casinos for anything—least of all to fund shortfalls at the cashier's cage. To cover the huge payout, Hicks and Jones turned to Lansky, "the mob's accountant." In return for a briefcase full of cash, Lansky extracted a significant share of casino ownership and a job for his brother. Jake Lansky not only got an executive's title but also the casino's best place to park his black Cadillac, just outside the Thunderbird offices.

The Lansky brothers' not-so-secret involvement in the Thunderbird would eventually put the casino license in jeopardy, but Hicks was still building up the business when he hired a musical act for his showroom. The act came with a young dancer from England named Jean Maree Hardy—a blonde with Grace Kelly good looks and that very British accent.

Hicks introduced his dancer to Kirk at the casino bar. They were very different. He was a financially comfortable divorcé in his midthirties; she was never married and barely old enough to drink. He was intense but shy; she was an outgoing, confident performer with a touch of blunt-spoken candor like Kirk's sister, Rose. He was deeply tanned with black hair; she was pale and fair-haired. So, of course, they fell in love. After a two-year romance, Kirk took out a marriage license in Los Angeles County and set a wedding date.

Their decision dashed any lingering hopes in the greater Kerkorian family that Kirk might one day end up with a nice Armenian girl. But the couple passed up a quickie Las Vegas ceremony for something more traditional back home in an Inglewood church. Kirk's family was there. His friend Jerry Williams was the best man. Little Johnny Hicks, Marion's son, was the ring bearer. And on December 5, 1954, a Catholic priest presided over the nuptials. Later, Hicks threw them a party back at the Thunderbird.[3]

Kirk was thirty-seven; Jean was twenty-three.

A s Kirk once again was feeling lucky in love, he tried to extend that streak into business, this time the gambling business. A surge in new casino openings promised to make 1955 the biggest year ever for Las Vegas expansion. Some friends were offering to let Kirk buy in to one of the new ones—he could own a percentage of the Dunes.

Originally envisioned as the Middle Eastern–themed Araby, the Dunes opened beneath a roof-mounted and lighted thirty-five-foot fiberglass figure of a sultan. It was on prime property kitty-corner across the Strip from the Flamingo. It boasted the widest stage in town—room for forty chorus girls—and the country's biggest swimming pool. What it didn't have, apparently, was experienced casino management and seasoned resort staff.

The timing was unfortunate, too. Four other hotel-casinos opened within a matter of weeks, with two more in advanced stages of development. There was a glut in the making. *Life Magazine* published a cover story questioning whether Las Vegas was growing too fast. One headline asked: "Is Boom Overextended?"[4]

All the new resort operations struggled that summer. Still, Kirk submitted an application to state gaming regulators seeking approval to buy 3 percent of the Dunes. He was willing to pay up to $150,000. He listed himself as an airplane dealer and easily passed regulatory review. After an investigation, Kirk was authorized to buy his first casino point (a one-percentage share) for $50,000. But the business was too far gone to be salvaged by his late investment.

If timing is everything, this deal had nothing going for it. "They were in such bad shape," Kirk later conceded.

The Dunes managed to stay open (unlike some others), but it went through a rapid series of ownership changes that left Kirk's equity share absolutely worthless. The good news for Kirk was that he lost only $50,000. But it was a bitter lesson. "I learned then not to invest in a business that I didn't run."[5]

Friends say the Dunes debacle even put a damper on Kirk's enthusiasm for big casino nights, at least for a time. But there were other possible explanations as well—for example, his new life with a new wife. And Kirk's air charter service was surging with new business. Business risks may have satisfied some of his gambling urges. He also became an avid sports bettor. And with friends in the casino business, Kirk remained a familiar figure on the Strip.

Despite the costly failure of his first foray into casino ownership, Kirk still harbored private ambitions to gamble again on the gambling business.

9

JACK MAGIC
AND THE BLADE

INAUGURATION DAY, 1961
WASHINGTON, D.C.

Politics had never been an interest or concern of the apolitical Kirk Kerkorian. Friends said that "if forced at gunpoint" to declare a party affiliation, he would probably say he leaned Republican. But in the 1960 presidential race, Kirk supported the young Democrat from Massachusetts, John F. Kennedy. It was, at least in part, a business decision.

Kirk was doing very well financially, but the charter business was often at the mercy of federal rules changes. One day the CAB was encouraging competition with bigger commercial carriers, the next it was protecting those same carriers. Sometimes, the frustration drove Kirk to contemplate cashing out of the business.

In that election year, however, he had been persuaded that a Kennedy administration might improve matters, that it might be more sympathetic to American charter operators. Kirk was also impressed with the senator's heroic war record. And at forty-three they were the same age, their birthdays only eight days apart. So the kid evicted from Weedpatch decided to bet on the kid who summered in Hyannis Port.

It probably helped that one of Kirk's new friends in Las Vegas was singer-actor Frank Sinatra, a regular at the Sands Hotel with his "Rat Pack," who happened to be a big Jack Kennedy backer. Kirk made a campaign donation sufficiently generous to score an invitation with wife Jean to the Kennedy inauguration celebrations.

Kirk and Jean were part of the crowd in tuxedos and gowns filing into the Washington Armory that snowy night before Kennedy's formal swearing-in ceremonies in January 1961. The star-studded Kennedy Inaugural Gala, a preinaugural ball, was organized and headlined by Sinatra. He crooned one of his standards to lyrics specially revised for the occasion: "That old 'Jack' magic that you weave so well . . ."[1]

The next day, a memorably cold and blustery winter morning in Washington, Kennedy famously proclaimed, "ask not what your country can do for you . . ."

Of course, Kirk was asking his country for a small favor—as he saw it, a chance to compete fairly with bigger commercial airlines. And there was no need to ask what he could do for his country. Besides his own heroic war service, Kirk's efficient little airline was contributing to the economy and to the nation's increasingly robust transportation system. His fleet had even helped the Eisenhower administration a few years earlier evacuate refugees fleeing strife-torn Hungary.

All the glamour and power brokers on display during those historic few days in the nation's capital had to mark a high point in Kirk's social life. He was seated with the elite of American society and politics. The junk-plane-dealing son of an illiterate Armenian farmer was sharing the same smoke-filled ballroom with a scion of the wealthiest and most influential of New England families. But Kirk came away disappointed.

"It was a waste of time and money," he told friends,[2] a specific reference to his lobbying campaign. In the end, he considered the

Kennedy administration no more friendly to his business interests than the previous bunch. Worse, he felt misled when promises were not kept. As a man of his word, Kirk naively expected politicians and their people to keep theirs.

Afterward, he declared himself "done with politics." Even the inaugural ball had annoyed him. Kirk complained that the handsome new president was a flirt who spent far too much time that evening "keeping his eyes on Jean."[3]

Six years into their marriage, Kirk and his beautiful young wife had a two-year-old daughter, Tracy, and a thriving business. Los Angeles Air Service had expanded to operate out of Burbank and Los Angeles, and adopted a new name—Trans International Airlines (TIA)—reflecting its more ambitious global intentions. Kirk had also added a maintenance operation center at suburban Hawthorne Airport. Business was good. He was making an annual income in the range of $300,000 to $350,000.

And he was bored.

The steady growth of LAAS/TIA had thrust Kirk into realms of affluence he could barely have imagined while selling two-cent newspapers on the streets of Los Angeles or clearing brush in the Sierras for a dollar a day. Nonetheless, he was still looking for new challenges, new risks, new thrills.

One of Kirk's guilty pleasures was sports betting. He especially loved wagering on professional football or boxing matches around the country. It often meant placing bets outside the legal sanctuary of Nevada. And that meant dealing with illegal gaming figures. Bookies. Guys with arrest records. Guys with "reputed mobster" in their press descriptions. Guys with monikers like "the Blade."

At the same time, Kirk's search for new and more interesting challenges was drawing him back to the fringes of the boxing world. A United Press International story published in April 1959 disclosed that Kerkorian, "a wealthy Los Angeles aviation executive," was considering buying the contract of a British fighter named Brian London—that is, if London did well in an upcoming bout against American Floyd Patterson.[4] The 204-pound Brit, described as "an aggressive mauler" with a face like a battered Elvis Presley, was knocked out fifty-one seconds into the eleventh round, and Kirk's interest apparently collapsed at the same time.

Kirk's name appeared again in 1960 press reports that he had taken over management of dethroned welterweight champion Don Jordan of Los Angeles. Kirk told reporters he was working to arrange a rematch with the new champ, Benny "the Kid" Paret of Cuba, who had beaten Jordan soundly in a unanimous decision at the convention center in Las Vegas.

However, a few weeks later the California State Athletic Commission yanked Jordan's state boxing license for "actions detrimental to the best interest of boxing." Jordan had acknowledged an earlier friendship with Mickey Cohen, a reputed Los Angeles mobster described by the Associated Press as "an ex-gambler."[5] But the fighter insisted that friendly association was long over. Kirk publicly championed Jordan's reinstatement and assured reporters that his man's personal life was beyond reproach. Jordan was finally reinstated seven months later, and in March 1961 he faced another former champion also trying to rehabilitate his career—Carmen Basilio.

Kirk was in the audience at War Memorial Auditorium in Syracuse that snowy night on March 11[6] when his protégé and rehab project went ten rounds only to lose by a unanimous decision. It wasn't official, and he would lose a few more fights, but that night Jordan's boxing career was over. So was Kirk's flirtation with a new career as a boxing manager. It was not, however, the end of his gambling on fights.

The next big event in the boxing world of 1961 was the rematch and grudge fight between dethroned welterweight champion Kid Paret and new champ Emile Griffith. The fight was set for September 30 in Madison Square Garden. Kirk liked Griffith, who had knocked out Paret to seize the crown back in April.

This time, both fighters were still standing at the final bell. But after fifteen rounds, Paret looked like the loser—bleeding from the mouth since the fifth round, with a bloody cut under his left eye and with both eyes badly swollen. Griffith looked untouched, not a mark on his face. But on a split decision Paret was declared the winner.[7]

And Kirk owed his bookie $21,300.

Five days later the phone rang at the Kerkorian residence in Beverly Hills. The operator said, "I have a call from Mister George Raft." Kirk knew it wasn't really Raft, the movie actor. It was a code name for Charles "Charlie the Blade" Tourine, Kirk's friend and bookie, known by the alias "Charles White." Kirk owed him the twenty-one grand and had been expecting his call. The question was where to send the money.

Tourine, whose criminal record included bootlegging and gambling convictions in New Jersey, wanted a check sent directly to him. Kirk offered instead to fly to New York and deliver the money in person. It would be best, Kirk suggested, if the bookie's name did not appear on the check—not even his endorsement on the back.

"The heat is on," Kirk tried to explain.[8] It was a possible reference to law enforcement crackdowns on illegal gambling, but also an indication that Kirk may have known something of "Charles White's" true notoriety. Tourine was known in some circles, including among federal investigators, as a mob enforcer for Vito Genovese.

It was finally agreed. Kirk would send the $21,300 check via airmail special delivery to George Raft at the Warwick Hotel in Manhattan. The understanding was that Raft the actor would endorse the check and turn the funds over to Charlie the Blade. No one would ever know that Kirk the aviation executive had any dealings with a bookie or a mob lieutenant or whatever he was with his ties to Vito "the boss of the bosses" Genovese.

No one would know except . . . the FBI. A court-approved wiretap on Tourine's phone had just captured and recorded every word of his conversation with Kirk.

10

A CRAPSHOOTER'S DREAM

EARLY 1962
NASSAU COUNTY, LONG ISLAND

K irk had been uncomfortable writing a check that might link him officially with Charlie the Blade Tourine, but at least paying a gambling debt didn't make him a partner. It didn't put Kirk in business with any of Charlie's shady associates. Kirk was having bigger doubts, however, about what he was doing riding along with his bookie buddy to meet a banker of sorts, a guy with access to a lot of cash—a vending machine tycoon.

So far it was just a shopping trip. Kirk was under no obligation. Neither was the guy with all the coin. Still, Kirk wrestled with whether he should even be here.

His latest brainchild was a big, bold, and risky plan that could make or break his charter business—stakes perversely big enough to excite the small-business owner. With commercial airlines all switching their fleets to jetliners, Kirk wanted his to be the first supplemental service to own one. He wanted to buy a state-of-the-art four-engine jet-propelled DC-8. And for that he needed at least . . . . $5 million.[1]

It turned out to be an especially difficult challenge. Kirk could buy a perfectly fine prop plane on the glutted used-plane market for a million to a million and a half. That was more easily in Trans International Airline's range. Its net annual profits hovered around a quarter of a million dollars. But TIA's corporate value was far from sufficient to secure a loan in the stratospheric neighborhood of $5 million.

Commercial banks were particularly leery of edging out on any limb with supplemental air carriers for fear the CAB might abruptly change its rules and shut down a profitable route or service. Regulators had done just that to TIA's California-Hawaii service the year before.

Kirk was getting signals from just about everyone that he might be out of his league, that even if his idea was sound, it was not financially feasible given his limited resources. So, he was out meeting people, testing the market, shopping for cash, riding out to visit Harold Roth at his Long Island residence near Hewlett Bay Park with Charlie the Blade.

Roth owned a tool-making firm, ran an East Coast vending machine empire that sprawled to St. Louis, and made loans through a corporate entity called Valley Commercial Corporation. Some of those loans were shady, as were some of his friends and clientele. One of those was Tourine, a.k.a. the Blade, a.k.a. Charles White, Kirk's friendly and well-connected bookie.

In arranging the meeting with Kirk, Tourine made it clear to Roth what mattered most: "He's a very good friend of mine." The emphasis was less on business than on personal favors. "He's a very nice guy. I like him a lot," he told the vending machine executive. So Roth opened his door, shook hands with Kirk, and invited him to make his pitch.[2]

The key to Kirk's grand plan was to go all in with TIA as a defense contractor. Since 1959 when the company landed its first government bid—ferrying U.S. soldiers and their families to North Africa—military business had become a steady and reliable source of revenue. But that wouldn't last if TIA had to compete with jets moving troops and cargo twice as fast as his prop planes.

Kirk also reasoned that if his company was the first supplemental airline with jets, he could sew up all the government business he could possibly handle and take a giant leap ahead of his competitors.

It wasn't exactly a crapshoot, but it was a crapshooter's dream—a big risk for a big payout. But Kirk wasn't taking a wild guess or betting on chance. He knew the business. He saw the expansion of U.S. military bases in and around the Pacific. And he was confident that future demand for troops and cargo would translate into strong returns on investment.

Roth listened to Kirk's enthusiastic assessment. Tourine was right. Kirk was a very nice guy. But Roth wasn't sure Valley Commercial could handle such a big investment. And across the coffee table, Kirk wasn't sure he wanted anything to do with Valley Commercial and whatever came with it.

Kirk headed back to California determined to defy the odds and parlay his numerous advantages with people he knew and trusted in the more traditional banking and aviation worlds.

I t was the right move. Back home Kirk's reputation was gold plated. His track record running Trans International, or LAAS, for nearly two decades was the envy of the aviation business. His credit was flawless. He had a loyal friend at the Bank of America. And he had a smart, ambitious idea.

His first stop was Walter Sharp at the Bank of America branch in Montebello—a Kerkorian fan since Kirk's Vail Field flight school days. Sharp said he would try to get his main office to go for a loan up to $2 million. It was no sure thing. It was an amount well beyond a branch manager's independent authorization.

With that request pending, Kirk drove out to Long Beach to look at a plane. He had learned that Douglas Aircraft Company was refurbishing a used jetliner—the very first DC-8 fuselage that came off the assembly line back in 1958: factory number N8008D. It was being upgraded with more powerful engines and reconfigured for passenger and cargo service as a Model 50 Jet Trader.

Kirk wanted *that* plane.[3]

He arranged to pitch his idea to Douglas executive Jackson R. McGowan, a familiar face to Kirk. They knew each other casually, having negotiated a couple of DC-3 deals in the past when McGowan was a Douglas vice president for sales. He was now vice president and general manager of the entire aircraft division where DC-8s were built.

McGowan was skeptical. A supplemental air service paying five million for a jet? Was he serious? But he knew Kirk's reputation. He knew his credit history. He knew his track record. And Kirk's quiet, controlled excitement describing his plans for the Jet Trader made sense. It got McGowan excited, too. There was even an escape hatch, a Plan B. If government contracts were slow or failed to materialize, Kirk could lease the plane to a commercial carrier. The Douglas exec agreed with Kirk—it was a good bet. And he wanted a piece of it.

McGowan crafted a special deal for N8008D (a.k.a. Fuselage No. 1), the upgraded Jet Trader. Kirk came up with some cash. Bank of America came through with the loan of about $2 million. And Douglas Aircraft Company financed the balance—an unprecedented move at the time—of about three million dollars.

On his signature alone, Kirk had assumed a personal debt load of nearly five million dollars. Default would wipe out everything he had built. Failure would give him a taste of his father's desperation back in those final days at Weedpatch.

But Kirk the gambling aviation executive was going all in.

The Jet Trader deal closed in June and Kirk moved quickly. He turned to Glenn A. Cramer, a sales executive at Lockheed and leading figure in the postwar charter business, and lured him over to

TIA—making him president of the company. Cramer's mandate was to keep the meter running on their DC-8, keep it making money.

The big jet's first steady work was flying high-priority military loads from Travis Air Force Base in Northern California to Guam. More contracts followed. And just like Kirk envisioned, TIA was scooping up the cream of new defense contracts. In its first partial year of operation, the Jet Trader single-handedly propelled TIA from earnings of a quarter-million dollars to $1.1 million. The company's net value surged into the multimillions of dollars.

To Kirk's everlasting relief, he managed to avoid sharing ownership of the airline or any of his businesses with the likes of Charlie the Blade or his crowd. He would later acknowledge to a friend that he had on occasion during that period been tempted by unspecified but shadowy moneymen.[4] In this case, history confirms that Kirk did it his way—not only protecting his personal reputation, but also leaning heavily upon it.

As for Harold Roth, the Long Island businessman, he was indicted soon after the Kerkorian meeting. He pleaded guilty to making illegal loans to a Teamsters Union official. He was also sued along with others for $41 million in Brooklyn federal court for looting his own vending machine company.[5] He was further accused of using Valley Commercial to fraudulently transfer funds to his own use. Roth resigned and his companies were placed under court supervision.[6]

There would never be any questions about who controlled Trans International Airlines. It was Kirk's company—lock, stock, and DC-8. That is, until a stodgy old Indiana-based carriage-and-car-making company made him an offer he couldn't refuse.

11

HIS FIRST MILLION

Sherwood Harry Egbert, the president of Studebaker Corporation, had flown out from South Bend, Indiana, to make a deal. He was an athletic, six-foot-four man on a mission—and in a hurry—to save his company through diversification. Studebaker already had a stylish new car called the Avanti and new investments in makers of a commercial ice cream refrigerator and other small appliances. Now Egbert and the board wanted Trans International Airlines.[1]

With the Jet Trader now flying mostly out of Northern California, TIA had shifted its operations center to the San Francisco Bay Area. That's where the man from Studebaker found Kirk. The two men had met before as twentysomething private pilots on some forgotten tarmac in Los Angeles. This time, in their forties, they were sitting down together as young captains of industry.

Kirk had shrugged off the carmaker's initial buyout feelers, but he also said he had time to talk. The aggressive Egbert took that as an invitation to negotiate. He plunged into discussions unaware of what a favor he was doing for the debt-sensitive Kerkorian.

It wasn't that Kirk was worried or even mildly anxious about be-

ing on the hook personally for the $5 million DC-8 owned by his
company. New business with the Military Air Transport Service
(MATS) already exceeded expectations. But big debt deprived Kirk
and TIA of room to maneuver, to take advantage of other investment opportunities, to expand, or to withstand unforeseen economic
slowdowns.

The plane and TIA were insured against a catastrophic accident,
but Kirk was a sitting duck in the event of any business slump. A
forced sale of the Jet Trader under such conditions most likely meant
bankruptcy. Debt is what broke his father four decades earlier. Kirk
pondered ways to minimize his personal exposure to financial ruin.
And then, Studebaker came knocking.

Egbert came prepared to make concessions. Kirk was a classic
self-made entrepreneur who ran his own company. He wasn't going
to relish having a boss. Egbert assured him that Studebaker wanted
Kirk to continue running the air service. Kirk would be a corporate
vice president and the president of Trans International, a Studebaker
subsidiary. Kirk's poker face disclosed nothing.

Egbert said that Kirk would receive more than 120,000 shares
of Studebaker stock, then valued at about $8.25 per share. The deal
would make Kirk a millionaire, at least on paper. Egbert agreed to
a proviso that if stock prices sagged, more shares would be added to
guarantee Kirk's sale price at a floor no lower than $950,000. Stude-
baker also would compensate Kirk with additional annual shares for
managing the operations.

And as Kirk acted the role of "reluctant bride," Egbert wrapped up
his offer with the promise of a brand-new Avanti every year. And, of
course, Studebaker would assume responsibility for Kirk's DC-8 debt.

Kirk had everything he wanted, plus his first million dollars—
and a new Avanti. The total deal was worth about $10 million.

The honeymoon didn't last long. Accountants and executives
in South Bend questioned marketing strategies and even the

smallest expenses. The struggling carmaker—only a few decades re-moved from manufacturing beer wagons for Anheuser-Busch and its Clydesdales—seemed wholly unprepared for competition in the jet age.

The board of directors imposed cost-control measures requiring preapproval by the full board of any TIA expenditure over $50,000. Kirk's accountant, Arnold McGraw, called to raise some practical concerns: "What do I do if there's a plane stranded in Guam, and I need to buy a $400,000 engine right away?" The answer: a long silence. Studebaker accountants had no idea that a DC-8 engine could cost so much. By comparison, a new Avanti engine went for less than $400.

Sometimes Egbert called Kirk directly to complain about costs, or whatever. On one occasion the exchange went something like this:[2]

Egbert: "What the hell do you think you're doing?"

Kirk: "What the hell do you think you know about running an airline?"

After so many years without a boss, Kirk's midlife encounter with supervision and second-guessing turned out to be about as wel-come as a patch of moderate to severe turbulence. But intrusions from South Bend declined as the able Glenn Cramer took on more of TIA's daily operations.

Kirk wanted it that way. He not only trusted and relied on Cra-mer's judgment, but he had also come to appreciate how much more he could accomplish by delegating management decisions. Besides, Kirk had a new passion—gambling on empty tracts of sand, other-wise known as investing in Las Vegas real estate.

To commute regularly between the Bay Area and Las Vegas, Kirk needed a plane. Studebaker owned everything in the TIA fleet, so it was time to buy his own set of wings. He found a twin-engine Cessna 310. Kirk's first private plane was a sleek five-seater that cost him $50,000—almost as much as he'd paid for his entire airline back in 1947.

Coincidentally, perhaps, $50,000 was also how much he might

wager in a night or on a single roll of the dice, though Kirk's casino gambling had changed markedly in the years since the Dunes investment failure. He was more patient now, more disciplined, no longer inclined to chase his losses. The new Kirk came with a plan: whether winning or losing, he walked away once he made his intended bets.

He still relished big risks. And he subscribed to the logic of his friend and casino owner Wilbur Clark of the Desert Inn: "The smaller your bet, the more you lose when you win."[3] Besides, what's the point—where's the thrill—winning a small wager? Betting the limit became Kirk's trademark.

He took a similar approach in real estate investing. After receiving nearly a million dollars in stock from Studebaker at the end of the year in 1962, Kirk turned around and invested most of that fresh income—$960,000—on eighty acres of sand and brush. The property was a potentially prime location near the Dunes and across the Strip from the Flamingo. The trouble was a cluster of small lots along the boulevard held by individual owners and blocking Strip access. Those small lots were unbuildable, but an eighty-acre lot without frontage on the Strip resembled an even bigger white elephant.

"We were taking a gamble,"[4] Kirk agreed. But the gambler had a plan. His cash purchase offer was still in escrow when he engaged those owners of small lots in separate negotiations. He offered generous property swaps—as much as four or five acres for virtually useless little plots—that improved everyone's land value, especially Kirk's.

No sooner had Kirk taken title to the land now fronting on the Strip than a motel developer from Atlanta rode into town. He was shopping for his own piece of the Vegas gaming market and wanted to build a Roman-themed hotel and casino. He called it the Desert Cabana and guaranteed it would be the biggest and most opulent joint in town. He wanted it on that big corner lot across the highway from the Flamingo.

Jay Sarno, the maestro behind upscale motel developments from Georgia to California, already had financing lined up through personal friendships with Teamsters Union president Jimmy Hoffa and Teamsters Central States Pension Fund honcho Allen Dorfman.

Now he needed to win over Kirk Kerkorian, the Strip's newest landowner.

They met over dinner on a summer night in 1963. The slim, fit Kirk with his wavy black pompadour had come to listen. The stocky, balding Sarno had come to make a deal. He proposed a lease agreement that would make Kirk a partner in the casino profits. Kirk wanted an old-fashioned lease with monthly payments he could count on in good times or bad. Sarno inhaled his meal and then launched into his pitch: "This is going to be the greatest hotel-casino in the world . . . Everything is going to be topnotch . . . We'll have the finest restaurant, the best entertainers, the most luxurious rooms . . . People won't want to stay anywhere else . . . It can't lose."[5]

Kirk was intrigued but unconvinced. His ill-fated Dunes investment had coincided with the end of a Las Vegas building boom that had remained stalled for nearly a decade. Not only was Sarno daring to end that development drought, but he also proposed to do so with an ultraluxury project that was unlike anything seen before on the Strip.

It was a very big play. Kirk wanted to hear more.

They agreed to meet a couple of days later on the Dunes's new golf course. Kirk preferred tennis. He considered golf a waste of time and a poor excuse for exercise. But from most of the lush fairways, golfers could gaze out beyond the greenery across open desert and see Kirk's empty lot. Sarno could stop, gesture with his arms and hands to fashion a make-believe high-rise hotel there . . . a swimming pool and cabanas over there . . . and through the magic of his imagination and the force of his enthusiasm pull Kirk ever deeper into his dream.

"I've done this before," he assured Kirk, citing the wide range of his investors—from actress Doris Day to the Teamsters pension fund.[6]

Kirk agreed to compromise. Final terms of the deal would take months to negotiate, but with assurances of a long-term lease in his pocket Sarno had the green light to round up investors for his $20 million project.

Over dinner at a restaurant in Nashville where Jimmy Hoffa was fighting federal jury-tampering charges, the Teamsters president used a cloth table napkin to scribble a note to Dorfman at the pension fund: "Give Jay Sarno $10 million per JH."

Then, traveling to Miami, Sarno tracked down an investment group that specialized in airport hotel developments. Burt M. Cohen, then an attorney for the group, agreed to hear Sarno's proposal and later described the encounter:[7]

"In walks a little fat guy who looks like a penguin, eyes bulging, a roll of plans under his arm and a commitment from the Teamsters and a long-term lease from (Kerkorian)."

It looked like a shaky deal to Cohen—a lot of debt and hefty lease obligations with a sketchy business plan. After his door shut behind the departing Sarno, Cohen dictated a note to one potential investor: "This afternoon I met with Jay Sarno and reviewed his plans for the Las Vegas hotel. I examined the terms of his lease, his loan commitment, and his business plan. If you put one penny into this deal, I promise I'll have you committed to a mental institution."

Undeterred, Sarno moved on, following various dead-end leads to New York and Washington, D.C., before arriving in Baltimore where Nate Jacobson was prominent in the Maryland insurance world. He was also an original owner of the Baltimore Bullets professional basketball team—and a gambler. He agreed to raise the additional $9 million needed for construction. Sarno made Jacobson president of his dream resort.

Back in Las Vegas, Kirk agreed to final conditions. His long-term lease would be subordinated to the Teamsters pension fund loan. Sarno and Jacobson would pay a relatively modest monthly lease of $15,000. Kirk would receive 15 percent of casino profits and have access to his own two-bedroom suite in the new hotel.

It would seem that Kirk was violating his first rule of business—to invest only in ventures he controlled—but he was finally gambling again on the business of gambling.

Members of the Armenian community of central California were among the first to learn about the deal. On September 13, 1963, the *Fresno Bee* reported that Fresno-born Kirk was providing the land for a multimillion-dollar hotel and nightclub on the Strip tentatively called the Desert Cabana.

Construction was still more than a year and a couple of name changes away. The Desert Cabana would become the Desert Palace but eventually open as Caesars Palace. Kirk was a partner and land-lord, licensed by the state gaming commission. The Gambler was now the House.

Kirk's biggest worry: if Caesars failed, he and the Teamsters pension fund might have to step in and save it. Kirk could end up largely responsible for running a failed hotel and casino. He wasn't ready for that . . . and he knew it.

THE ARMENIAN CONNECTION

EARLY IN 1963
THE TROPICANA HOTEL, GOURMET ROOM

When Kirk and Jean Kerkorian arrived for dinner that night it caused the usual buzz among the service staff. Kirk was known up and down the Strip, in the casinos and the restaurants, as a generous tipper. His table was in a section served by a Persian-Armenian waiter named Emmanuel, an immigrant by way of Chicago. Everyone called him Manny. He greeted the couple with a confident air, saw to their immediate needs, and withdrew to afford them maximum privacy.[1]

Manny was a pro. He had trained in the Pump Room at the Ambassador East Hotel on Chicago's State Street. He started as a busboy and worked his way up to waiter while studying math and engineering at nearby Roosevelt College. His old Pump Room boss now ran the Tropicana's popular Gourmet Room. Manny followed him to Las Vegas where his salary almost supported a wife and two small children. He made a little extra giving private tennis lessons on the Tropicana's courts.

This was Manny's first time serving the tanned and polite Armenian businessman and his blond and friendly wife. Kirk liked a cocktail before dinner—scotch, no ice. His menu favorite was the Dover sole—deboned, please. Manny was especially solicitous to Jean, and he chatted easily with the couple between courses. Kirk wanted to know more about the waiter's Armenian roots.

Manny was born in Tehran to Armenian parents. He left Iran after twice representing his country in the Olympics of 1948 in London and at the 1952 summer games in Helsinki. At age twenty-two he followed his older brother to Chicago where he married, started a family, and never looked back. His Olympic sport: boxing.

Rifle Right Kerkorian was stunned. He had stumbled upon an Armenian two-time Olympic boxer over Dover sole in the most unlikely of places. It was like finding a long-lost cousin. Kirk treated his waiter with more than a generous tip—he embraced Manny Agassi as "my friend."

It was the beginning of a special association that would segue naturally from dining in the Gourmet Room to a few lessons months later on the Tropicana tennis courts and beyond.

Kirk had just discovered tennis. What would blossom into a passion was the perfect physical exercise for a middle-aged businessman. It also suited his appetite for competition. And with Manny Agassi, his tennis instruction came with shared tales from their fighting days in the ring. In fact, both men recognized striking similarities between singles tennis and boxing.

Tennis has been called "boxing without the blood."[2] Both sports feature two solitary athletes facing each other alone, relying equally on power and finesse, swinging gloved fists or rackets until one wins and the other loses. Both men savored such lonely struggles. And the friends shared a powerful self-confidence that extended well beyond the lines of any sport.

It was Manny's fighting skill that would endear him even more to Kirk and Jean in the months after their first encounter. Manny happened to be walking past the Riviera Hotel one afternoon when he noticed someone in the window of the cocktail lounge waving urgently for his attention. It was Jean Kerkorian.

Moments later Manny was at her side. Jean, in obvious distress, had been having lunch alone while waiting for Kirk in the lounge. She pointed to two men at the bar a few steps away. They were young, drunk, and lewd. "Manny, they're bothering me," she whispered. One of them still sat facing Jean, his legs splayed, zipping and unzipping his fly and leering at her.

Both men were bigger than Manny. In Iran he had fought as a featherweight. More than a decade later, he was still a lightweight compared to the pair of six-footers. Manny stood five foot five. Maybe. But he wheeled around to confront them. He got their attention shadowboxing as he approached—firing off a lightning-fast sequence of menacing jabs that eventually stopped just short of their startled faces.

"Turn your ass around and zip up," he barked.

Then, lowering his voice, he warned the men in a cold and convincing tone, "I'm going to knock the shit out of you. I will put you on the floor and you will crawl out of here with ten thousand dollars in dental expenses." The drunks zipped up and scrambled for the nearest exit.

Jean asked Manny to stay until Kirk could join them. A short time later, she was calm and relaxed when her husband arrived. Kirk's seething anger over his wife's rude treatment by those strangers was matched by his enormous gratitude to Manny—gratitude that would last a lifetime.

Kirk would later take Manny aside. He was hardly a boastful man. Friends and competitors alike invariably described him as humble and gracious. But after his new Armenian friend rescued Jean at the Riviera lounge, Kirk shared the rarest of insights into his own very private ambitions, "Manny, I'm going to be a big man in this town, and you're always going to have a good job."

For his part, Manny honored their friendship by naming his next child after Kirk: *Andre Kirk Agassi*. The baby that came home from the hospital to find a tennis ball dangling over his crib would grow up to make tennis history bearing the middle name of his father's Armenian friend.

Kirk's Armenian connections were growing in his aviation business, too. After selling Trans International Airlines to Studebaker in 1962, he was introduced to an enterprising young stock trader from Fresno with an eye on Kirk's fat portfolio of Studebaker stock. George Mason, whose grandfather had changed the family name from Elmassian, sent one of his cousins as an emissary to get an audience with Kirk.

The cousin happened to be the most famous Kerkorian of that day—Gary Kerkorian (no relation to Kirk), an All-American football quarterback who took Stanford to the Rose Bowl in 1952. He later played for the Pittsburgh Steelers and Baltimore Colts. Gary was already a friendly acquaintance of Kirk's after they met during a 1960 gathering of Armenians in Los Angeles. Kirk agreed, of course, to meet with Gary's cousin George Mason.

Mason at age thirty-two was a very busy man. In Fresno, he represented the San Francisco trading firm Schwabacher and Company, was a night school law student, and published a weekly English-language Armenian newspaper called the *California Courier*. But after prematurely advising Schwabacher executives about his personal connection to the Studebaker stockholder, Mason was chagrined to learn that his boss had made a personal call on Kirk. George was getting "big footed."

In a follow-up wire, boss Albert Schwabacher described his contact with Kirk: "Just had a friendly chat. He's a very nice fellow. Spoke highly of you. We'll take it from here."

Mason hadn't even met Kirk yet, but he was already getting shoved aside. He also was behind with Schwabacher accountants— taking salary advances against yet-to-be-earned commissions. Mason chose a bold response. He immediately called Kirk, invoked the name of cousin Gary Kerkorian, and said he wanted to handle Kirk's Studebaker stocks.

Always open to doing business with friends—if the business seemed like a good idea—Kirk asked how the brokerage relationship would work. He wasn't eager to make trips to Fresno delivering paperwork every time he sold a block of stock.

"Absolutely not," Mason reassured him. "All you have to do is put the order in through me." Stock certificates and transaction paperwork could all be exchanged at the office in San Francisco near where Kirk maintained a residence.

"Then I'll tell you right now, that's the way I'll do it."

Mason could finally breathe again. Kirk's reputation as a businessman who kept his word was already well established, enough to further embolden Mason. He immediately wired his head office on Market Street: "Spoke to my friend, Kirk, and he assures me that he will let us handle the business through me at this office. I'll take it from here."

The call to Kirk had taken only a few minutes, but through that brief exchange George (Elmassian) Mason had picked up more than an investment client. He had just gained lifetime admission to the Kerkorian inner circle.

Kirk's sale of Studebaker stock began in 1963. It had to be handled . . . delicately.

He summoned Mason to San Francisco where the broker checked in to the elegant Fairmont Hotel atop Nob Hill. When his room phone rang the next morning, it was still dark in San Francisco, but Kirk was already downstairs waiting in the hotel coffee shop. The New York Stock Exchange was about to open on the East Coast, and Kirk's goal was to cash in more than a hundred and twenty thousand shares of Studebaker. And it had to be accomplished without inciting a sudden sell-off that could send share prices plunging.

On the phone in a room overlooking the city, Mason placed

orders in small increments—a few thousand in one hour, another
ten thousand a little later. Prices fluctuated in the low-to-midseven-
dollar range with each sale authorized by a nod from Kirk. The
plan was working, but it was a very slow process. Mason returned
to Fresno, and Kirk had business in Los Angeles, but each day they
resumed phone contact for three-way conversations with the trading floor in New York. Nearly two weeks after the sell-off began,
Kirk still had thirty-five thousand shares left. The trading specialist
Mason had been using at the NYSE offered to buy the remaining
lot for a lump sum.

"Dump it all," Kirk said.

Mason had no idea what Kirk had in mind, but he figured his
new client must be getting ready to make some sort of major move.
One thing was clear by the end of the year: Kirk had cashed out of
Studebaker just in time.

The carmaker was in free fall. It was on track to lose $16 million
in calendar year 1963—and that was despite the fact that TIA and
several other nonautomotive subsidiaries were all profitable. In December the struggling company announced it was closing its South
Bend plant, eliminating thousands of jobs, and moving all Studebaker car production to Canada.

Kirk's boss, Sherwood Egbert, who was also undergoing debilitating cancer surgeries, was ousted as president and replaced by a
senior bean counter and former bookkeeper, Byers A. Burlingame.
Behind the scenes Burlingame had authorized quiet inquiries with
potential buyers of the company's various subsidiaries. He was especially eager to get out of the airfreight and charter business.

Frank Sinatra and Barron Hilton, the son of hotel mogul Conrad
Hilton, were approached as potential buyers of TIA. Nothing came
of those efforts, but talks with Robert Six, founder of Continental
Airlines, were getting serious when Kirk intervened. He refused to
approve any merger or takeover involving Continental, a unionized
airline, complaining that it would have cost most of his nonunion
TIA employees their accrued seniority.

"I can't do that," Kirk protested to the Studebaker board of directors. He insisted that TIA crews be protected. "They've come this far with me, and I can't sell them out that way."

He offered instead to buy it back. Besides, his original deal with Studebaker included an approval-of-purchaser clause. Kirk flew to Indiana and launched negotiations with Burlingame. The new president had just started selling off everything from idled factory machinery to corporate subsidiaries in a desperate campaign to slash Studebaker debt. Kirk left South Bend with a $150,000 option to buy back TIA for $2.5 million cash.

With Studebaker in its death throes, it was a good deal for everyone. However, Kirk still needed Walter Sharp and Bank of America to finance the deal with a $2 million loan. It was granted only after a split vote of the skeptical loan committee and after Kirk put up every piece of property he owned as collateral. Kirk was once again flirting with financial ruin. He covered the rest of the cash deal with most of his personal savings.

By September 1964, after less than two years under Studebaker control, Trans International was back under the direct ownership of Kirk with his managing partner, Glenn Cramer. They promised to expand TIA service and make it even more profitable.

The year 1964 would be a year of many landmarks for Kirk. He had negotiated his Las Vegas lease deal with Jay Sarno for the Caesars Palace land only days after his mother, Lily, had died in January. That fall, just as press reports announced his repurchase of TIA, Kirk had to bury his father, Ahron. The Kerkorian siblings naturally assumed their roles as family elders. But it was Kirk, the youngest, on whom they all relied for financial and familial leadership.

He remained especially close to sister Rose, the diminutive and blunt-spoken mother of two, who idolized her little brother. Her ex-husband had complained in divorce filings that he had always suffered by comparison to Kirk. During Kirk's extended residence in Las Vegas, he bought Rose a home on the Las Vegas Country Club's eleventh tee, not far from his own. She filled it with an enormous doll collection. It seemed a poignant response to her deprived childhood.

"We didn't have toys like children do now," she said, recalling having few playthings aside from "chickens and ducks."[3]

In Las Vegas she played at the roulette wheel and slots with decidedly mixed results. Once when she double-downed at the blackjack table in an almost certain losing situation, her friend Gene Kilroy exclaimed: "Rose, what are you doing!" She replied with a shrug, "I'm giving my brother some of his money back."[4]

Since their teen years Rose had always been Kirk's confidante and sounding board, one of the few people he trusted with his secrets—personal or professional. She had been Kirk's first partner in Los Angeles Air Service. And she knew before anyone, even before Kirk's Armenian broker in Fresno, that a much bigger wager was coming.

Kirk was ready to open TIA to Wall Street investors—his nearly two-decade-old charter business would be the first supplemental airline ever taken public.

Trans International Airlines—now with a pair of DC-8 Jet Traders, two Constellations, and assorted other planes in its relatively small fleet—was barely known outside the aviation industry. Still, it was well run. Profits and revenue were steadily growing. And it paid its bills.

In San Francisco, Albert Schwabacher agreed to consider underwriting TIA's public offering. But after careful consideration, he finally told Mason, "Well, George, probably not."

Mason hated bringing such bad news, but Kirk seemed indifferent. He said that another brokerage was interested, too. Mason studied Kirk's poker face. Not a clue. He was pretty sure that claim was an exaggeration. Nonetheless, Mason seized the opening and rushed back to gain Schwabacher's hasty reconsideration. It worked. In April 1965, TIA stock went on the market.

And investors yawned.

It was, at best, a modest beginning. TIA stock opened at $10.375 per share, dropped to $10, and didn't move for weeks. In occasional spurts of trading, it sold in a narrow range—up or down no more than a dollar from its original offering.

One of TIA's earliest investors was a precocious recent high school graduate from Encino named Mike Milken. He was at the time working for an investor before starting college at Berkeley and had met Kirk through business associates of the boy's family. Milken's father was a prominent accountant and financial adviser in the San Fernando Valley.[5]

But what finally started moving the stock were Kirk's Armenian connections.

Kirk had already been getting a lot of press attention in the pages of Mason's *California Courier*. The airline-owning Armenian may as well have owned a fleet of flying carpets. To the *Courier's* readers, Kirk was an Armenian celebrity nearly on a par with J. C. Agajanian, the race car owner and designer whose team had two years earlier won its third Indianapolis 500.

Mason promoted TIA stock sales to fellow Armenians he knew through the newspaper. It was as if the entire Armenian community was getting an inside tip about a sure thing. It was hardly that, but favorable word spread. Armenians started buying. After two quarters of sluggish sales, a surge in the third quarter was almost entirely Armenian driven. Stock prices doubled, then tripled. TIA business boomed, making Mason look like a prophet. TIA stocks split two for one. One Armenian farmer from Fresno—who like so many other San Joaquin Valley Armenians invested in Kerkorian's airline—named a farm he bought with those profits the "TIA Ranch."

In a matter of months, Kirk had paid off the $2 million bank loan with which he had bought back TIA from Studebaker. Kirk himself was now sitting on stock worth more than $66 million, a vast fortune by any measure. And no one was more surprised than he was.

"I thought after the war, 'God, if only I could get up to having fifty thousand, that would be great.' Then it was a hundred thousand. It just kept going," Kirk would recall.

"A lot of people ask me, 'Did you have any idea that you would do this?' The answer is: Absolutely zero!"[6]

II

THE
MAKING
OF A
BILLIONAIRE

"WHEN YOU'RE A SELF-MADE MAN YOU START
VERY EARLY IN LIFE . . . YOU GET A DRIVE THAT'S
A LITTLE DIFFERENT, MAYBE A LITTLE STRONGER,
THAN SOMEBODY WHO INHERITED."

—KIRK KERKORIAN

13

TROUBLE WITH MOBSTERS

DECEMBER 29, 1966
LAS VEGAS, NEVADA

On a chill winter day the somber crowd filing into St. John the Baptist Greek Orthodox Church could have just stepped from the pages of a Damon Runyon tale or the cast of *Guys and Dolls*. It was a mix of swells in silk blend suits, down-and-outs with holes in their soles, reformed rumrunners, unreformed bookies, blackjack dealers, bar girls, celebrities, politicians, mobsters, newspaper reporters, casino owners, cops, and croupiers—in other words, a cross section of Las Vegas society.

With the exception of a couple FBI agents filming the parade of arrivals from an unmarked car across the street, everyone there was paying respects to the memory of one Nicholas Dandolos, better known on the Strip and around the world as the professional gambler "Nick the Greek."[1]

Kirk was there, too. He hated funerals, but he had a reserved seat for this one. He was a pallbearer. He also helped pay for the ceremony and the burial plot. A lot of people had chipped in to rescue Nick's earthly remains from a pauper's grave and provide him a royal send-off.

Years earlier, long before the massive heart attack that killed him at age eighty-three, Nick Dandolos had gone bust. It was a familiar end for lifelong gamblers. He died living alone in a small Beverly Hills apartment—the kind of lonely existence in the end that no one plans for or even cares to contemplate. But everyone in the town where he gambled had a soft spot for the old man.

In many ways, Nick the Greek could have been a role model for Kirk. Both men were gentlemen gamblers—suave, gracious, and good-looking. Both were generous tippers. Both faced winning and losing with the same serene demeanor. Both regarded money with a certain indifference. It was a stake, not the measure of a man's character or genuine worth. Or, as Nick would say whether collecting winnings or shrugging off a loss, "It's only money."[2]

Nick also set an example performing random acts of charity,[3] details of which he routinely kept secret. He shared little about his personal life, even with his most trusted friends. No one ever knew where Nick got the millions of dollars he ultimately lost at the tables, no one, including the other pallbearers like casino owner Benny Binion. And Binion once asked. "He wouldn't tell me!"[4] Kirk, of course, considered the question impolite.

The standing-room-only crowd of mourners gave proof to the notion that the dearly departed had touched many lives. And over the years, much of his private benevolence had become known. He had funded businesses for hundreds of friends, sent dozens of kids to college, and donated more than half a million dollars to local charities. Everyone remembered how he preached the wisdom of Plato and Aristotle and further endeared himself with good-natured pranks and jokes. "He was a kinky old guy," recalled Binion with affection. "He'd put a snake in your pocket and ask you for a match."[5]

Hank Greenspun, editor and publisher of the *Las Vegas Sun* and another designated pallbearer, eulogized Nick with soaring oratory as a courageous risk taker comparable, he suggested, to the Founding Fathers. He went on to characterize leaders of the American Revolution as "noble gamblers," to defend gambling in general as a metaphor for free enterprise, and he called Nick the Greek one of the great assets of postwar Las Vegas.[6]

According to the publisher, Nick had once been "the reigning king of gamblers." Now, the king was dead, and his realm was looking for new royalty.

If gambling royalty needed a luxury residence, it was getting a new $25 million palace on the Strip. Nineteen sixty-six was the year that Caesars Palace moved from the drawing boards to its construction site on Kirk's property. Work started with plenty of naysayers critical of its projected daily overhead ($40,000), its debt load, its location, and its design. Its unprecedented operating costs meant that Caesars would have to attract the highest of high rollers, the biggest of big players from far and wide and definitely from out of town. It could not expect to survive on local action or the nickel slot players rolling in on a Greyhound.

Kirk was never among the skeptics. He always thought the idea of Caesars Palace was a winner. At the same time, he wanted what he called "a back door" if anything went wrong. If the Sarno team blew it somehow, Kirk needed a Plan B to step in and operate the place . . . to protect his property investment. Construction was barely under way when Kirk reached out discreetly to the boss of the highly efficient and successful Sahara. Despite a prickly personality, Alex Shoofey was supposed to be the best operations man in Las Vegas. He wasn't remotely flattered by Kirk's interest.[7]

"I'm happy doing what I'm doing," Shoofey said. "I'm not going anywhere else."

Kirk patiently wooed him, but Shoofey understandably was a hard sell. Kirk was asking him to leave his $80,000 a year position (among the highest in town) at one of the Strip's best hotels to stand by in case Caesars Palace flopped. And while awaiting that uncertain outcome, Kirk would pay him at the rate of $30,000 a year.

Shoofey wasn't particularly sympathetic with Kirk and his fear that he might get the keys to Caesars. It wasn't Shoofey's problem if Kirk got into something he couldn't handle. Shoofey certainly wasn't dumb enough to take a $50,000-a-year pay cut to sit around keeping company with Kirk.

And then Kirk offered to loan him the $50,000 difference. "That's a stupid proposition!" Shoofey snapped. "You're gonna loan me what I'm already making? That's ridiculous."

Kirk decided it was about time to let the Sahara boss in on what was driving his persistent courtship. It turned out that Kirk's Plan B was a disguise for a much grander scheme. Shoofey was invited on a private cruise of Lake Mead aboard Kirk's new forty-five-foot yacht, the biggest party boat in the marina. It was Kirk doing his impersonation of the freshly minted tycoon. And it was impressive. But the secret he shared with the only other passenger on his boat was even more impressive.

"I intend to build a one-thousand-room hotel in this town," Kirk confided.

A thousand rooms was unheard of on the Strip. Shoofey's Sahara had only four hundred at that time. Caesars Palace would open with no more than seven hundred rooms. Kirk was proposing something to rival the biggest hotels in the world. Such a project could bring dramatic change to Las Vegas. He asked Shoofey to work up a financial analysis projecting the profitability of his dream resort.

"I suppose you want me to do this for what . . . for free?"

Kirk smiled. He knew he had finally reeled in Shoofey.

Alex Shoofey had grown up between orphanages in Montreal and Brooklyn. He was trained as an accountant and worked as the head of payroll for a Manhattan department store before going to war. He ended up in Las Vegas in the spring of 1947.

He was driving back to New York from Los Angeles when his

old Buick blew its engine on Main Street. It was going to cost $1,000 to fix it. Shoofey had paid only $150 to buy it off a used car lot. He couldn't afford to fix it or even to replace it. He checked into a cheap motel and took an accounting job at a new bingo and dice place. The job came with a free meal. He never left. And a Las Vegas hotel management career was born.

It was his self-reliance, blunt honesty, and up-from-the-bottom origins that a self-made millionaire from Weedpatch could especially appreciate.

The grand opening of Caesars Palace was one of the most anticipated events in Las Vegas history. Sarno planned to spare no extravagance. There would be scores of toga-clad women, champagne to fill fifty thousand glasses, Ukrainian caviar, three hundred pounds of Maryland crabmeat, and two tons of filet mignon. Then came bad news on the doorstep. Newspaper headlines from Chicago to Los Angeles alleged secret mob ownership of the newest star on the Strip. Caesars had hoods in the house.

One of the biggest challenges facing any of the legitimate gambling operations in Nevada was finding experienced casino managers without a criminal record. Many an able pit boss or credit manager got his early career experience in illegal gambling joints elsewhere in the country. Nevada offered them a chance "to go legit," but it could be hard to escape their pasts. Then, too, since major mob organizations ran some of the biggest illegal gambling rings in the country, a lot of gamblers were likely to find themselves much closer than six degrees of separation from the unwelcome label "mob associate."

Editions of the *Los Angeles Times* trucked across the Nevada state line on the morning of August 4, 1966, carried a big front-page headline: "Gang Ownership in Casino Charged." The companion story quoted the *Chicago Sun-Times*, alleging not only that Caesars Palace had mob figures in high places, but also that hoodlums were skimming profits at casinos up and down the Strip.

This was troubling news to Kirk. It wasn't news at all to Sarno. When Nate Jacobson was raising the final $9 million to fund Caesars' construction, he had encountered investors willing to make substantial contributions but only if the casino hired their friends and associates, people trusted to protect the investors' interests. Teamsters president Hoffa and the union's heavily invested Central States Pension Fund had their favorites, too. Certain special people were expected to come along with the money, as a condition of investment.

That's how Jerome (Jerry) Zarowitz became Caesars' credit manager and Elliott Paul Price landed a job as a casino host. Zarowitz was a former bookie and noted oddsmaker who did prison time for trying to fix the 1946 National Football League championship game between the New York Giants and Chicago Bears.

Without investing a dime of his own, Zarowitz controlled one-third of Caesars Palace, and he handpicked the entire casino crew— giving the place a certain ambiance that comedian Alan King once said was less Roman than "early Sicilian."[8] Sarno got the clear message that *Mr. Z* ruled the gaming floor and that he had dangerous friends.

In the face of news reports, Caesars partner Stanley Mallin expressed alarm about Zarowitz and what hidden interests he might represent. The harried Sarno cut him off. He didn't care, he said.

"We need the money. We've got to make some concessions."

Mallin persisted, noting that Zarowitz tried to fix games: "He's a crook."

"We're not betting against him," Sarno said. "Relax."[9]

But Mallin didn't relax, and neither did Kirk. More bad headlines were coming. But then a more immediate crisis threatened their grand opening—a nationwide airline strike. High rollers and investors alike were grounded. Kirk dispatched one of his Trans International jetliners to the East Coast. It collected gamblers and financiers and invited guests from New York and Baltimore and delivered them to the Caesars gaming tables in time for a strong opening-night take.[10]

One of those who hopped a ride on the TIA DC-8 was a University of Pennsylvania frat brother of Nate Jacobson's son—a precocious gaming entrepreneur named Steve Wynn. At the age of twenty-four, Wynn was already running his late father's illegal bingo parlors in Maryland. And in Las Vegas, he owned a small interest in the troubled Frontier Hotel, then closed for major renovation. Wynn was married to Elaine Pascal, the daughter of a prominent Miami hotel operator.

The Caesars Palace opening was Wynn's chance to schmooze and mingle with important gaming associates. Jacobson provided the formal invitation and a room behind the pool area. It wasn't quite finished. There were rolls of carpeting in the halls. Wynn's bathroom had no shower curtain. He got a seat at the big opening show with headliner Andy Williams. His was the seat farthest from the stage. But his fortunes turned after tracking down Zarowitz in the casino and introducing himself.[11]

Mr. Z knew Elaine's father, Sonny Pascal. He was also a friend of top management over at the Frontier. And the kid impressed him. They had a drink together. The next day Zarowitz moved Wynn into bigger and better accommodations, complete with a shower curtain. It was room 1066—Jimmy Hoffa's just-vacated suite.

For the quiet and reserved Kirk, who regarded big public events with the same dread that he did funerals, the Caesars grand opening had to be an ordeal to endure. He was especially uncomfortable being the focus of attention. As the landlord and one of the licensed gaming partners, it would have been difficult to avoid introductions to strangers, the inevitable small talk, and the awkward silences.

His usual haunt on such occasions was a corner in the back of a room. But Kirk in this case had a handy retreat—his own private two-bedroom suite. He had it outfitted as an office. It was his favorite perk. But it wasn't comped. It was negotiated under their original lease and partnership contract.

Kirk made it a rule never to accept complimentary food, drink, or other gifts from any company in which he was invested. He had the money. He paid his own way. That's why in private he was more bothered than most by the continuing stream of media stories about casino mob links. He was no prude about gamblers having criminal pasts or nefarious friends. He disapproved of guilt by association. He figured a man should not be held responsible for the mistakes of his friends. But all the press reports about skimming to pay off mobsters posed a threat to public confidence in Nevada gaming generally—and to Kirk and his fellow legitimate investors quite directly.

And there was likely some déjà vu from the decade-old Dunes investment. Kirk never blamed anyone but himself for that bad investment in 1955, but others faulted a toxic combination of mobsters, kickbacks, hidden interest, and poor management. The headlines of 1966 were reminders to Kirk of the perils that arise when management is in someone else's control. At Caesars Palace he was again at the mercy of forces and managers beyond his control.

It had taken Alex Shoofey more than a month to work out financial projections on Kirk's hypothetical one-thousand-room hotel and casino operation. They met to compare notes after the triumphant grand opening at Caesars Palace. It was unchallenged as the hottest spot in town and exceeding all financial expectations.

"I guess you got no worries about Caesars," Shoofey joked. Kirk smiled. He never shared his private worries. The only item on their agenda that day was a rundown on the numbers. Shoofey cut immediately to the bottom line. "It comes to about ten million dollars . . . a year," he said.

Old poker face broke into a big grin. For the next several minutes they bantered about the implications, about economies of scale, about how the numbers would look if the room count was even bigger, about how it might change the hotel business, Las Vegas, and the gambling world at large. Shoofey was swept up in Kirk's enthusiasm. He was surprised to realize that he, too, was getting excited.

"Where would you put a hotel like this?" Kirk asked.

There were possibilities on the Strip, near the airport, downtown—and one that seemed to intrigue Kirk the most. It was about sixty-five acres on the site of a defunct horse track off Paradise Road, well off the Strip but adjacent to the new Las Vegas Convention Center. Ominously, the ill-conceived Landmark Hotel stood empty and uncompleted across the road, but a golf course and country club were planned nearby. Shoofey strongly endorsed Kirk's instincts. A big hotel and the convention center would be natural allies.

A few weeks later, Caesars Palace was back in the news with a front-page report in the *Los Angeles Times* about a new federal grand jury investigation. The U.S. Justice Department was looking into an October 1965 gathering of mobsters in Palm Springs. Two of those named in the account were Caesars executives Jerry Zarowitz and Elliott Paul Price. Others included Anthony (Fat Tony) Salerno and Vincent (Jimmy Blue Eyes) Alo, alleged members of the Vito Genovese crime family in New York.[12]

Mob lawyer Oscar Goodman, the future mayor of Las Vegas, would step in to defend Zarowitz, and no criminal sanctions were ever imposed. But Kirk had already seen enough. Shortly after the grand jury investigation was disclosed in Los Angeles, Kirk moved out of his Caesars Palace office. He still had more than a year on his free lease. Mallin knew what troubled Kirk was "the Mafia, or whatever." He and Sarno understood completely. It was their problem, too.

Kirk was now ready to take full control of his very own Vegas hotel and casino. He hadn't shared the news with anyone but Shoofey and his most intimate insiders. But on the day they buried Nick the Greek, Kirk embraced another confidant—a fellow pallbearer. He asked *Las Vegas Sun* publisher Hank Greenspun to take a ride around town with him. It became a tour of hotel building sites.[13]

The tour ended on Paradise Road by the convention center. Kirk was going to change the face of Las Vegas and he wanted his friend the newspaperman to know what was coming. A month later the news was a headline: "$30 Million Vegas Hotel Near Convention Center."

According to published accounts, Kirk had paid $5 million cash for about sixty-five acres. He planned to break ground on the city's tallest high-rise hotel project later in 1967. The casino would feature the largest gaming floor in Nevada. The hotel would have fifteen hundred guest rooms—making it the world's biggest at the time. Hotel guests would have access to an adjacent country club and eighteen-hole golf course then under development. And at $30 million, Kirk's International Hotel would eclipse Caesars Palace.

The news seemed to wake a sleeping recluse. From seclusion in his penthouse suite at the Desert Inn, billionaire Howard Hughes made his own headlines a few weeks later when he bought the entire hotel for $13.2 million in cash and loans. Then he bought the Sands . . . and the Frontier . . . and more. A buying spree was on.

Kirk had gambled big on Las Vegas real estate and on the gambling business itself. It didn't bother him to have another player at the table. He still held Hughes in high regard. And the superrich businessman's interest reinforced Kirk's own hunch that Las Vegas was a very smart bet.

Political leaders were delighted. Neither Howard Hughes nor Kirk needed unconventional lending sources such as Meyer Lansky or the mobbed-up Teamsters Central States Pension Fund. With illustrious captains of industry investing heavily in the state's gaming business, Nevada was getting what some leading citizens likened to "the *Good Housekeeping* seal of approval."

But in shadows behind those perpetually drawn curtains in his penthouse, Hughes was plotting a one-sided rivalry to undermine Kirk's grand plans. To the hermit billionaire, Las Vegas wasn't big enough for two kings of gambling.

A CLASH OF TYCOONS

Kirk Kerkorian's business fortunes had just taken a sudden turn toward complicated. Not bad. Not yet. Back on Nob Hill in San Francisco he was in secret negotiations for the sale of his airline, Trans International. The deal that a day earlier had promised to put $150 million into the pockets of TIA shareholders—about $100 million of that into Kirk's own—was teetering on the verge of collapse. Kirk and his small team of advisers retreated to his suite at the Fairmont to consider their options.

At the same time in Las Vegas, Kirk was several million dollars into what was widely seen as a risky hotel and casino venture. His plan to build the International Hotel a half mile off the Strip on Paradise Road had old-timers shaking their heads. Common wisdom regarded the project as a potential flop. And not just any flop, but the biggest-hotel-in-the-world kind of flop. Already he was having unexpected trouble getting construction loans. And groundbreaking ceremonies were barely three weeks away. The project needed his full-time attention.

And then there was Howard Hughes.

Kirk tried to ignore the feeling, but he sensed an onerous weight from the famous industrialist's unspoken disapproval of the superlative-rich International Hotel. It would be the biggest, the tallest, the plushest, the costliest . . . and a prominent challenge to Hughes's status as the giant of the Strip. A yearlong $100 million buying spree had made Hughes the owner of five gaming resorts and most of the vacant land along the Strip. And he was still shopping.[1] No one challenged him for the biggest of anything in Las Vegas— except Kirk Kerkorian and his world's biggest hotel with its world's biggest gaming floor. Even its swimming pool promised to be the state's largest man-made body of water after Lake Mead.

No one told Kirk directly that Howard's ego was in a twist. But there were signs. Some local bankers would barely talk to Kirk for fear of offending Hughes.[2] Even Kirk's well-earned loyalty at Bank of America had its limits. The bank declined to finance the International. It didn't make loans to casinos. But Kirk's aides always suspected it was Hughes and a threat to move his billions that chilled those prospects.

Kirk learned from Hughes aide Robert A. Maheu that the billionaire wanted his help lobbying the U.S. Atomic Energy Commission (AEC). Hughes was intent on halting underground nuclear testing in neighboring Nye County, and he had sent off letters of protest and alarm to the AEC and President Lyndon Johnson, among others. Kirk, however, didn't share Hughes's fears or obsession. He simply ignored the Hughes entreaties. In the process, what Kirk still considered a friendly rivalry turned into something darker.

With lending uncertainty plaguing the hotel project, Kirk was under mounting pressure in Las Vegas to delay construction—maybe indefinitely. It was getting late, but no concrete had been poured yet. Kirk had, however, raised expectations. And not just in headlines. He also bought the Flamingo for $12.5 million to use as a training ground for management and staff moving into the International.

Still, without financing for the hotel's construction, he had to reconsider whether he was betting a losing hand. He tried not to let ego cloud his judgment, but even "the Perry Como of the craps tables" would be hard-pressed to conceal the humiliation of a very public bust.

Now, through a quirk of fate, Kirk was gambling on two fronts simultaneously over separate deals, either one of which was big enough to make or break any ordinary financier.

Intermittent rain and patches of fog outside fit the dreary mood inside the Fairmont Hotel suite where Kirk and five advisers conferred in January 1968. The $150 million sale of Trans International Airlines to financial services giant Transamerica had been so close that lawyers on both sides had been summoned to oversee final conditions and formal signatures. Then the New York Stock Exchange (NYSE) refused to recognize a new class of stock central to the Kerkorian side of the deal.[3]

Kirk had wanted a tax-free stock transfer. The deal was fashioned around a convertible, preferred stock in Transamerica that would be more like common stock and retain its tax-free benefits. With a dividend and other sweeteners, this newly crafted equity would be worth 20 percent more than equivalent common stock. It would be a new kind of stock that had never before been traded. And, as it turned out, the NYSE wasn't interested in getting that creative at the moment.

The deal was off as originally negotiated. A final meeting was scheduled for the next morning when both sides could reconvene with any suggestions as to how or whether to proceed. Kirk and Transamerica president John R. Beckett would be across the table from each other one more time.

Kirk's group spent the afternoon gaming out various scenarios. The advisers included two lawyers from Los Angeles, TIA president Glenn Cramer, Walter Sharp from Bank of America, and Fred Benninger, a recent addition to Team Kerkorian from Flying Tiger Airlines where he was general manager and executive vice president.

Benninger, a former accountant, was Kirk's man running hotel development in Las Vegas, but this was a more pressing matter. All five advised Kirk of drawbacks to every option.

Asking Transamerica to increase its stock swap offering by 20 percent to cover Kirk's lost benefits was the most obvious option. But that invited a reduced counteroffer. And any eagerness to get the deal done with a compromise might indicate weakness or worse . . . desperation. That could invite second thoughts, almost certain delay, and put the entire transaction in jeopardy.

Kirk abruptly ended the group analysis. He was going for a walk around the block, he said. No one else moved. No one else was invited. And the door slammed behind him. About thirty minutes passed. It was getting late in the afternoon when the waiting advisers heard Kirk letting himself back into the suite. He had made up his mind.

"We're going to make a deal," he said. The meeting was over. Just how Kirk planned to broach the delicate matter of a compromise, he didn't say. And nobody asked.

The next morning Team Kerkorian was early, as always, arriving as one for an 11 A.M. meeting at Transamerica's headquarters on Montgomery Street. The group was led to a windowless third-floor conference room where men in dark suits waited at a massive oak table. All eyes were on Kirk as he took the chair across from Transamerica's president. He said nothing as his colleagues took their seats. His poker face revealed nothing. Finally, his piercing gaze settled on Beckett. It was a signature moment. With an unreadable look, aides would say, Kirk could make a snowman sweat. In the silence after the last squeak and scuff of a chair, Kirk said: "Well, Jack—I guess we're not going to be able to make a deal."

Kirk stood, scooped up the file folder on the table in front of him, and reached out smiling to shake hands with Beckett.

It had taken Beckett a moment to process what was happening. He may have been expecting Kirk to suggest the most likely alternative—the extra common stock to cover his tax liability. But, no, Kirk was walking out.

"Wait a minute!" The Transamerica president waved off the handshake. "We can give you a deal and give you the same value we talked about."

Kirk sat down. His advisers who were rising to follow him out the door sat down.

Transamerica offered to provide extra common stock to cover Kirk's increased tax liability. Beckett was offering the same terms that Kirk hoped for—terms that might have betrayed weakness had Kirk been forced to request them himself. Now, Transamerica was trying to convince Kirk to take the very deal he'd wanted all along.

Back at the Fairmont bar later that evening one of Kirk's lawyers congratulated him on "playing a helluva poker hand." There was general agreement among the celebrants that Kirk must have ice water in his veins.

"They thought you had aces back to back," chortled attorney Ronald J. Del Guercio. "And all you had in the hole was a deuce. They really thought you were ready to walk out."

Kirk was amused. But if his young lawyer was probing to find out whether Kirk really intended to walk out, he never got an answer. It didn't really matter. Kirk's theory on walking out of negotiations was adaptable to almost any occasion. "You can always walk back in again," he used to say.

Closing the deal left Kirk the single largest shareholder of Transamerica stock. The little charter airline he bought for $60,000 with the help of a $5,000 loan from his sister, Rose, had returned more than $100 million in that one transaction. Kirk could also expect a seat on the TA board of directors.

Shortly before the final signatures on the deal, Beckett took Kirk aside for a heart-to-heart. The historically conservative Transamerica Corporation had a problem with Kirk's heavy involvement in Las Vegas. The gambling business was . . . well, embarrassing to the stodgy bunch in San Francisco. Would Kirk mind putting his TIA man Cramer on the board instead?

In truth, Kirk wanted as little to do with board meetings as possible. The freshly minted megamillionaire from Weedpatch with his eighth-grade education and a budding empire in Las Vegas agreed not to seek his own seat on the board, happy to let Beckett off the hook without so much as a blush.

T urning his attention back to Las Vegas and the challenges of developing the International Hotel, Kirk was hit almost immediately by stunning news. Howard Hughes announced to the local media his plans for a mammoth expansion of the Sands.[4] He proposed a $150 million makeover adding four thousand rooms and a posh transformation of the Sands casino.

"It is our hope that this hotel will be something completely unique and novel," Hughes wrote in a three-page typed news release, "like nothing anyone has ever seen before—a complete city within itself." He promised entire floors dedicated to shops, family amusements, the world's largest hotel bowling alley, and an indoor golf course. In a contest of superlatives, Hughes had emphatically raised the ante.

Well before Kerkorian's project was finished—if that day ever came—the Hughes property would surpass it as the most luxurious . . . the biggest . . . the best . . . the priciest. In fact, the Hughes press release alone could scuttle Kirk's chances. And unbeknownst to Kirk, that was part of the Hughes design all along.

In a separate handwritten note to aide Maheu, Hughes confided: "The disclosure of my new [$150 million] establishment will make it much harder for [Kerkorian] to get financing."[5]

Prospects of a sudden addition of four thousand rooms also raised prospects of a glut that could swamp the entire Las Vegas market. It raised the risk factor especially for Kirk. His planned off-the-Strip giant was considered a pioneering venture and its unprecedented fifteen hundred rooms a likely test of market capacity. Already difficult-to-secure construction financing might have to be shopped among the likes of loan sharks or the mobbed-up friends of Jimmy Hoffa.

An unusually shaken Kirk turned to publisher friend Hank

Greenspun of the *Las Vegas Sun* for counsel. They had a series of evening conversations. The newspaperman was sure his friend had "spent a few sleepless nights worrying about Hughes's new plans." Kirk acknowledged he was pondering whether to fold and walk away from the International, but Greenspun pressed him to call his rival's bluff. Hughes, he said, "doesn't build—he merely buys."[6]

In the end, Kirk bet on that assessment, shoving more of his chips onto the table. Groundbreaking ceremonies went on as planned. Now he needed to raise between fifty and sixty million dollars to complete the project. He flew off to New York with Fred Benninger where more doors were slammed in their faces. They managed to land about half the construction cost closer to home when the Nevada National Bank of Commerce accepted his nearly sixty-five-acre site as collateral. That would get it half-built. Kirk was going to raise the rest on the fly. It was a financial high-wire act—without a net. The International Hotel's grand opening was set for midsummer of 1969.

At the Sands, nothing happened—no architects hired, no plans submitted for approval, no dates set for groundbreaking or completion. After a few months, it was clear that the "unique and novel" Hughes plan was dormant or abandoned. It was, however, a continuing centerpiece of Hughes's campaign to stop Kirk and the International Hotel.

In another note to Maheu, who played tennis with Kirk on occasion, Hughes discussed his latest ploy.

"Please tell Kerkorian that I postponed the new Sands because I learned of the possibility that the (underground nuclear bomb) testing would be resumed in this area on a heavier than ever basis," Hughes wrote.[7] The recluse also wanted Kirk to be convinced that architectural and geological experts were advising Hughes against building high-rise structures while such testing continued.

At 7 A.M. on April 26, 1968, a 1.3-megaton blast—the largest underground explosion recorded to that date—was felt in four states and the Desert Inn penthouse where Hughes said he gripped the sides of his bed in fear. His appeals to President Johnson and the

AEC had succeeded only in delaying the test for forty-eight hours. Now Hughes was hoping to persuade Kirk to suspend construction of the International to show solidarity against the common threat of more bomb tests.

"Please further tell him that the high rise of our Desert Inn, only nine stories, has been very definitely damaged in a number of places," Hughes continued with growing exaggeration, "and that we firmly believe the Mint, the Sahara and the Riviera have also been damaged very seriously."[8]

It wasn't true, but Hughes suggested his aide go even deeper into realms of fiction, telling Kirk the lie that other hotel owners were keeping secret widespread structural damage. Maheu should explain, said Hughes, that the silent owners didn't want to scare away customers fearful that Las Vegas hotels were unsafe and "might come piling down on top of them" from future test-induced quakes.

Kirk kept building.

Howard Hughes had moved into Las Vegas after a midnight arrival by private railcar in late November 1966. He was delivered to the Desert Inn on a stretcher. The town was packed with Thanksgiving holiday gamblers. Hotels were overbooked. It took the personal intervention of Teamsters boss Jimmy Hoffa, making a call to his friend Moe Dalitz who ran the Desert Inn, to free up rooms and the ninth-floor penthouse. The $250-a-night suite reserved for high rollers was available for only ten days. They moved in . . . and stayed . . . and stayed.[9]

When Hughes was still there four months later, Dalitz was fuming and threatening eviction. Hughes was hardly a high roller. He never ventured into the casino. He never left his room. And while his entourage had grown, taking over the top two floors of the hotel, many were Mormons. They weren't big gamblers, nor did they spend big at the bar. So, even with such high occupancy, Dalitz was counting his losses.

For Hughes, who was once treated to a ticker-tape parade in New York for an audacious three-day flight around the world, who once ran the RKO film studios and romanced the most glamorous leading ladies of his day, and who just sold his controlling interest in Trans World Airlines for a staggering personal fortune, the primary goal of his life in March 1967 seemed to be keeping his bed in the Desert Inn. So he bought it—his ninth-floor penthouse and the entire hotel—for $13.2 million.

The transaction turned out to have enormous tax advantages. Hughes had just deposited a check for $546.5 million on that TWA sale—what he called "the largest check that any single individual ever carried out of Wall Street." It was generating passive interest income at such a high rate as a percentage of the billionaire's total income that Hughes faced a twenty percent tax penalty.

But when an infusion of active income from his new Desert Inn casino abruptly shifted the tax math more to his favor, Hughes declared a new investment strategy: "Hell, let's buy them all." Maheu immediately went shopping and by the end of his first year in town Hughes had bought five casinos on the Strip, including the Sands. He was also promising huge financial gifts to the University of Nevada for a medical school, new jobs, and industry to spur the local economy and development of a new international airport capable of handling future supersonic aircraft.

While Hughes was making headlines with every new purchase, Kirk drew only modest attention when in August 1967 he bought the Flamingo. It was a strategic move. He wanted a moderately sized hotel and casino where he could train a staff to run the biggest hotel in the world—once the International was ready for business.[10]

Kirk also was still wooing Alex Shoofey to finally quit Sahara, then one of the most successful hotel and casino operations in the state. The Flamingo purchase provided immediate employment for Shoofey and any staff he could recruit through the next two years while the International was being built.

Shoofey was still a bit skeptical when Kirk offered him a 10 per-cent piece of the Flamingo profits. "Hey, what are you talking about? Ten percent of zero is zero," he protested.[11]

The Flamingo that Bugsy Siegel built in the 1940s had been through various owners, renovations, and expansions, but over the years one thing remained the same—the skim. Payoffs, kickbacks, and underworld favors left big gaps in its profit margin. The Internal Revenue Service, among other federal agencies, was curious enough to be secretly investigating where all that cash was going. They also were tracking a $200,000 "finder's fee" paid to mob financier Meyer Lansky for his behind-the-scenes role in a previous sale of the casino—fees paid through a charitable foundation headed by an unwitting U.S. Supreme Court justice, William O. Douglas. Investigators were closing in.

Kirk didn't know anything about secret federal probes when he penciled out what he thought should be a reasonable rate of return on a well-run Flamingo. He showed Shoofey his numbers, scribbled on a paper napkin. First year projected profit: $1 million. Shoofey's share: $100,000. And beyond the Flamingo was the promise to run the brand-new International, the biggest hotel in the world. Shoofey signed on.

But Kirk's projections proved dramatically wrong. Under Shoofey's management and with the elimination of skimmed casino revenues, Kirk's reorganized Flamingo cleared nearly three million that first year. And it was still growing. It seemed too good to be true—at least to federal investigators who quietly added the name Kerkorian to their persons of interest list.

Meanwhile, Hughes remained the toast of Nevada's political elite. When he needed special considerations from state gaming officials, he counted on Governor Paul Laxalt to declare the favors "good for Nevada."[12] When he needed gaming laws changed to allow corporations to be licensed, the state legislature made it a bipartisan priority.

It never seemed to bother Kirk that he was operating in the shadow of Howard Hughes. He still admired the man, still honored his genius and past contributions as an engineer and intrepid aviator. "He's a mountain; I'm a molehill," the soft-spoken Kirk said.[13]

But such respect was far from mutual. Among thousands of memos scribbled to Maheu, Hughes grumbled that Las Vegas "was fine until the place was invaded by Kerkorian . . . and a few others." He compared the gambling haven to a jungle hill and Kirk to a rival tiger. "It just does not work out to have more than one tiger to each hill."[14]

Hughes offered to buy Kirk's land on Paradise Road just before construction began. Once major work was under way, the billionaire came up with a scheme to trade Kirk the Stardust Hotel (Hughes had an option to buy it at the time), reimburse Kirk for the unfinished hotel's full midconstruction costs, buy the land at full market value, and then scrap the project.[15]

When all manner of financial incentives and bomb-test fearmongering failed, Hughes encouraged Maheu to dangle offers of personal friendship. He even scripted Maheu's lines: "I think [Howard's] friendship, and he has very few friends, is yours for the asking."[16] The script also offered future blockbuster partnerships, suggesting Hughes and Kerkorian might join forces to buy Western Air Lines (WAL) where Hughes was secretly engaged in talks. Kirk demurred again and again. He later professed to be completely unaware of any friction between them, or that they were proceeding on a course that a frustrated Hughes privately lamented "can only lead to a disastrous collision."[17]

In October 1968, with steel girders of the future International Hotel already rearranging the Las Vegas skyline, Hughes invested $20 million in a bankrupt hotel with a seemingly cursed history. The Landmark Hotel had stood empty for eight years, never quite completed, collecting creditors, critics, and dust. What made this monument to financial calamity attractive to Hughes was its location. It was directly across the street from Kerkorian's construction site.

Hughes was setting up to challenge Kirk head-to-head, hotel versus hotel, the Hughes Landmark pitted against the Kerkorian International—a demolition derby of casino owners. The collision on Paradise Road was set for July 1969.

15

A $73 MILLION SIDE BET

Alden W. Clausen, vice chairman of Bank of America, had been a big fan of Kirk Kerkorian since those days shortly after the war when Walter Sharp, his Montebello branch manager, brought the young aviation entrepreneur to the bank's attention. The bank's relationship with Kirk had been mutually profitable for more than two decades—an uninterrupted series of successful loans and repayments that also resulted in friendships transcending business.

They hit a rough patch earlier in 1968 when the bank declined to make a construction loan on Kirk's International Hotel and Casino. Kirk blamed an industry-wide bias against casino lending and harbored no hard feelings.

But on a Friday afternoon late in the year, Clausen was trying his best to be helpful to Kirk in other ways, interceding personally to introduce him to another of the bank's major clients—Terrell C. Drinkwater, hard-charging president of the nation's oldest commercial air carrier, Western Air Lines.

The banker reached Drinkwater by phone at his office in Westchester just before the executive headed out for the weekend. "Terry,

Kirk Kerkorian wants to see you this weekend," said Clausen. "Do you know him?"[1]

Drinkwater was familiar with Trans International. He knew Kerkorian by name, but they had never met. "I don't know him personally," he said.

"Well, I've raised Kirk from a pup," Clausen went on. "He's a nice guy. He wants to see you about something important."

But Drinkwater had plans for the weekend. "I'll see him Monday," he said.

"He wants to see you right away."

"What about?"

"I can't tell you."

"Then it'll have to wait until Monday."

With that, Drinkwater blew off a friendly introduction to the man most widely known at that time as a Las Vegas financier. Three months earlier Kirk had sold his interest in the land beneath Caesars Palace for $5 million—bringing to about $9 million his total five-year return on that former sandlot. He held a million-dollar second mortgage on the newly opened Circus Circus resort built by Caesars Palace impresario Jay Sarno. And just a few weeks earlier he had acquired the bankrupt Bonanza Hotel and Casino. Kirk already owned the Flamingo and was building the world's biggest hotel just off the Strip. But Drinkwater wasn't interested in Las Vegas except for the paid passenger volume the town generated for Western Air Lines. And he couldn't be bothered with a Vegas financier on that weekend in December 1968.

Kirk was dealing with a number of uncertainties at the time. The massive International Hotel was already under construction, but financing to complete it was not yet in hand. To make that happen, he was counting on a public offering of stock in his new International Leisure Corporation, even though the national economy was cooling and market prices were sagging. The Bonanza needed costly renovation or demolition. And Circus Circus was a month-to-month risk to default.

Yet Kirk picked this unsettled time to surprise friends and the financial world with a hefty side bet on assets beyond Las Vegas. He had arranged a $73 million loan from Bank of America to fund his bid for controlling interest in Drinkwater's Western Air Lines. He had wanted to talk to Drinkwater about it first, as a courtesy, before the executive read about it in the news. Kirk also hoped to allay any fears about his investment motives. He had no immediate plans to change management.

The Western Air bid had plenty of logic going for it and at least a dash of sentiment. The company dominated short-haul routes throughout the West and was, in Kirk's words, "a darn good routed airline." It was about to open nonstop service out of the Midwest to Las Vegas and was expecting to win lucrative routes to Hawaii soon.

On a more personal note, for the first time since Kirk's postwar investment in the air charter business, he found himself at the end of a calendar year without an airline of his own. It turned out not to be as easy as he thought it would be to sever ties—and his personal identity—with Trans International and the wider world of aviation. At heart, he was still an airline guy. And it all started with Kirk's first flight nearly thirty years before out of Western Air Express Airport in Alhambra, the original Southern California home of the airline he now hoped to control.

He had talked it over with Fred Benninger, his right-hand man on the Vegas hotel projects. Fred had also been a pilot during World War II and a longtime executive at Flying Tiger Airlines where he started as an accountant. He wasn't a visionary so much as Kirk's guardian of the bottom line, but Kirk consulted Fred on most business matters.

What did Fred think about the future of leisure travel? Benninger hadn't given it much thought. He was trying to get the International Hotel built. Kirk envisioned leisure travel on the verge of booming growth. He saw a surge in leisure spending benefiting Las Vegas tourism and a well-run airline right along with it.

Kirk had another question. What did Fred think of Los Angeles–

based Western Air Lines as an investment target? Benninger shrugged. "From what I know, it's a good little airline with potential," he said, just as it dawned on him what the boss was thinking.

"But Kirk—if I were you," he quickly added, "I wouldn't buy any airline at this time."

Inflation was starting to sap the economy. Some newspaper commentators were even speculating about future currency revaluations. The naturally conservative Benninger was growing more bearish as well. He also had his hands full overseeing the Flamingo and building the International. Not only was construction financing still a work in progress, so was delivery of plans to the hard hat crews. As fast as plans came off the drawing boards for installing pilings or erecting steel or whatever, that's when work installing pilings or erecting steel or whatever began. But it was also too late—too late for trying to talk Kirk out of another gamble.

A tender offer for Western stocks, enough to make Kirk the company's single largest shareholder, was announced on Monday morning, December 9, with half-page advertisements in the *Los Angeles Times* and other major papers around the country. Unlike Howard Hughes who seven months earlier toyed with bringing Kirk into his secret talks with Drinkwater, Kirk was going in alone—and directly to the stockholders.

Drinkwater didn't see it coming. He hadn't even read his *Los Angeles Times* yet that morning. In traffic, inching toward Western's corporate offices at the edge of LAX, the executive was catching up on the latest news—and traffic reports—listening to his favorite all-news radio station. In local business news, said the voice on his car radio: Western Air Lines may be the takeover target of Las Vegas financier Kirk Kerkorian. The casino owner was seeking 1.5 million shares at $45 each, a $10 per share premium over Western's recent trading range.

In an age before cell phones, Drinkwater had to contain his rage until reaching Western Air headquarters on Century Boulevard, closing the door to his private office and grabbing the phone to dial his friend, the vice chairman at Bank of America. "You sonuvabitch!" he greeted Alden Clausen.

Drinkwater was a big man with a big personality, prone to loud tirades whenever his patience was tested and not one to worry much about business niceties. He once saved his company from a $150,000 aviation debt by wagering a double-or-nothing coin flip with a Douglas Aircraft Company executive. In his twenty-year tenure running Western, Drinkwater had dragged his ailing company back from the grave, put it on sound financial footing, and made it a model of aggressive marketing and management. Western was his airline. It wasn't for sale. And he was feeling betrayed.

He was also shouting into the phone: "Every bank in California's been after our business . . . I told them we'd stay loyal to [Bank of America]. Now you guys come along and try to cut our throats."

The bank's $73 million loan to Kerkorian had not been disclosed in the published tender offer or in the news radio report. But Drinkwater knew the score and the math of 1.5 million shares at $45. He knew that Clausen and Bank of America were standing behind Kerkorian's bid, and that's what elevated his decibels and his blood pressure.

"I'll bet you loaned him God knows how much to make a corporate raid," Drinkwater seethed.

"It's not a raid, Terry!" the banker interrupted. "Kerkorian is acquiring the stock as a good investment."

"Bullshit," roared Drinkwater, and he slammed down the phone.

That same Monday afternoon Kirk flew into Los Angeles International Airport from Las Vegas aboard his private DC-9 jet. Western's corporate offices were a ten-minute cab ride from the private plane terminal on Imperial Boulevard, Drinkwater was waiting for Kirk wearing an angry scowl and his customary bow tie.

Introductions were strictly perfunctory. Kirk either didn't notice or ignored the icy reception. He obviously considered the meeting a formal occasion. He was wearing a tie instead of his customary turtleneck and sport coat.

"I'm sorry I couldn't get in touch with you prior to the offer," Kirk began in a confident but friendly tone. Drinkwater's personal assistant was struck by Kirk's commanding presence in the room—his cold electricity—despite the fact that Drinkwater towered over him as they shook hands.

"I'm sure you want to know who I am, what I'm like, and what my interests were in making this investment," Kirk continued. "We have many friends in common. You can check me out through them—"

"You dirty sonuvabitch!" Drinkwater cut him off.

The fact is that they did have many friends in common. Some of them were Drinkwater associates and members of Western Air's board of directors. Most had only good things to say about Kirk.

One of those was Arthur G. Woodley, former head of Pacific Northern Airlines until it merged with Western and he joined the board with Drinkwater's team. Woodley once bought a used DC-4 from Kirk only to have his maintenance people complain it was leaking fuel so badly that it was a safety hazard simply parked on a tarmac.

"Art, so help me, I didn't know it was in that kind of shape," Kirk apologized. He returned the entire purchase price without debate. And Woodley considered Kirk one of the most honest businessmen he'd ever known.

But that afternoon in Drinkwater's office, the airline boss saw Kerkorian in only the starkest of terms—as an interloper and a pirate trying to loot his domain. He barely took a breath for the next fifteen minutes as he spewed invective and condemnation in rapid fire.

Kirk was surprised by the tirade, though he wasn't angry. Not yet. But like Las Vegas, it was becoming clear that Western Air Lines wasn't going to be big enough for two tigers.

There was one important factor underlying Kirk's confidence in opening a second investment front in the risky aviation business. Back in Las Vegas, day-to-day operations were under control. He had absolute trust in a team temporarily headquartered at the

Flamingo to manage things on the ground, at the construction site, behind the front desks, and on the casino floors. His key hires were Benninger and Alex Shoofey. They weren't exactly a close-knit team. They could barely tolerate each other.

Benninger was a German by birth and frugal by nature. He earned his nickname "the Prussian" from his hard-nosed negotiations with contractors and suppliers and from an unrelenting aversion to spending money. The former accountant never spent a dime he didn't first try to save. Fred was the gatekeeper protecting Kirk's millions and he embraced that role with fierce loyalty—playing the tough guy to Kirk's soft-spoken nice guy.

The front office at Circus Circus already had its fill of Benninger barely three months after it opened in the fall of 1968. The new resort was wrestling cash flow and start-up troubles but one thing it could count on—a monthly call from Benninger wanting assurances that Circus Circus would make its next interest payment on Kirk's million-dollar loan. "I just want to go over there and hit the guy," one of the partners confessed.[2]

Benninger was Kirk's top financial adviser, but Kirk wanted Shoofey to pilot the Flamingo. His mission was to make it profitable and at the same time build up a staff that could transfer directly to the International Hotel the day it opened. In order to lure him away from Del Webb's Sahara where he had been the best-paid and most-sought-after resort operator in town, Kirk offered Shoofey more than a title and generous share of the profits.

"Alex, I want you to run the (Flamingo). Promote it. Whatever expense you need—I don't care if it's five dollars or five million dollars—if it's for the benefit of the hotel, go ahead and do it."[3]

A day after taking over the Flamingo, Shoofey was driving to his first meeting as president of the hotel. He stopped for a morning car wash and fill-up. With an appropriate Vegas-sized tip, the tab amounted to twenty dollars. He put it on his expense account. Benninger summoned him to his office. His reimbursement claim was rejected as inappropriate.

"It's not right," said a very serious Benninger from behind his horn-rimmed glasses. "If you can do it, then anyone else could."

Shoofey, the president of hotel and casino operations generating millions in revenue and expenses every week and accustomed to handing out twenties like they were nickels and dimes, was silent, dumbfounded, in total disbelief—for about five nanoseconds—before unleashing a string of epithets.[4]

"I can't take this shit," he barked and reached for Benninger's desk phone to dial the boss. Kirk answered and Shoofey exploded, "This sonuvabitch is questioning me . . . he's annoying me!"

Kirk hurried over to calm the tempest. He told Benninger, "Listen, my deal with Alex is this . . ." and he repeated Shoofey's carte blanche authority to spend "five dollars or five million" to promote the hotel.

The rejected expense account was promptly reinstated. Shoofey got his twenty bucks back. Far more importantly, the point had been made. Kirk had cleared the air and freed Shoofey of what he considered bean counter constraints. But the two executives would never reconcile.

On another morning weeks later, Benninger summoned Shoofey again—this time to confront him with a report that the casino had been ripped off the night before. Based on the tip of a watchful friend, Benninger said the casino probably lost forty thousand dollars at a certain craps table. Shoofey immediately ordered the drop box from the suspect table. But its contents matched receipts. Its weight was normal. If anything, it appeared to have been an exceptionally good night at this particular table.

Benninger conceded his friend must have gotten it wrong. Shoofey was in no mood for apologies. He warned the finance chief to stay out of the casino and out of his hotel operations or someday, "I'm going to knock your head off."

In Las Vegas, the chronically unfriendly partnership between Benninger and Shoofey served Kirk's purposes just fine. Both were honest, competent, and loyal to him. And that left Kirk free amid all the turmoil to turn his attention to the increasingly bitter fight over Terry Drinkwater's airline.

K irk had tried to reassure Drinkwater and his team that he had no intention of making major management changes, that all he wanted was two places on the Western board of directors. It was a modest request reflecting his 28 percent ownership. But Drinkwater was adamant. He didn't want Kirk or any of his people on the board. This, despite the counsel of his closest friend and the president of operations, Stanley R. Shatto, who said of Kirk, "I don't know anything bad about him, Terry. He seems to be an honest, capable guy, and people who've had dealings with him say he's straightforward."

Even Shatto drew the line, however, when Kirk said he wanted to put Benninger on the Western board. Shatto regarded the Prussian as "that damned hatchet man."

Stubborn resistance to his request for board positions prompted Kirk to increase his investments by $6.1 million—boosting his holdings to about 31 percent. Drinkwater finally agreed to a compromise, opening one board position. Kirk rejected the gesture. Drinkwater and his board then agreed to expand from fifteen to eighteen members, making room for Kerkorian, Benninger, and Kirk's lawyer William Singleton.

It was as if Drinkwater was determined to keep peppering Kirk with jab after jab to wear down and discourage the new majority stockholder. Instead, it made him angry. And when Rifle Right Kerkorian finally had enough, he fired back.

In a demonstration of power and impatience, Kirk demanded five seats on the board and a title enabling him to challenge Drinkwater directly. He wanted to be chairman of the board. Now the feud was personal on both sides.

16

HELLO, WORLD!

From his ninth-floor penthouse at the Desert Inn, Howard Hughes could watch Kirk Kerkorian's dream come true, keeping an eye on every phase of progress as his rival's International Hotel rose from the sand off Paradise Road. Week after week it took on the shape of the world's biggest hotel and casino with more steel, more floors, and a more prominent profile in the desert sky. Instead, Hughes shut out the view. Day and night he kept his curtains drawn.

What no one could see was the drama behind the scenes. A worksite crawling with tradesmen and bulldozers disguised the fact that although Kirk had financing to get the International Hotel started, his limited loan package would be exhausted at roughly the halfway point of construction.

Kirk's plan was to issue stock in a new Nevada corporation called International Leisure, a holding company for both the Flamingo and the rising International Hotel. The Securities and Exchange Commission (SEC) had authorized the public offering, a tribute to Kirk's solid reputation and the success of his earlier Trans International Airline public offering. And when the markets opened on a Valentine's Day Friday, International Leisure Corp. was on the trading block.

For would-be investors—or those with their curtains closed—a company prospectus described the International's state of completion: "At the present time the outer framework for 22 of the hotel's eventual 30 stories has been completed in accordance with the company's time schedule. If construction continues on schedule, management expects completion of the hotel and its opening to the public in the summer of 1969."

Investors were offered a mix of stocks and bonds in units—each of the twenty-five thousand units on the market included twenty shares of stock valued at $5 each and a $1,000 bond offered at 8 percent interest for a total purchase price of $1,100 per unit. Even in the face of a deteriorating national economy, the offering was an immediate success. International Leisure raised $26.5 million. Completion was assured.

Kirk was especially encouraged by how smoothly the stock sale had gone. He planned to repeat the exercise later in the year, once the hotel was open and showing its anticipated profit. He was confident, too, that a second public offering would raise substantially more cash. And that confidence was reinforced almost instantly.

Within a few hours after markets opened the following Monday, the hotel's five-dollar stocks had jumped 600 percent to nearly $30 per share. And by summer they were trading as high as $50. Kirk's winning streak was suddenly gaining national attention. It was Kirk's "hello, world!" moment. Reporters from both coasts flocked to Kirk's Las Vegas office for interviews.

"Can an honest and ambitious Armenian boy start out in the Civilian Conservation Camps and wind up with nearly $200 million and everybody still his friend?" asked the *New York Times*.[1] "He can, if he's Kirk Kerkorian, biggest Las Vegas hotel and landowner next to Howard Hughes, and who is in a strategic position to control an airline that just received some lush rights to serve Hawaii."

The *Los Angeles Times* predicted that Kirk could end up a bigger player in Las Vegas development than leading landowner Howard Hughes and "controlling a whole lot more hotel space." The newspaper called him "such an unobtrusive sort of guy it's difficult to believe he's built a $200 million fortune."[2]

From his office with a window on the hotel construction site, Kirk shared a key element of his investment strategy with the visiting *Los Angeles Times* financial editor, preferring a few "big ventures" to many smaller ones. "Something with a lot of meat on it."[3] In business, as in gambling, Kirk still relished the thrill of the biggest bets.

B ack in Los Angeles, the Kerkorian-Drinkwater feud was still boiling. With the approach of Western's April 24 stockholders' meeting Drinkwater continued his all-out resistance to anyone from the Kerkorian faction joining the board. His latest delaying tactic came with a demand that the CAB investigate Kirk and disqualify his WAL stock purchase over certain alleged conflicts of interest. Among other things, Drinkwater charged that Kirk's holdings in Transamerica stock made him an owner of a competing airline in Trans International. The Western boss said Kirk's ownership interests in the Flamingo also disqualified him since the hotel regularly employed charter services to provide junkets for high rollers.

The CAB wasn't buying any of it. Investigators found no evidence that Kirk asserted any influence over TIA and tossed out the Flamingo claim saying simply that the hotel was not in the aviation business. Kirk kept batting away Drinkwater's challenges, but the relentless attacks and delays had pushed his patience to its limits. He finally demanded a list of stockholders, serving notice that a proxy fight was next.

In the months since Kirk's tender offer made him nearly one-third owner of WAL, the federal government had announced plans to award Hawaiian air routes to several airlines, including Western. Drinkwater had reacted aggressively, placing orders for a dozen new jets—including three Boeing 747 jumbo jets set for delivery in 1970. The bold play created a bad case of airline overcapacity, a jump in personnel costs, and further fueled the feud at the top.

Kirk demanded that Western corporate officers turn over their plans for financing the fleet expansion. And he called for a suspension of new jetliner orders pending his review of the company's financial status. Now he had poked Drinkwater in the eye. The enraged Western president made a second try to get the CAB to investigate Kerkorian. Again, it refused.[4]

Drinkwater could see a proxy fight going badly against him. One clue was Art Woodley, the former Pacific Northern Airlines executive who considered Kirk one of the most honest businessmen he'd ever met. In response to Drinkwater asking him for his proxy in the Kerkorian fight, Woodley growled, "I'll vote my own shares, Terry!"

Drinkwater got the message. And if Woodley was not a reliable vote, he had to assume he might not have anything near full support from his own board. Besides, the entire board and Drinkwater combined controlled less than 5 percent of Western shares.

Bank of America vice chairman Alden Clausen, with a stake in both sides of the Kerkorian-Drinkwater match, summoned the factions to a conciliation conference a few days ahead of their annual meeting showdown before shareholders. He proposed a compromise that required any three of Drinkwater's directors to step aside in favor of three from Kerkorian's group. It might preempt the proxy war, he suggested. And before Drinkwater could object, his closest friend and adviser, Stan Shatto, waved him out into the hall along with two other loyal directors. They offered to resign to end the feud, leaving Drinkwater unscathed by a devastating and likely vote against him and still running the company. He reluctantly agreed.

Minutes later, back in the meeting room where the banker, Kerkorian, and the rest of the board waited, Shatto announced his resignation along with those of Art Kelly and J. Judson Taylor—each of them veteran insiders of Western. All eyes turned to Kirk.

"I appreciate what you're trying to do, Stan," Kirk said in his soft, rumbling baritone. "But I won't go along with any of you resigning from the board." He considered the trio of insiders top aviation men and critical to Western's future. He didn't want to lose them.[5]

Instead, after further discussion, all agreed that the WAL board would be expanded from eighteen to twenty-one members. Drinkwater would remove three outside directors of his choice. And Kirk would appoint nine representatives, giving him slightly less than 50 percent of the board.

The proxy war was resolved before it could be waged, but peace did not reign in Western world. Recently inaugurated U.S. president Richard M. Nixon, responding to wage and price inflation and a teetering economy, had suspended all CAB-authorized route expansions for the airlines, among a number of executive actions. At Western, Hawaii service was delayed and then, when it started, the airline was competing with established carriers. Some had widebodied planes. Western didn't. Others had in-flight movies over the wide Pacific Ocean. Western didn't.

"Absolutely not! There will be no movies on our flights. We don't need them," Drinkwater insisted.[6]

Business was tanking. The Western shares that Kirk purchased for $45 had plunged to about $15 by June. Kirk turned to the Prussian. "Well, I guess you're elected," he told Benninger. "See if you can straighten things out."

Benninger had strong feelings about how to run an airline. He'd run Flying Tiger. And he wasn't particularly happy to be pulled away from the late stages of the Las Vegas hotel project. He canceled Western's orders for 747s. He also wanted other new plane orders suspended until airline financial health could be restored. He soon replaced Kirk as the most hated man in Drinkwater's executive suite.

If it bothered Benninger, he wasn't going to show it. He acknowledged sometime later, "There was ill feeling right from the start and, as Kirk's alter ego, I had to take the brunt of it."

In fact, Benninger reflected his boss's values right down to the financier's penchant for punctuality. Kirk was never late. His staff and business associates were never late twice. So, when Western's on-time performance as an airline slipped badly, Benninger ordered daily 8 A.M. meetings involving all key departments to review what happened the day before. Howls of protest among the affected vice presidents were ignored. And Western's on-time performance rankings soared to the top of the industry.

The airline was in good hands, a tribute in no small measure to Kirk's delegating skills. The recalcitrant President Drinkwater notwithstanding, Kirk and the Prussian also were starting to win admirers among Western's executive team, especially as the company's finances improved—along with its on-time record.

Everywhere he looked, Kirk saw things humming along according to plan. The gambler was getting that itch again for another big bet. And in the summer of 1969 he was already looking around for the next challenge. But first, back in Las Vegas where the world's biggest hotel was about to open, it was showtime!

17

CARY AND KIRK
AND BARBRA AND ELVIS

K irk entered the packed International dinner theater on July 2, 1969, without an entourage, without a spotlight, without most in the crowd of two thousand even noticing as he slipped into a chair at his reserved table. It was near the stage but less than a prime location.

It was opening night of his $60 million International Hotel, the world's biggest hotel and casino, the one he built with borrowed money and cold-blooded daring. He'd made it happen. And he was proud of it. But instead of drawing attention to himself he was sticking to his comfort zone—in the background, basking in the shadows. This was singer-actress Barbra Streisand's night, the richest opening act in the history of nightclubs. Kirk had lingered out of sight for as long as he could, avoiding the big crowd and small talk of the party scene. Now he waited for his close friend and actor Cary Grant who was about to step out and introduce the hotel's much-anticipated headliner.

Grant's cultivated cool movie star persona belied the fact that he hated public speaking almost as much as Kirk did. It was a shared phobia that helped bond the friendship dating back seven years to their first introduction at the Dunes. Now they also shared the experience of being older fathers with young daughters of similar age. The girls brought them together for father-daughter horseback riding.

It had been the International's new president, Alex Shoofey, not Kirk himself, who pestered Grant to take the stage that night. "Whadaya mean, you don't give speeches?" said an incredulous Shoofey when Grant declined his first request.[1] But it was for Kirk that Grant had come to Las Vegas for the opening-night celebrations, and it was to honor his friend that Cary Grant agreed finally to Shoofey's request.

The audience of invited guests and celebrities was settled at their dinner tables, most of them greeted personally by the hotel's music director, Bobby Morris. They included Raquel Welch, Natalie Wood, Rita Hayworth, Red Skelton, the Smothers Brothers, and basketball legend Wilt "the Stilt" Chamberlain. Bobby Morris already loved his job as Kirk's celebrity greeter. Whenever Kirk was in the house, Bobby could count on getting his first hug of the evening from Kirk himself. Tonight he was wearing his first custom-made tuxedo, a gift from Kirk and fashioned by his personal tailor.[2]

The Bobby Morris Orchestra had taken its place onstage. A standing-room-only crowd of VIPs watched from the cocktails-only balcony level as the tuxedoed Cary Grant strode out to an explosion of applause. As the ovation subsided, he spotted his friend out in the shadows.

"Kirk," he began. "I know you don't like this kind of thing, but . . ."

Grant's introductory detour immediately alarmed Kirk, who cringed at any kind of public attention. His custom-made tuxedo was suddenly feeling tight around the collar. His face felt hot as Grant continued, "I want everybody here to see the guy who made this spectacular hotel possible." A spotlight followed Grant's wave toward Kirk's table.[3]

Kirk could have savored the moment, taken a bow, waved to the dinner crowd on his left and right, maybe even joined Cary onstage to welcome everyone now offering another ovation for him. Instead, Kirk stood up, smiled sheepishly at his friend, and sat right back down again. People in the room later swore that, despite Kerkorian's deep tan, they could see he was blushing.

Grant then introduced Streisand, who swept onstage in a fuchsia chiffon gown to officially open the world's biggest and most expensive resort hotel with her opening song, "I Got Plenty of Nothin.'" Her pay for that four-week run actually set its own records for that time. Besides a weekly fee widely reported to be more than $100,000, Kirk presented her with stock in his International Leisure Corp., which soared from $5 a share to $100 immediately after the hotel's strong opening. She could have made at least $2 million depending upon the timing of her stock sales—a sum, by any form of accounting, that added up to plenty of somethin' for Streisand who remained a good friend of Kirk's through the years.

While Streisand's opening-night performance received mixed reviews, she continued to sell out the dinner theater as she tweaked and refined her act. She went on to set Vegas showroom attendance and box office records, finally leaving to effusive reviews by some of the same reviewers who had been most critical of her before the International showroom performances.

For Kerkorian it was one unmitigated success—big, profitable, and filled with class and glamour. And that was before Elvis Presley arrived at the end of July to rewrite all those same attendance and revenue records again.

Across the street at the $20 million Howard Hughes Landmark Hotel, opening night one night earlier had been a bit slapdash and seemed pulled together at the last minute.[4] In fact, Hughes didn't approve the July 1 date for his grand opening until June 29. Hughes had won the race to open first by twenty-four hours—but no one else seemed to care. And the billionaire recluse didn't even attend his own grand opening. In the public relations contest over who had the biggest whatever, Kirk dominated in press coverage, star power, and cash flow.

It was probably best that Hughes missed his own grand opening because the casino lost money from day one,[5] and his celebrity comedians mocked him, though ever so gently. Singer-actor and noted boozer Dean Martin said he could be just as rich as Hughes: "All I got to do is return my empties."[6]

Hughes top aide Robert Maheu delivered best wishes to rival Kerkorian and good luck at his grand opening, prompting television and nightclub comedian Danny Thomas to quip, "It's so touching to see money congratulating money."

On its big opening night, the Landmark suffered by comparison to the International in almost every way. The popular but overmatched Danny Thomas couldn't possibly compete with Streisand and Peggy Lee, the International's secondary act in its five-hundred-seat casino lounge. An indecisive Hughes had failed to approve a VIP guest list until two days before the event—and then provided only forty-four names. Maheu added four hundred at the last minute, most of them in town already as guests of Kerkorian.[7]

Cary Grant, for one, also made it across Paradise Road to the Landmark opening. He had no formal role, but he did draw inadvertent attention when he boarded the tower's glass elevator for the ride thirty-one floors to the upper-level casino. A distracted elevator operator swooning over Grant in such close proximity reached a gloved hand for the up button but instead she accidentally set off a loud alarm.

July turned out to be one incredibly hot month in town, temperatures in triple digits outside and standing-room-only crowds inside the International as Elvis Presley—Streisand's follow-up act—blew the lid off every expectation. He was selling out every show twice a night seven nights a week, including the big showroom's balcony. He was pulling in gamblers and hotel reservations from around the world.

After Presley's opening night, Kirk's man in charge of the International took one look at the overnight numbers and the exploding reservations switchboard and went hunting for the rock 'n' roll star's manager, Colonel Tom Parker. Shoofey and the colonel ended up together huddled over cups of coffee at a quiet table.

There had been internal debate months earlier about whether to open with Streisand or Elvis. Colonel Parker himself had expressed reluctance to put that kind of pressure on his kid to carry the opening after being off the road doing movies for a dozen years. Kirk's team shared that same doubt. And Kirk himself said he believed that "Streisand would be a bigger opening act than Elvis."

But a stunning surge in ticket sales and public excitement was obvious to everyone without a hangover first thing in the morning after Streisand gave her closing performance. Guy Hudson reported for his regular 8 A.M. to 4 P.M. shift in the International cashiers' office and stopped dead in his tracks. "What the hell!" A line had formed outside the showroom box office that wouldn't even open for another two hours—a line out the door "that never stopped."[8]

"We made a mistake," Kirk had to admit. "Streisand didn't do quite as well as we thought. And Elvis tore the hotel apart."[9]

Shoofey was determined to correct that mistake even before all the ashtrays were emptied the morning after Presley's debut. The man with Kirk's carte blanche to "spend five dollars or five million" for the hotel, immediately shot the wad—all five million.[10]

"Listen, I want to extend your contract," Shoofey told Presley's manager.

"Let's wait," the colonel cautioned. "It's too early. Let's find out whether he can make it or not. There's no telling if Elvis is going to collapse."

In fact, Elvis had taken on a grueling schedule—two shows a night every night for two weeks—for which he was being paid $100,000 a week, plus incentives. Presley's stamina was certain to be tested in the days ahead.

"Well, I'll take that gamble," Shoofey said without hesitation. "Right now."

Parker eyed the International's president and finally asked, "What do you want?"

"Five more years. Twice a year. A month each year. Five hundred thousand per engagement. Five million dollars." He threw in unspecified advertising expenses and a $100,000 bonus to sign immediately.

"You're crazy!"

Parker was dumbfounded. But when Shoofey made no move to back down or qualify his offer, Parker moved quickly. Clearing aside half-empty cups and saucers, the colonel asked Shoofey to repeat the terms of the Elvis deal so he could jot them down on the rose-colored tablecloth. The coffee-splotched restaurant linen covered with crumbs and random spots and smears would become the official record of their negotiations.

When he was finished, Parker rolled up the tablecloth, stood up, and tucked it under his arm. "You've got a deal," he said and walked off to confer with Elvis.

That masterstroke of deal making would do more than guarantee the International's long-term entertainment dominance in town. It would also clinch Las Vegas as the Elvis performance capital of the world.

One notable side effect would only become clear decades later with the rise of a timeless entertainment niche: the Las Vegas–styled Elvis impersonator. Untold thousands of performers with black pompadours and white jumpsuits probably owe their gigs from birthday parties to nightclub acts directly to Kirk Kerkorian, Alex Shoofey, and the deal consummated on that pink tablecloth.

The International Hotel's heavy reservation traffic, healthy casino business, and headline-grabbing series of shows provided a baptism in positive public relations. Its early financial returns were sensational. International Leisure stock steadily climbed. Kirk's original 82 percent ownership, held by his Tracy Investment Company, had been worth a modest $16.6 million before the hotel opened. It jumped to $180 million on the strength of steady profits at both the International and the Flamingo.

It was time to take advantage of all the good press and potential investor enthusiasm by preparing for another public offering of International Leisure stock. The second offering figured to be wildly more successful than the first stock sale, which raised $26 million to finish construction. Beyond that, and beyond raising enough cash to pay off about $50 million in high interest loans, Kirk expected this public offering to raise his next fortune—something that could make the Trans International Airlines deal seem modest by comparison.

While his legal team applied to the Securities and Exchange Commission for authorization to offer a second issue of stock, Kirk went shopping for his next business challenge. The gambler needed a new thrill.

18

THE SMILING COBRA

JULY 22, 1969

NEW YORK CITY

It was a Tuesday, after four in the afternoon. The markets had closed. Edgar M. Bronfman, chairman of the MGM board of directors, took a call from one of Hollywood's biggest lawyers, Gregson Bautzer. They had residences a few blocks from each other on Park Avenue. The two men had been talking for months about Bautzer's client Howard Hughes and the billionaire's supposed interest in acquiring the film studio. It wasn't a popular prospect. Hughes was regarded as the human wrecking ball that destroyed RKO Pictures, so Bronfman and the MGM board were polite, took Bautzer's calls, and otherwise let his famously indecisive recluse of a client take his sweet time. They were busy trying to save an ailing icon of the movie industry.

That Tuesday afternoon, however, Bronfman and the board discovered that a year's worth of Bautzer inquiries about MGM financials and assets and strategies had not been solicited on behalf of Hughes after all. Contrary to their assumptions, it turned out that since 1968 Bautzer had been quietly consulting with Kirk Kerkorian. And, more to the point of the Tuesday phone call, he now wanted to announce that Kirk would be launching a tender offer in the morning. His bid: $35 each for a million shares. His goal: management control.

Did Bronfman want to sell?[1]

The forty-year-old head of the Seagram Company in the United States was stunned by the news and outraged to be confronted with the uninvited takeover bid. He declared his opposition immediately. The offer was inadequate "and not in the best interest of shareholders." Beyond that, Bronfman was taking the challenge personally. An associate told *Forbes* magazine: "He blows up whenever anyone mentions Kirk Kerkorian."

Clearly, Kirk would have to fight for MGM.

MGM board vice chairman George L. Killion, a San Francisco Bay Area shipping executive, had been completely taken in by the Hughes ruse. He felt betrayed. "I had meeting after meeting with (Bautzer). He set up half a dozen dates with me to meet Howard Hughes. He even made reservations at the Desert Inn . . . but always they were canceled at the very last minute." Killion heard from Bautzer that same Tuesday afternoon, letting him know that Hughes had "decided not to acquire control of MGM, but that Mr. Kerkorian of Las Vegas was going to do it tomorrow morning at 9:00 A.M."

Unlike the Western Air Lines bid in which Kirk hoped to be a partner with management—until bitterly resisted by Drinkwater and his loyalists—this time he was declaring war on management from the start. Under Greg Bautzer's guidance, Kirk was setting up to play the role of a big, bad corporate raider. And in taking on the Bronfman organization, he was challenging one of the giants of North American business. Bautzer had warned him, "Are you sure you know what you're getting into?" But Kirk relished the fight, and he wasn't going to waste any time playing Mr. Nice Guy.

Another difference that distinguished the MGM tender offer from Kirk's previous Western bid was the price. Its eight-dollar premium over the prior day's market price was based on a greatly reduced value. The studio was hemorrhaging cash and its share price was sliding. Officials had just reported a forty-week operating loss of $14.4 million. Kirk's $35 a share offer—if accepted by Bronfman and Time, Inc.—would have cost MGM's two biggest shareholders a combined loss of $30 million.

Once again Transamerica Corp. was standing behind Kirk, guaranteeing his $35 million tender offer. But that was a problem, too. Transamerica owned most of rival studio United Artists, posing a potential conflict of interest. Kirk sold his own shares of Transamerica stock in June. It went to pay off the $73 million Bank of America loan he'd used to buy Western Air Lines—a loan that wasn't even due for nearly two years.

Transamerica's possible role financing an MGM purchase gave Bronfman and the board a way to challenge Kirk in court. Days later, he agreed to find alternate financing. On the verge of being debt-free once he was free to issue stock in International Leisure, the Transamerica challenge seemed a minor nuisance.

Kirk immediately flew off to London where Europe's top bankers were eager to make his acquaintance.

W hat Kirk saw in a tired old MGM with its run of box office losers was something beyond the view of most investors. He saw hidden value. With a market price wallowing around $25 a share, investors were missing hundreds of millions in existing value, not even considering any turnaround potential. Kirk and Bautzer figured the company's actual value to be closer to $400 million, or about $69 a share. What they saw was MGM's vast library of classic films—*Gone With the Wind, Singin' in the Rain, The Wizard of Oz.* The company owned music publishers, a record company, overseas studios, and tens of millions of dollars in real estate.

And then there was the priceless cache of its legendary name. For many, MGM spelled class—as in old Hollywood glamour, gowns and tuxedos, klieg lights and red carpets. What was Leo the Lion worth? No one had ever imagined putting a price on the MGM logo. Not until Kirk Kerkorian.

Kirk's alliance with Bautzer brought together two supremely competitive men with scrappy youths and bold careers. Bautzer was a kid from the tough waterfront town of San Pedro who became a noted Hollywood lawyer and playboy. He represented and romanced such stars as Ingrid Bergman, Ginger Rogers, Lana Turner, and Joan Crawford.

In the 1940s Bautzer was a friend, legal adviser, and frequent clubbing buddy of nightclub impresario Billy Wilkerson, founder of the *Hollywood Reporter*. Wilkerson also owned the famous Ciro's on Sunset and the land under Bugsy Siegel's rising Flamingo hotel and casino in Las Vegas. Bugsy and Billy were having a serious money dispute two weeks before the resort's scheduled Christmas 1946 grand opening.

Bautzer came along as friend and lawyer to a contentious meeting at the construction site. The mobster, accompanied by two silent lawyers of his own, demanded that Billy surrender a share of his interest in the Flamingo to help pay off mob financiers that included underworld accountant Meyer Lansky. He didn't say "please."

"You're gonna have to do it," Siegel said.

"Just a minute," Bautzer interrupted. His client didn't "have to do" anything.[2]

"I've sold one hundred and fifty percent of this deal and I don't have one hundred and fifty percent—only one hundred percent. Everybody's gonna have to cut, including Wilkerson."

Bautzer calmly waved him off. "You better figure another way out, 'cause he ain't gonna cut."

Siegel was on his feet in a rage. Unnamed people "in the East" needed to be satisfied or Bugsy was gonna be killed. Then, turning to Wilkerson, he said in a thoroughly convincing tone, "I'll kill you if I don't get that interest."

"Sit down and shut up," Bautzer barked at Siegel.

The lawyer ordered his client out of the room and then turned back to the mobster's two lawyers, who still had said not a word.

"You'd better shut this guy up 'cause I'm gonna make an affidavit . . .

on the remarks Mr. Siegel has made at this meeting and who was present. I'm sending one copy to the attorney general. And I'm sending one copy to the FBI. And if Siegel is wise, or his associates are, they'd better make sure Mr. Wilkerson doesn't accidentally fall down a flight of stairs. They'd better make sure he doesn't sprain an ankle walking off a curb. . . . So, you'd better be goddamned sure Mr. Wilkerson enjoys a very long and happy life."

At Bautzer's urging, Wilkerson spent most of the next few months at the Hotel George V in Paris. He was there again on June 20, 1947, when news of Bugsy Siegel's murder in Beverly Hills reached the banks of the river Seine.

Kirk loved telling people how his lawyer once told Bugsy to shut up and sit down. By the time Kirk signed on with Bautzer, his Beverly Hills law firm—known simply as Wyman Bautzer— had emerged as a political powerhouse as well. Two of the partners covered both sides of the local partisan divide. Eugene Wyman was chairman of the California Democratic Party, and former U.S. senator Thomas Kuchel had been the GOP minority whip before losing a primary election in the summer of 1968.

The firm was already becoming a magnet for some of the top young legal talent in Southern California, fresh recruits to join the growing ranks of Team Kerkorian.

MGM was in court on Friday, July 25, 1969, to block Kerkorian's use of Transamerica funding to buy its stock shares. That same day Kirk flew to London, heading out over one of the North Atlantic air routes he helped pioneer as an RAF contract pilot nearly a quarter century earlier. This time, however, he relaxed in plush leather lounge chairs and a private bedroom cabin aboard his own personal jetliner. The four-million-dollar twin-engine DC-9 was custom fitted with long-range fuel tanks that took most of the adventure out of such a crossing. No boost from the "hurricane express" required.

Credit was tightening in the United States, but Eurodollars were available—at a price. Interest rates were in double figures and edging upward. In his pocket on the flight over, Kirk carried a copy of the Teletype message his friends at Bank of America had sent ahead to leading European banking houses on Kirk's behalf. They recommended him for his strong reputation in the financial world. And the Bank of America said it considered Kerkorian good for $70 million on his signature alone.

Kirk checked into his suite at the London Hilton overlooking Hyde Park. It was a Saturday. His phone rang that same morning. Burston & Texas, a London banking firm owned in part by the Texas National Bank of Commerce in Houston, wanted a piece of the MGM action. First thing on Monday Kirk met with bank officials and settled on terms for a one-year, $12 million loan at 12.875 percent.

The old-line West German financial firm Bankhaus Burkhardt & Company was so eager to participate that it flew one of its partners to London, sparing Kirk the inconvenience of a trip to Essen. In their meeting, Burkhardt partner Otto Schoeppler agreed to loan up to $50 million. Kirk accepted a smaller initial deal of $20 million.

Kirk's casino investments prompted questions in the European media about the staid old German bank's new financial ties with a prominent Las Vegas gaming figure. Schoeppler dismissed any doubts about Kerkorian's reputation: "We consider Mr. Kerkorian forthright and a man of good standing. The fact that he has an office in Las Vegas has no bearing on the nature of the man."

In little over two business days, with bankers rushing to see him, Kirk lined up $70 million in European funding. He was back in New York on Wednesday where MGM lawyers thought they might have blocked the Kerkorian menace by blocking his Transamerica line of credit. Kirk didn't break the news of his success just yet. He was busy getting ready for a flight the next day to Las Vegas for the International's big Elvis Presley opening on Thursday night, July 31.

His DC-9 was on the ground in New York only long enough to be refueled and filled with East Coast rock music writers and critics.

Kirk waited a few days before disclosing publicly that he had dropped the Transamerica loan. He didn't need it. Instead, he would rely on a consortium of European banks to make the MGM buy.

But Kirk also was upping his ante. He announced that he would seek 1.74 million shares, about 30 percent of MGM stock and enough to guarantee working control of the company. Again, MGM lawyers went to court, arguing that Kirk lacked the collateral to support those loans. But a federal court refused to intervene.

At $35 a share, Kirk's offer had attracted more than a million sales. But it was too low to spark the sales volume necessary to acquire 30 percent. Too many shareholders were waiting for something better. As the final numbers came in, it looked like a nail-biter of a close election: Kirk ended up with 1,263,950 shares, falling about a thousand shares short of matching the Bronfman-Time Inc. bloc at 1,265,000 and well short of the 30 percent range.

Kirk headed back to Europe to renegotiate his Burston & Texas loan. He had yet to draw any funds from that original $12 million package, but now he wanted to raise the limit to $22 million. With that additional funding secured, Kirk raised his ante again—now offering $42 a share for an additional 620,000 shares, a $17 premium from MGM's summer low.

Results were unambiguous. Nearly a million and a half shares flooded in, but Kirk at first took only his declared 620,000-share limit. He ended September with 32 percent of MGM stock. Then, after market prices fell back in October, he bought more, inching toward a position at which no one could challenge his dominance.

For nearly a month, Kirk and Bronfman observed a truce of sorts. During that period Kirk met with members of the Bronfman team, who described Kirk as "a very gentlemanly, quiet man."

But in late October Kirk moved to fire Bronfman's handpicked president, Louis "Bo" Polk. Bronfman capitulated and quit the board. Kirk had offered the MGM presidency to mild-mannered United Artists executive and former literary agent Herb Jaffe. They played tennis together when Kirk was in Southern California. Kirk liked the United Artists business model. It operated more as a film distributor. It had no costly studio to operate and support. But Jaffe decided against taking on the demands of the salvage mission that clearly loomed for the ailing MGM.

At Bautzer's urging Kirk named one of his lawyer's clients to run the studio, the controversial former CBS president James T. Aubrey. Known as "the Smiling Cobra," Aubrey seemed better suited to play the bad guy and manage a campaign of painful cutbacks to save the company from financial collapse.

And MGM was Kirk's company to save. He now controlled nearly 40 percent of MGM stock—40 percent of *Gone With the Wind*, 40 percent of Leo the Lion, 40 percent of the boulders he and Norman Hungerford shoved around that sound stage one long night back in their teens for $2.60 each. Bautzer, for one, could see that MGM mattered more to Kirk than a typical investment.

"Kirk felt he'd bought himself a little immortality."[3]

A KICK IN THE ASS

It was the dream of at least two generations of federal agents to indict, convict, and finally imprison the little man with the biggest name in the American underworld, the infamous Meyer Lansky. They called him the mob's accountant, the wizard of Mafia finance, the chairman of the board of organized crime. Journalists wrote how he laughed at the law.

So, when a team of Internal Revenue Service investigators hit the Doral Beach Spa in Miami Beach with a subpoena seeking Lansky's testimony in a big gambling and tax evasion case, the intrusion was greeted more as an inconvenience than a concern by the old man trying to relax that fall afternoon in the steam room.

The unimposing Lansky certainly didn't look the part of a dangerous gangster. He stood barely five feet tall in his prime—and he was long past those hale and hearty days. He was pushing seventy with a heavy smoking habit, stomach ulcers, and clogged arteries. About the only exercise he got was walking his small dog, a shih tzu fur ball named Bruiser. He and his wife, Teddy, lived modestly on what appeared to be his Social Security stipends. If he was worth

$300 million, as some speculated, he was spending it on kibble and Maalox.

Still, investigators suspected that with records and testimony they could find Lansky's hidden fortune. They wanted to know more about the bad old days at the Flamingo casino in Las Vegas, back before Kerkorian bought it—back when the skim took four to five million dollars a year off the top of casino profits and redistributed the wealth among Midwest and East Coast mobster investors. Lansky was among those investors, an early partner in the Flamingo with his friend Bugsy Siegel.

Everyone knew that in the decades since Bugsy was killed, the Flamingo casino kept right on skimming. It was part of the hidden value that Kirk recognized before he offered to buy the place in 1967. In his earliest discussions with Alex Shoofey about coming to work for him, Kirk had penciled out his expectation that simply ending the skim would produce an easy million-dollar profit for owners and stockholders. He underestimated. Kirk and Shoofey cleared nearly $3 million in profit that first year.

The IRS noticed—primarily because Fred Benninger dutifully reported the profit as profit. The Flamingo had never before reported a profit greater than $500,000—and sometimes it was half that. But when the IRS asked for two prior years of financials, from the years the casino was owned by Sam Cohen and Morris Lansburgh, Kirk couldn't comply. He didn't have them.

Cohen and Lansburgh were Miami hotel guys with financial ties to Lansky. They had ended up having trouble with their Nevada gaming license. They were under pressure to sell when Kerkorian stepped up with $12.5 million in cash. Kirk declined to hire their management personnel, bringing in thirty of Shoofey's team from the Sahara. Cohen and Lansburgh declined to provide business records—not that Kirk didn't try.

"I asked them, but they looked at me like . . . 'where do you want your bullet?'" Kerkorian confided to close associates.

Of course, Kirk didn't really care personally about obtaining those numbers. He wanted their assets, not their spreadsheets. So when the IRS asked Kirk for the business records of prior owners, all he could offer were a few notes he'd jotted on a paper napkin. Suspicious federal investigators weren't satisfied. They served a search warrant on the Flamingo's New York offices looking for records of gambling payouts under the previous owners. At that point, the Lansky tax investigation started becoming a nuisance to Team Kerkorian. But Kirk wasn't going to be distracted. He was on a roll.

He not only controlled Western Air Lines but he had also just sold his Transamerica stock and paid off the big Bank of America loan that financed his airline takeover. Control of MGM was also in sight. And in Las Vegas the International Hotel had opened to stunning numbers and great reviews. Even a looming national recession and tight credit didn't seem to discourage Kirk.

The first inkling that federal pursuit of Lansky might ultimately inflict serious collateral damage on Kerkorian came shortly after his International Leisure Corp. filed for SEC approval to sell stock—its second public offering. Responding to pressure from the IRS and the U.S. Department of Justice (DOJ), the SEC demanded additional financial reports predating Kirk's 1967 purchase of the Flamingo—records that Kerkorian again explained he never received and never reviewed.

The SEC was skeptical that Kirk had accepted such limited information. What kind of due diligence was gut instinct? How could Kirk agree to spend $12.5 million without more detailed financials? The agency suggested that Kirk's people renew their request for more pre-1967 Flamingo data. Cohen and Lansburgh, now facing the same skimming and tax evasion suspicions as Lansky, stonewalled Kirk again, just as they were also stonewalling the IRS and DOJ.

The law of unintended consequences delivered a punishing blow to Kirk shortly before Christmas 1969. A second public offering of stock in International Leisure was blocked indefinitely. The SEC wouldn't budge from its insistence that the current Flamingo management was responsible for providing financial documents its predecessors had lost, destroyed, or failed to maintain.

Those federal bloodhounds on the scent of Meyer Lansky had successfully rousted the old mobster from his steam room. But now they were forcing Kirk Kerkorian into financial hot water when it appeared that the only thing he did was take a former Lansky property legit.

The stock sale had been Kirk's ace in the hole for retiring much of the high-interest European debt accumulated in his pursuit of MGM. Kirk couldn't help feeling victimized by the SEC's intransigence. He was being held responsible for past cover-ups of Meyer Lansky's secret interest in the Flamingo—secret interest that Kirk ended and replaced with straightforward recordkeeping. He was frustrated. Friends noticed a darker, angrier Kirk. His treatment by the SEC wasn't fair. It wasn't right. It shouldn't have happened.

And then, things got worse.

Kirk was staying at the Regency in New York on January 15, 1970, when he got a call from MGM president Jim Aubrey asking, "Have you seen the papers?" He immediately rode an elevator down to the lobby to find his own copy of the tabloid *New York Post* and its front-page headline: "MGM Head Talks to Mafia."[1] It was based on a wiretap recording of that long-forgotten telephone call between Kirk and his bookie, the man he knew in 1961 as "Charlie White."

As Kirk read the *Post* account, it all came flooding back—his betting on football and boxing . . . the check for $21,300 that he endorsed to actor George Raft, a friend of Charlie's . . . that he sent to Raft, care of the Warwick Hotel . . . *because the heat was on.*

The sensational press accounts came out of evidence submitted to a New York legislative committee hearing testimony about organized crime in the state. Featured that day were various intercepted phone calls involving Charles "Charlie the Blade" Tourine (a.k.a. Charles White), an enforcer for New York mob boss Vito Genovese. "It was strictly a gambling debt," Kirk insisted. "Is that a big deal, you know, betting on a sporting event?"[2]

Kirk's choice of bookies looked especially questionable in retrospect. By 1970 Tourine had a rap sheet with arrests ranging from illegal gambling, bribery, and tax evasion to murder, robbery, and kidnapping. Kirk was embarrassed by the disclosures, deeply and awkwardly embarrassed.

"I knew a guy named Charlie White but suppose it was Charlie Tourine?" Kirk tried to explain to a friend. "Who knew who these people were . . . then? Like Meyer Lansky? I'd never heard of Meyer Lansky."[3]

His Las Vegas attorney, William Singleton, finally issued a media statement "flatly denying" that Kerkorian "has ever knowingly been associated with any member of a criminal organization." But that did little to quell the controversy. There was new speculation that Kirk may have borrowed money from the mob. "Mafia Tie Again Denied" said the *Wall Street Journal,* keeping the unsupported allegation alive.[4]

Tourine appeared before the committee and refused to testify, invoking the Fifth Amendment again and again. That didn't end it, either. Worse, Tourine's voice was heard repeatedly on the wiretap recordings.

On one tape, "Charlie the Blade" can be heard touting Kerkorian as "a real nice guy. I like him a lot." Kirk could only cringe. For a financier controlling three publicly traded companies and hoping for the SEC to ease its ban on the second offering of International Leisure stock, such glowing words from a mobster were no more welcome than that attack of appendicitis he had years ago riding horseback with Sheriff Lamb.

Part of the problem facing Kirk as the story spread in those first weeks of 1970 was his sudden appearance on the big stage of American high finance. Little was known about his background, and Kirk's reluctance to seek publicity only added to the public curiosity. He was what's called a media virgin. Unfamiliar with public controversy and with no public relations people to guide him, he was suddenly caught up in a press feeding frenzy.

"To some, Mr. Kerkorian is a mystery man," said the *Wall Street Journal* in a story about Kirk's links to the mob wiretaps. "Most of his fortune has been accumulated since 1965, and there are people who ask how a man could get so rich so fast." But the paper also reported that federal investigators across the country with "a direct knowledge of the Mafia" said they found no evidence of business ties between Kerkorian and the underworld. And Frank Johnson, chairman of the Nevada Gaming Commission, which investigated Kerkorian before granting him his gambling license, called any suggestion that Kirk had mob ties "nonsense."[5]

But as the negative news coverage continued, there was no question that any publicity that put Kirk in the same headline with the mob was very bad publicity. By spring, International Leisure was forced to withdraw its application for the second public offering. And Kirk had to hang FOR SALE signs . . . on everything.

Talks began with a very aggressive Barron Hilton of the Hilton hotels chain. He was a big fan of Kirk's investment strategies and still kicking himself for being too slow to buy into Trans International Airlines. This time, Barron was eager for a partnership with Kirk as joint owners of the International Hotel. He had to be aggressive. The Hyatt's Pritzker family was also interested in breaking into Las Vegas.

Team Kerkorian was disappointed that Kirk was selling any portion of the hotel business they had helped launch. They had brought up the International from a hole in the sand. It was their baby. Benninger favored selling off the movie company. Unfortunately, both MGM and Western stock prices were badly depressed. Besides, Kirk wanted more time to mine the hidden value lurking in both the airline and the film studio. And he had special plans for MGM that he wasn't sharing yet—not even with Fred Benninger.

It appeared that a fifty-fifty split of International Leisure with the Hilton chain was likely to satisfy Kirk's immediate cash needs, paying off the most pressing of those high-interest European loans. But Alex Shoofey didn't like the deal and said so in his own typically unvarnished way: "That's a stupid agreement!"[6]

Clearly, Kirk didn't hire Shoofey to be a "yes man." Kirk hired experts to tell him things he didn't know, to be straightforward and honest with him, and to do what was best for the company. Shoofey put that priority to the test more than once.

"With a fifty-fifty deal, you have no say. You'll be arguing constantly," insisted the disdainful hotel president. He pressed Kirk to sell only 49 percent.

"They'll never go for it," Kirk said.

The sale ended up coming together in stages, which had the effect of delaying an actual fifty-fifty outcome for months. One reason for the protracted transaction was the dreadful condition of the stock market. It was heading to record lows and taking with it the paper savings of millions of Americans—and a big chunk of Kerkorian's net worth. In just a few months, International Leisure stock had fallen from about $65 a share to less than $6.50. Kirk had no choice but to sell at the worst possible time.

Hilton paid only $19.4 million for roughly half of Kerkorian's holdings—nearly three million shares that a few months before would have brought $180 million. "I got a good kick in the ass,"[7] Kirk conceded to a close friend. But his share of a stockholders' dividend put another $5 million in his pocket, allowing Kirk to pay down half of his largest European bank loan.

And Kirk kept on selling things. His million-dollar yacht, the 145-foot *Tracinda Jean*, was sold suddenly after an unexpected offer from a Saudi Arabian businessman. A *Chicago Tribune* columnist reported that Kirk sold the boat out from under his last charter customer, *Playboy* publisher Hugh Hefner, who had leased it for a week off St. Tropez in the French Riviera.[8]

A year later, after a chance encounter at the Madrid airport with Saudi playboy and businessman Adnan Khashoggi, an impromptu negotiating session on the tarmac led to the $4 million sale of Kirk's DC-9.

One outgrowth of Kirk's unpredictable childhood—of constantly being on the move, dodging landlords and creditors, in and out of money—was his personal detachment from material things. "Things" didn't matter in the Kerkorian home—loyalty and family were the only "possessions" that came along on every move.

"I'm not married to any 'thing,'" Kirk would say. And whether in times of crisis or just to make a good deal, almost every "thing" in Kirk's possession throughout his life was for sale; some of those things ended up bought and sold over and over again.

Kirk's deal with the Hilton chain faced modification in the weeks after he sold off half of his personal share in the International. The Hilton company required an eventual 50 percent plus one share of stock to satisfy its own corporate rules. The problem was that not enough other International Leisure stockholders were willing to sell to Hilton at the $6.48 per share price that existed when Kirk sold.

The mostly amicable transaction could not be closed without Kirk finally agreeing to dip into his personal holdings again, this time for nearly 400,000 shares that he again sold at the $6.48 per share price, although the market price had more than doubled by then. The Hilton chain's full 50 percent threshold was reached at a cost of $21.4 million—a bargain in any market—but worth nearly $50 million even in the bear market of 1969–70.

Kirk remained the largest single stockholder of International Leisure, personally controlling 38 percent compared to Barron's individual holding of 3 percent. Kerkorian and Fred Benninger represented half of the four-member board of directors. Barron and Hilton executive Stanley Zax were the other two. Both sides agreed not to fill a jointly appointed fifth director. It was a concession to Kirk, who was smoldering over his lost autonomy. At least with two slots on a four-member board, Kirk did not fear being outvoted.

He didn't care, he said, if they changed the name of the International to the Hilton. And he shrugged off questions about his staggering paper loss on the deal. But in a rare public display of temper, Kirk let his feelings show when asked about sharing management control with his friend Barron Hilton and his team:

"They can talk all they want. They can call it Hilton Hotels. I have no ego problems. But we own equal voting control. . . . We have two directors. They have two. I hate even that. I like to call my own shots. It's my place more than Barron's and Conrad Hilton's. So, I'm not going to dance to their tune . . . and they can go whistle."[9]

Like any sane gambler, Kirk never looked back. He wanted no part of what-if speculations, no second-guessing about past decisions. Learn a lesson from mistakes and move on, that was Kirk's way. But Kirk's legal and financial advisers wanted to blame the SEC. They estimated that Kirk lost $100 million as a direct result of the stock offering denial.

Kirk blamed Kirk. He had let himself become vulnerable. He hated that. He hated feeling helpless and at the mercy of forces beyond his control. It took much of the fun out of his life and out of his business in 1970. He vowed never to let anything like that happen again.

20

MAKING DEBBIE REYNOLDS CRY

MGM was in the second week of a massive auction of props, costumes, and equipment when Item W-1048 was called. It was the moment a crowd jammed into soundstage 27 had been waiting for, the moment that defined all that was magical—and miserable—about Kirk Kerkorian's financially ailing film studio. More than half a century and two thousand movies after inventing Hollywood, the Metro-Goldwyn-Mayer dream factory was more closely imitating a C-47 falling out of the sky as the company plunged toward bankruptcy. Whatever wasn't bolted down was being tossed overboard, and that included Item W-1048: the ruby slippers Dorothy wore in *The Wizard of Oz*.

"What do I hear for the shoes?" called out David Weisz, the auctioneer. "Somebody start it out."[1]

"One thousand dollars," said a loud voice, and the bidding erupted.

In a few seconds the high bid reached ten thousand dollars. By that point a group of Culver City schoolkids had to withdraw. They were the "Committee to Save the Ruby Red Slippers." They had raised a few thousand dollars in nickel and dime contributions, parent donations, and even a city council pledge of $2,500 more in taxpayer support. It wasn't enough.

"Eleven thousand!" The bids resumed. Twelve thousand . . . and then, a jump to fifteen. The crowd went silent.

"Fifteen thousand, I'm bid—once," said the auctioneer. "Twice . . . Are you all through?"

And thirty-six seconds after asking somebody to start the bidding, Weisz declared the ruby slippers "sold for fifteen thousand dollars" to the lawyer for an unidentified millionaire. Thirty-six seconds to dispose of the holy grail of movie memorabilia. Thirty-six seconds to move on to the next item in what many called the biggest and saddest yard sale in Hollywood history.

The studio that Kirk took over had been in far worse shape than anyone dared admit when he was pouring tens of millions of borrowed dollars into buying its stock. A few months earlier, at the first stockholders' meeting under the Kerkorian administration, newly installed president Jim Aubrey announced a previous year loss of $35 million. More box office duds were in the pipeline. Drastic cutbacks, layoffs, and the sale of real estate and corporate body parts seemed the only option. Those concerned about preserving film history were trying to hold back a mob of desperate bean counters.

Fred Benninger was one of those who knew just how bad MGM's numbers were—and how much worse they could get. On a tour of the studio's Culver City back lot, he was impressed with how much "stuff" was lying around unused. Instead of historic props and sets, he saw an enormous and continuing storage expense. "How often is this stuff used?" he asked. For the Prussian, it was a polite way of broaching the question: What to do with all this junk?

The new owners saw little intrinsic value in back-lot stuff. After all, even the famous ruby slippers were just used shoes with red sequins. They cost the costume department no more than fourteen dollars back in 1938. The studio agreed to pay auctioneer Weisz a flat fee of $1.5 million for everything—from an Esther Williams swim-suit and Clark Gable's trench coat to a working steam locomotive that once hauled President U.S. Grant and last appeared on-screen in *How the West Was Won*.

Under the Kerkorian-Benninger-Aubrey scheme to save MGM, much of the back lot located on the pricey West Side of metropolitan Los Angeles was going on the block. The land itself was worth tens of millions to developers. To use it for costly warehousing to preserve the old stern-wheeler from *Showboat* or the racing chariots from *Ben-Hur* or *The Unsinkable Molly Brown*'s brass bed or Civil War cannons from *Gone With the Wind*. . . or Greta Garbo's hats . . . or Dorothy's old ruby slippers—well, that penciled out very badly in a cost-benefit analysis. The stuff had to go. Soundstages had to go. Andy Hardy's hometown, Scarlett O'Hara's Tara plantation, the streets of Old New York, and Tarzan's jungle all had to go.

It would take twenty days to complete the auction. Actress Debbie Reynolds was there most days. She spent a reported $600,000 buying up costumes, pieces of sets from award-winning movies, and various props hoping to preserve them for a future Hollywood museum. She considered the massive auction a "sad and stupid" waste of Hollywood's priceless past. "I sobbed every day," she said.

The MGM liquidation campaign started months before any opening bids in the auction that would make Debbie Reynolds cry. The studio's entire camera department was shut down and its equipment sold to Panavision. It was cheaper to rent cameras as needed than to store idle equipment and pay camera operators whether they were shooting or waiting for their next project. The New York executive offices on Avenue of the Americas were shut down and returned to Culver City. Aubrey had a sign marking his parking spot. Kirk requested that his be marked simply with his lucky number "21."

Hundreds of layoffs made parking easy even without reserved

spots. And the entire top floor of the Thalberg Building, now called the Administration Building, was left vacant. Maintenance workers were instructed to turn off the heat on that empty floor, proving that no expense was too small to save.

The company sold its theaters in South Africa, Australia, and Europe for more than $6 million. Its Boreham Wood studio in London went for $4.3 million. Sixty-eight acres of back lot—the setting for numerous westerns and Judy Garland's home in *Meet Me in St. Louis*—went the way of bulldozers via developers Levitt & Sons.

Jim Aubrey got a fast start spreading heartbreak and fury with a flurry of canceled film notices. The Smiling Cobra showed no sentimental biases. It was a matter of dollars and sense. MGM was in financial shambles. Its library of classic movies was hugely valuable. The rest was expendable. "Kirk and I decided we had to get rid of everything else. We really had to claw our way back," he said.

Among his earliest cancellations was the $10 million *Man's Fate* film project of the revered Fred Zinnemann—director of such earlier classics as *High Noon, From Here to Eternity,* and *A Man for All Seasons.* Beyond its then-astronomical budget, Aubrey didn't see box office potential, either. *Man's Fate* was a story of existential quandaries based on a French novel about a failed Communist insurrection in 1927 Shanghai.

Aubrey flew to London a week before the movie's first day of principal photography. In a meeting at the Dorchester Hotel he disclosed MGM's grave financial state and explored ways that Zinnemann might be able to cut costs—like taking a large pay cut and convincing his actors and production crews to do the same. That was a nonstarter. Nonetheless, Zinnemann left that evening feeling cautiously optimistic he could complete the project that he had been developing for nearly three years.

Three days later the director received a cable from the Smiling Cobra—*Man's Fate* was dead. The stunned company of actors that included Peter Finch, David Niven, Liv Ullmann, and Max von Sydow insisted on completing the last week of dress rehearsals—knowing no film was to be made—"just for the satisfaction of seeing how it was going to go," recalled Zinnemann. "Then, we all went home."[2]

Adding insult to indignities, Aubrey refused to reimburse Zinnemann or producer Carlo Ponti for nearly four million in preproduction costs. And there were guaranteed salaries to actors that were suddenly not guaranteed. *Taipan*, another Asia-set period piece produced by Ponti and Martin Ransohoff, was among another dozen film projects that Aubrey axed in rapid order, wiping away at least $45 million in prior commitments.

Ransohoff confronted Aubrey, accusing the MGM executive of reneging on time-honored pay-or-play deals. That was how Hollywood had always guaranteed payments to big-name stars and A-list directors. This was betrayal, he complained.

"Marty, you're missing the point," Aubrey interrupted.

"What's the goddamned point? You have a firm pay-or-play deal."

"The goddamned point is that we have no goddamned money!"

The most immediate result was litigation—in the end, a lot of litigation. The long-term effects of such drastic steps were more complicated. For a time, MGM was distrusted and shunned. It became the studio of last resort. Up until Aubrey rewrote the rules that Kirk's lawyers then had to litigate, Hollywood had been a place where handshakes and verbal assurances were considered ironclad contracts. Those days were changing, driven in part by financial crisis but also in this case by Aubrey's ruthless enforcement of Kerkorian's directive to pull MGM out of its dive.

Still, there was bitter irony in the fact that Kirk Kerkorian of all people would turn out to be such an important agent of that change. Kirk himself never changed. His signature would always be worth millions of dollars. His handshake and a promise would always be sacred.

Handed responsibility for protecting MGM from the messy fallout from Aubrey's last-minute cancellation of *Man's Fate* was a scrappy young associate at the Bautzer law firm, a recent ex-Marine named Terry Christensen. He was, as he liked to say, "just minutes out of the Marine Corps" when he was taking on some of the biggest names in show business.

Contract law hadn't been a big part of his military experience as a lawyer in the judge advocate general's office at Quantico, but Hollywood deal memos were notoriously imprecise and larded with special favors—as he soon discovered for himself: "Even a newbie like me could find a dozen holes in those thirty-page memos."[3]

Kirk left Aubrey alone to run and rescue MGM. As delegator-in-chief, he was mindful of results, not process. And like Shoofey at the Flamingo and the International, Kirk trusted Aubrey to manage the details at MGM. That meant no muddied chain of command, no interference from above.

But then the phone rang. It was attorney Sidney Korshak, a noted Hollywood fixer with particularly close ties to Paramount Studio bosses. He was also a social friend to Kirk—and to every other studio chief in town. Kirk and Jean were on the elite guest list for Korshak's who's-who-of-Hollywood annual Christmas party.

He was calling for a favor on behalf of Robert Evans, the president of Paramount. "Bobby" wanted to cast some unknown thirty-year-old actor in a big movie with Marlon Brando. The problem: Jim Aubrey had just signed the guy to a contract for some MGM fluff—a mobster comedy called *The Gang That Couldn't Shoot Straight*.

"This schmuck Aubrey won't let him go," Korshak said.[4]

Could Kirk please get Aubrey to release the guy?

"Sidney, I'd do anything for you," Kirk replied. "You know that, but my deal with Aubrey is he's got total control. It's Aubrey's call. I've got no say in it."

Korshak, who cultivated a tough-guy image and encouraged speculation about his supposed ties to Chicago mobsters, liked to joke that he made Kirk an offer he couldn't refuse—"I asked if he wanted to finish building his hotel," he told Evans. But Kirk wasn't building a hotel at the time. The International was already two years old and no other project was even on the drawing boards.

Whatever Korshak said, and it's just as likely that he simply played the good friend card, Kirk folded. "Who's the actor?" he asked. It was an unfamiliar name. He asked Korshak to spell it.

"Capital A, punk l, capital P, punk a-c-i-n-o."

"Who is he?"

"How the fuck do I know," Korshak said. "All I know, Bobby wants him."

A short time after the Korshak-Kerkorian conversation, an irate Aubrey got through to Evans at his Paramount office. The Smiling Cobra had just heard from Kirk and was spewing epithets. According to Evans's account in his book *The Kid Stays in the Picture*, he could only listen in silence. Aubrey's tirade lasted only a few seconds and ended with, "I'll get you for this!" And the phone went dead.

Kirk's rare intervention changed history. The unknown Al Pacino was released from his MGM contract, permitting him to break into superstardom playing Michael Corleone in Paramount's instant film classic *The Godfather*.

Under Aubrey's continued cold-blooded economizing, Kirk still got precisely what he wanted for MGM. The financial hemorrhaging slowed. Strict budget and spending limits were established and aggressively enforced. Aubrey kept selling off MGM assets, but in the process he was also retiring debt.

So, with MGM no longer in free fall, Kirk focused on the other pieces of his leisure empire, the Vegas hotels and Western Air Lines.

K irk had been getting what he considered bad press since early in 1970 for standing in the way of a possible merger between Western and American Airlines. He did oppose it at a time when Western was struggling. He preferred talking merger from a position of strength, not weakness. But to many it appeared that he was simply holding out until American paid him more money for his 30 percent.

At the company's annual meeting in April at the Beverly Hilton, shareholder Flint Rainey asked about published reports that

Kerkorian was standing in the way of a share-for-share deal with American. He held the floor for several minutes, noting:

"It seems to me this would be a very good merger for Western at this time . . . because American is profitable and Western is not. American pays a dividend and Western does not. American stock is about twenty-five dollars and Western's is about . . . thirteen dollars. American possesses the ability to modernize their fleet of aircraft to compete in today's market and Western apparently does not."

He concluded with more personal remarks directed at Kirk.

"If Mr. Kerkorian is the stumbling block here—and that's been reported in the press—then I think he is gambling not only with his own money, which is fine with me, but also with the investments of the other seventy percent stockholders in Western, and I think that's wrong."[5]

Behind the scenes it was deposed president Terrell Drinkwater, now the titular chairman of the board, who was stirring up stockholder unrest. He had continued meeting secretly with American president George Spader and stoking press speculation about a possible merger.

Now Kirk was furious. He had moved slowly against Drinkwater's insults and recalcitrance. The man was Mr. Western Air Lines, the unchallenged boss for twenty years. Kirk valued his experience, his loyalty to the company, and his leadership. But an insurgency against Kirk's agenda was intolerable.

He had tried to warn Terry. "You know what I'm going to have to do, and you know I can do it. I don't want to, but you're forcing me."[6] As corporate raiders go, Kirk had to be among the most polite.

After the stormy annual meeting, however, Drinkwater was doomed. Kirk called a special meeting of the board and summoned Terry home from a trip to Hawaii and Asia. As the last hours of the MGM auction were ticking down in Culver City, Kirk was a few miles away at Western's headquarters near LAX negotiating generous terms of Drinkwater's forced resignation.

Kirk's good friend Cary Grant replaced Drinkwater on the Western Air Lines board of directors.

Back in Las Vegas, Kirk was losing interest in the hotel and casino business. Or so it seemed. The Hilton "H" had gone up on the side of the International building, and Kirk's enthusiasm for management decisions had evaporated. He left everything to Benninger.

A year after selling off the first half of his holdings to pay down European loans, Kirk sold the rest of his shares. It wasn't out of financial necessity this time. He simply wasn't interested in being a partner. Hilton got a bargain. But Kirk profited, too—despite bad timing and lost paper value. The Hilton stock sales and the $5 million dividend brought Kirk a total of $50 million, a two-year profit of more than $30 million.

Kirk refused to look back at what might have been. He told a reporter: "We built the number one hotel in the world. It was an excellent enterprise. I have no regrets."[7]

21

THE RIVAL VANISHES

A twin-engine Lockheed JetStar swooped down out of a moon-less black sky, banked to the north skirting the neon glitter of the Strip and downtown gambling houses, and lined up for an approach into Nellis Air Force Base. It was a blustery night, Thanksgiving eve. The civilian JetStar, the largest class of business jet in the air, was avoiding busy McCarran International about sixteen miles south. Its mission was secret. And its 8:00 P.M. touchdown at the military airfield immediately set in motion a sequence of actions across town that would end the four-year Howard Hughes Era in Las Vegas—and his one-sided rivalry with Kirk Kerkorian.

The historic importance of bold investments in the city by both men was already altering the future of Las Vegas. Individually, and sometimes at odds with each other, Hughes and Kerkorian had started the transformation of Las Vegas from a mob-influenced gambling town to a corporate-controlled gaming resort. State licensing laws had been changed overnight to accommodate them and what Governor Paul Laxalt considered their "showpiece" corporations. Casino investing, though still dominated by the Teamsters Central

States Pension Fund and other mobbed-up "East Coast investors," was nonetheless going mainstream as federally insured banks shed their inhibitions over lending to Nevada gaming operations. Stockholders were soon to be the modern Vegas heavies, demanding profits instead of kickbacks.

But on that night a small crowd gathering nine floors up in the Desert Inn was not there to contemplate Hughes's contributions to Las Vegas. They were there to spirit him away—part of an internal power struggle led by the Hughes faction known as "the Mormons." With confirmation of the JetStar's arrival, they went into action getting the sickly man secured on a stretcher, his emaciated six-foot, four-inch frame clad in blue pajamas and wrapped in blankets.

To avoid his own security guards and any witnesses, Hughes was lifted through an open window and then carried down an exterior fire escape—nine flights of narrow stairs exposed to gusting winds and frigid temperatures, his stretcher maneuvered like a sultan's sedan chair.[1]

If the scene looked like a prison break, the similarities started with Hughes becoming his own drug-addled jailer. In four years he had never been seen outside the confines of the 255-square-foot bedroom in his sprawling penthouse apartment.

Waiting in the shadows behind the hotel that night were two getaway cars and a minivan to accommodate six passengers and the escaping invalid. When the little caravan reached Nellis Air Force Base, Hughes was quickly transferred into the ten-seat JetStar. Minutes later, no more than an hour after its landing, the private jet was back in the sky, leaving behind the lights of Las Vegas.

The recluse billionaire's sudden and stealthy departure remained a secret for several days, until copies of the *Las Vegas Sun* hit the streets in early December. "Howard Hughes Vanishes!" headlined a front-page story by publisher Hank Greenspun. "Mystery Baffles Close Associates."

It took close associate and chief aide Robert Maheu more than a week to track his boss to Nassau in the Bahamas—only to learn then that Hughes had fired him as part of an abrupt reorganization elevating "the Mormons" at Maheu's expense. It was in the aftermath of his dismissal that Maheu finally shared with Kirk the secret that Hughes had been working behind the scenes all along trying to scuttle the International Hotel.

Proof was in the Hughes memos. Maheu turned over copies to Kirk. "Dear Bob, we've got to address the Kerkorian situation again," began a typical handwritten note. For Kirk, who had always dismissed suggestions that Hughes was trying to sabotage his hotel project, the memos seemed to be a big disappointment. "I didn't realize this . . . not at the time. No."[2]

But he also didn't seem to hold any sort of grudge against either Hughes or Maheu. Kirk expressed sadness and sympathy for Hughes, whose bizarre behavior was widely blamed on an addiction to pain medications from injuries suffered in various plane accidents. "I had a lot of respect for him," Kirk said. "That was before he went bad with drugs and got hooked on that stuff . . . because of all the crashes."[3]

He called Maheu "a sweetheart of a guy" even after discovering the misleading roles the aide sometimes played trying to manipulate him at the behest of Hughes. The former Hughes man continued to be a frequent tennis partner with Kirk. They were neighbors for a time, living across a fairway from each other at the Las Vegas Country Club, in the shadow of the old International Hotel, soon to be renamed the Hilton Las Vegas. By whatever name, it would always be the hotel that Kirk built.

Lawyer Bautzer, who represented both Hughes and Kerkorian, had always reassured Kirk that there was nothing to the rumors of Hughes's animosity toward him. The attorney was more ambiguous in his public statements, telling the *New York Times* that the two men "neither hate each other nor are they partners."[4]

On the surface Kerkorian and Hughes presented similar profiles as aviators and gamblers. Both pilots had operated airlines, though Kirk's Trans International charter company was hardly comparable to the Hughes-run commercial giant Trans World Airlines (TWA). But Kirk's controlling interest in Western, a major regional airline, was an impressive acquisition. And Kirk's takeover of the struggling but venerable MGM film studio mirrored Hughes's former control of RKO Pictures.

"Our lives had a lot of parallels," Kirk acknowledged to close friends. "I even understand some of his phobias and paranoia. I have a little of that myself."

It was a bit of self-awareness that acknowledged his sometimes debilitating shyness and certain increasingly obvious obsessive-compulsive traits. He was fixated on punctuality. His closets were as orderly as the racks at a fine men's boutique. A tissue box left in the wrong place could get the cleaning staff a stern reprimand. But he hated to be compared to Hughes as a recluse, once chiding friend and business colleague Lee Iacocca as "that no good son of a bitch" for making just such a comparison about him in public. His closest friends called him a homebody with a touch of social anxiety, but all agreed emphatically that "he's no Howard Hughes." Not even close.[5]

When provoked enough to talk about it, Kirk was defensive: "I'm far from being reclusive. Just because I don't go to a lot of social events, it doesn't mean I'm antisocial. I have old friends—thirty- and forty-year friendships. I go out to dinner three or four nights a week."[6]

Legal gambling brought both Kerkorian and Hughes to Las Vegas as early as the 1940s. But they later returned and invested their millions of dollars for very different reasons—Kirk's was a dream, a plan to build a company around the leisure lifestyle boom; Howard's was a whim that morphed into a tax break and then enticed him with opportunities for political influence.

Hughes didn't come to Las Vegas to get into the hotel and casino business. He started his four-year occupation of the Desert Inn simply looking for privacy and a temporary place to sleep. When he overstayed his reservation and his welcome, of course, he had to buy the place.[7] In avoiding eviction, he stumbled upon an unanticipated tax windfall. And that, in turn, ignited a spending spree on hotels and casinos that brought him widespread media attention.

Oddly, the recluse loved the attention and the favors of fawning politicians that came with it. He created more headlines and more fans among the political elite when he vowed to fund a medical school, restore production to the state's idle mines, build an ultra-modern airport to accommodate commercial supersonic flight, and make Las Vegas as respectable as Lloyds of London. In memos intended for state officials who were receiving his financial support, Hughes wrote: "We can make a really super environmental 'city of the future' here. No smog, no contamination, efficient local government."

Hughes had come to see Nevada as a place where he could buy influence, so he expanded his shopping spree into heavy spending on vacant property along the Strip, tracts of ranch land outside of town, and mining rights all over the state. But he developed none of them. Rather, like a brooding mother hen, Hughes sat on his holdings and invested almost nothing in expanding or improving them.

Kirk, by comparison, came to town eager to build and expand. The fact that he used the Flamingo as a training school for the future staff of his proposed International Hotel was no whim. It was a cold and brilliant calculation, part of a broader vision to develop Las Vegas as a mecca for the modern leisure lifestyle.

"I thought it was going to become an adult Disneyland," he said. And he put his wealth and reputation at risk to serve that vision, plunging into building the International even before he had the cash to complete it.

An indecisive Hughes could never really compete with Kirk—and beyond plotting or committing sabotage, Hughes never really engaged head-to-head with Kerkorian. Their rivalry, to the extent there was one, existed mainly in the mind and ego of Howard Hughes.

As Maheu would say: Hughes never wanted to be in the hotel and gaming business, but once he was in both he didn't want anyone to be bigger than he was. So Kirk became a constant source of irritation, or worse.

"That damned Kerkorian," Hughes once complained to Maheu. "He's the only guy I couldn't buy or break."[8]

PUTTING ON THE MOVES

OCTOBER 24, 1971
LOS ANGELES, CALIFORNIA

It appeared that Kirk had dodged a financial crisis that could have forced his early exit from the ranks of American tycoons and movie moguls. More than simply surviving, he had his swagger back. He was generating headlines again about bold plans and ambitious ventures. Another world's-largest resort hotel was on the drawing board. His views on the economy and the future of Las Vegas were making national news. His choice of restaurants and his dining partners were making local society news . . . and the gossip columns.

All that attention, most of it friendly and positive, had a downside. It finally exposed the previously private fact that Kirk was also dealing with a marital crisis at home. He and Jean—married nearly seventeen years and now with two daughters, Tracy and Linda—had already discussed divorce but neither had taken any action. A few friends knew there were serious strains in their relationship, but Kirk was openly seeing other women.

Back in July, a gossip item in *Parade* magazine suggested that Kirk was seeing actress Claudine Longet, the ex-wife of singer Andy Williams. Kirk's lawyer Greg Bautzer and actor Ryan O'Neal were also mentioned as recent companions of Ms. Longet. One Sunday morning a more prominent and suggestive piece appeared in *Parade*—in Walter Scott's popular Q & A column "Personality Parade"—asking the very snarky question: When would Kirk Kerkorian be "trading in Mrs. Kerkorian for actress Yvette Mimieux?"[1]

Photos of Kirk in his trademark pompadour-styled dark hair and the blond Yvette in a sultry publicity pose were published side by side with the nondenial answer: "Mr. Kerkorian and Miss Mimieux are friends and do not engage in trades of that type."

Kirk was the married fifty-four-year-old multimillionaire; the actress—who had starred a decade earlier in the films *Where the Boys Are* and *Time Machine*—was single and twenty-nine. Friends say they met in New York City, that romance led to talk of marriage, but that Kirk honored Jean's pleas not to divorce.[2]

Whatever was happening in his private life, Kirk felt strongly that it was none of the public's business. He resented every word published about his family or his friendships. When a paparazzi photographer snapped a shot of Kirk with his daughters, he confronted the cameraman about his concerns as a father for the girls' safety and security. He insisted on a promise that the pictures of his children would never be published. They weren't.

But Kirk was fighting a losing battle if he expected to keep the gossip and celebrity writers completely at bay. As the wealthy owner of a movie studio he was infinitely more interesting to such columnists than he had been as the head of a charter airline. Now his lunches at Ma Maison, often with lawyer friend Bautzer, rated regular notice in gossip columns—as did his trips to Acapulco, whether with family or pal Cary Grant. When he danced with "ball of fire" Jacqueline Bisset in her "clingy white halter top jersey dress"[3] or came alone to a party or failed to show up at a black tie affair, it made ink somewhere.[4]

The world was suddenly a fishbowl for the very private Kirk Kerkorian. He was intrigued and insecure all at the same time. The shy tycoon turned increasingly to Bautzer for help navigating what were for Kirk the unfamiliar realms of Hollywood and celebrity. Bautzer's history as divorce lawyer and romancing playboy to the stars made him a staple in Hollywood gossip items, pictured with such beauties as Lana Turner, Ginger Rogers, and Joan Crawford. Bautzer knew how to handle celebrity. He knew the moves, and Kirk needed a mentor.

"We hit it off," Kirk said. "I like to talk to Greg whether it's about business, politics, or just about anything." Another lawyer at Bautzer's firm said "Kirk worshipped Greg" and that the playboy lawyer would often make dates and reservations to show Kirk "how to have a good time."[5]

After getting his various foreign loans paid off, paid down, or renegotiated, Kirk was once again building up cash reserves in 1971—topped by the summer sale of his last million shares of stock in International Leisure. Even MGM was accumulating cash rather than bleeding it—not so much from making movies as from moving real estate. The company sold off another piece of its back lot earlier in the year for $20 million. Movie production costs had been slashed. And the box office flop rate of recent film releases had been improved from 70 percent duds to 50 percent. President Aubrey was predicting MGM's best revenue numbers in many years.

Things looked sufficiently promising to Kirk that earlier in October he had convened a private meeting of his closest advisers and MGM executives for a strategic brainstorming session. How could the studio survive and thrive making movies in an entertainment market dominated by free consumer programs on television? How could it hedge its bets? Where could it go for a more reliable, steady, and growing stream of revenue?

Kirk had an idea: modified diversification of sorts. Combine the movie side of the entertainment business with the gaming side. This could be achieved if MGM borrowed about $75 million and built its own grand new Las Vegas hotel and casino. Fill it with movie memorabilia. Name the rooms, restaurants, and menu items after the stars. And call it the MGM Grand Hotel, after the 1933 classic *Grand Hotel* featuring Greta Garbo telling the world: "I want to be alone."

In disclosures that set off dire predictions from movie nostalgia buffs, Jim Aubrey came out of Kerkorian's brainstorming session to announce that Leo the Lion was moving to the Strip. He would preside, one wag suggested, as the new "king of the green felt jungle." Aubrey put it in business management terms: "We've reached the conclusion that it's silly to rely on the motion picture business as the only business that a corporation of this size should be in."[6]

MGM, the film studio, was going to build the hotel, own it, and operate it as a subsidiary. It would need stockholder approval, but that was never in doubt. Kirk owned 40 percent and was buying additional shares. And Edgar Bronfman, the second-largest shareholder, announced wholehearted support for the plan. MGM would take on debt for construction costs through debentures, interest-bearing unsecured bonds. Unlike public offerings of stock, debenture funding would not dilute share values.

The hotel would be built on prime Strip-fronting property—sixteen acres already occupied by the then-defunct Bonanza Hotel at the same intersection shared by Caesars Palace, the Dunes, and the Flamingo. Kirk owned the Bonanza, so MGM would pay him about $5 million, based on an independent appraisal. MGM would also purchase an adjacent twenty-six acres for $1.75 million, making room for another big Kerkorian footprint in Vegas gaming.

The MGM Grand would be even bigger than Kirk's International Hotel. For the second time in a couple of years, he was launching construction of the world's-biggest resort hotel—twenty-six floors with more than two thousand rooms, a casino 140 yards long with more than a thousand slot machines, ninety blackjack tables, and ten oversized craps tables, and trimmed with real imported Italian marble and genuine crystal chandeliers. And once again Fred Benninger would wear the hard hat as Kirk's man on the site.

Critics accused Kerkorian of disrespect toward a national treasure. Ann Rutherford, who played Scarlett O'Hara's little sister in *Gone With the Wind*, likened MGM's financial shift into Las Vegas gaming to selling superstar racehorse Secretariat for dog food. It made Debbie Reynolds sad all over again. "It's like going back to your old hometown and it's been torn down," she told gossip columnist Joyce Haber, herself an ardent critic of the MGM Vegas move.[7]

Kirk was emerging as a man with conflicting reputations—as a cad in Hollywood where he stood accused of dismantling a sacred icon of the arts, but as a class act in Las Vegas where his new hotel would create more than three thousand new jobs and advance the city's stature as a leading resort destination.

More than that, the Kerkorian-directed MGM Grand investment represented a very big bet—the kind of high-roller wager that a gambling town like Las Vegas especially admired.

On the evening of April 15, 1972, traffic to groundbreaking ceremonies for the future hotel created limousine gridlock around the intersection of Flamingo Road and the Strip. Cary Grant was back like a good-luck talisman to support his friend's latest and greatest hotel venture. Actress and sex symbol Raquel Welch, Aubrey's girlfriend at the time, was in charge of detonations.

Among the crowd entering a big red-and-white circus tent erected for the champagne and caviar party, Kirk and wife Jean slipped in barely noticed. As usual they were without an entourage, accompanied only by Kirk's personal secretary—the bald and tattooed ex-cop Bob Garn. He nursed a beer in a bottle and stayed close to Kirk.

In a room full of tuxedos, Kirk was dressed in black slacks and a black blazer over a white turtleneck that emphasized his trim physique. Jean wore a black dress with an open back revealing her well-maintained tan, perhaps a remnant from the family's recent stay in Acapulco. The couple's personal troubles were not in sight.

Aubrey and most of the MGM board of directors, already in

town for an earlier closed-door meeting to review prospective plans and architectural renderings, stayed for their MGM-hosted party. Though Aubrey was publicly supportive of the hotel project, his enthusiasm seemed more reserved. The studio chief was still trying to restore MGM as a profitable filmmaker, an act of wizardry that relied mostly on cost-cutting and asset sales. But this was not the night for such talk.

Kirk's brother Nish was there, too, in his working tuxedo. He ran Nishon's, a Las Vegas restaurant and nightclub that he operated in a brotherly partnership with Kirk. The wealthy little brother had bought stakes in Circus Circus and made other Las Vegas investments for all his siblings.

Outside the big tent, security for celebrities and the business elite was provided by a brigade of uniformed Clark County sheriff's deputies, all under the supervision of Kirk's close friend—now the sheriff—Ralph Lamb. On this night in a crowd of VIPs and strangers, Kirk was also surrounded by family and friends. Still, he was hard to find.

When Cary Grant tried to invite him up on a makeshift stage to take a bow, Kirk was nowhere to be found. When Raquel Welch detonated the fireworks, Kirk was chatting near the bar with a young woman in a designer dress. She said he was fortunate to be so rich. For Kirk, who considered small talk something close to torture, her comments were ironic.

"What good does it do being rich?" he said, consulting his scotch, no ice. "I can't do what I want to do. I don't like getting dressed up and going to see bankers. I hate that sort of thing."

He surveyed the boisterous crowd around him with big, sad eyes and added, "I don't want to be here right now. I'd rather be someplace else."

"Where?"

"I honestly don't know. Just someplace else."[8]

It really didn't matter that Kirk wasn't enjoying his own party. On this night, he owned Las Vegas.

23

A VIEW TO THE ABYSS

LATE FALL, 1973
CULVER CITY, CALIFORNIA

As it turned out, Kirk still had a few loose ends to worry about in his financial world—a six-million-dollar German bank loan, for one, left over from his borrowing spree to build the International Hotel. It was a loan secured only by the Kerkorian signature. Past renegotiations had already exhausted the bank's long-running patience. There was no ill will, but it was time to settle the account. The bank had formally demanded payment in full under terms of their original agreement.

Kirk gathered his team of personal advisers, his inner circle from the private holding company Tracinda Investment that he named for his daughters, Tracy and Linda. Fred Benninger and accountant Jim Aljian came down the hall to Kirk's modest MGM office. Lawyers Frank Rothman and Terry Christensen from Bautzer's law firm drove over from Beverly Hills.

What they saw in Kirk's new predicament was the abyss.

He had plenty of assets, most of them tied up as collateral for other loans. But he had nowhere near six million in cash. He was weeks away from defaulting on the German loan. And that was just for starters.

A perfectly sound $50 million Bank of America loan, fully se-
cured by MGM stock, contained a clause that if Kirk were to default
on any other credit agreements, it would trigger default on the Bank
of America loan. That in turn would put Kirk's controlling shares of
MGM stock securing the B of A loan in immediate peril.

It was a nightmare version of the domino theory. Kirk needed
something close to $6 million in short order or he faced the very
real possibility that he and his team could be run right out of the
MGM building. Risking default would be like playing Russian roulette. Not that Kirk's demeanor gave away any trepidation. The Perry
Como of the craps table was holding court, discussing options, as if
he were playing for chump change.

Someone in the room did some quick calculations. If MGM were
to declare a special dividend of $1.75, Kirk's share of a $10.5 million
payout to all shareholders would amount to $5.25 million—enough
that he could pay off the German loan. But it would also be controversial.

Diversification into the hotel and casino business had yet to prove
itself. The MGM Grand wasn't set to open until December and was
already running at least $20 million over budget. There remained
substantial resistance, inside and outside MGM, to what was per-
ceived as the cannibalization of a beloved filmmaking studio. Its
financial recovery was based mostly on revenue from onetime sales
of assets. And recent revenue numbers offered little to brag about.

Kirk turned to Christensen, the junior lawyer in the room, who
was already handling a nettlesome shareholder's suit. It stemmed
from MGM's purchase of Kirk's Bonanza Hotel property where
the MGM Grand was going up. Kirk liked the thirty-one-year-old
former military lawyer and referred to him regularly as "that cocky
Marine." About that dividend idea, he wanted to know: "Can we
handle that?"

"Absolutely," said Christensen without hesitation. "We will be
sued. We'll probably settle somewhere along the way. But it should
be reasonably inexpensive."[1]

And it would buy time.

Benninger and Aljian endorsed the idea and went to work on a full-blown financial analysis to present to the board of directors. It was obviously good for Kirk. But it also had to be good for shareholders generally.

O utside of periods during intense negotiations, Kirk tended to keep regular hours at the MGM headquarters at that time. He was comfortable working nine to four, then retiring for an hour or so of vigorous exercise—tennis or jogging most likely—and then a shower and a cocktail before dinner. He rarely took work home with him. That's why when he summoned Greg Bautzer unexpectedly to his Benedict Canyon home one evening just before Halloween, the lawyer arrived already sensing trouble.

It had been a busy several weeks for everyone on Team Ker-korian, but especially for Kirk. Quite apart from dealing with his own very private cash flow issues, he had been heavily engaged in di-rect negotiations to sell MGM's foreign distribution operations to a consortium that included Paramount and Universal. The final terms were worked out at the Bistro on Canon Drive, across a table from Paramount power lawyer Sidney Korshak. Kirk had earlier made a deal with United Artists, turning over all MGM domestic distribu-tion to UA for the next ten years. MGM was now the only big studio in Hollywood without its own distribution arm.

The back-to-back transactions brought in more than $20 mil-lion for MGM but came with a substantial downgrade of status in the entertainment world. *Los Angeles Times* columnist Joyce Haber declared the studio "all but closed." What was once among "the major-major" players in Hollywood, she wrote, "is now a mini-minor."[2] Similar sentiment came from the *New York Times,* where Vincent Canby reported that MGM as a feature filmmaker had all but "ceased to exist."

Kirk didn't see it that way. The company's distribution operations could be outsourced on a per-movie or as-needed basis at a fraction of the cost. Besides, MGM also needed the cash. It was financing the twenty-one-hundred-room MGM Grand Hotel and trying to stay viable as a movie studio.

President Jim Aubrey continued to play the role of good soldier—and bad cop—as Kirk's front man to the press and public, putting a positive spin on what was widely seen as the continuing liquidation of MGM. He said MGM would remain in feature film production by doing fewer but higher-quality projects. He also touted a shift to television production even as he blamed TV for radically changing the entertainment business. He repeated the new company mantra: diversification into the leisure field will help MGM.

He blamed a changing film market for MGM's troubles, telling reporters that "the bottom has fallen out of the movie marketplace," prompting collective skepticism. Charles Champlin, entertainment editor at the *Los Angeles Times*, said the only thing wrong with the market was bad movies.[3] "The bottom dropped out of the marketplace for Edsels, not for automobiles," he wrote. And Canby in New York said Aubrey had demonstrated to Hollywood how not to improve matters. "He made inexpensive films . . . but they were almost uniformly bad."[4]

Behind the scenes, however, Aubrey had argued against selling off distribution assets, argued strenuously at times against the very strategies that he defended in public—especially the deal Kirk negotiated with United Artists. Aubrey was so unhappy with the domestic distribution deal that he told friends, "If I was a regular stockholder, I'd sue us."

Kirk had been glad to hear Aubrey's opinion in the privacy of the MGM boardroom. He valued pushback during the executive meetings. But when Bautzer reached the house in Benedict Canyon that late October evening, he found Kerkorian in a rare fury. Kirk wanted to talk about an unsolicited letter from Aubrey detailing the studio executive's continued opposition to the sell-off of MGM divisions. It was a letter that Aubrey said pointedly he wanted "on the record."

It was more than a "cover your ass" exercise for Aubrey. It was also direct criticism of Kirk's judgment and an affront to his leadership. Under Kirk's demanding code of conduct, the letter represented betrayal. A team, like a family, always pulled together once decisions were made. That is what Kirk expected and demanded. He was already disappointed in Aubrey's feeble box office returns. The letter, however, was a capital offense.

Bautzer had persuaded Kirk to hire Aubrey in the first place. Now he had to play executioner. The next day in his law office, Bautzer greeted Aubrey with a polite round of drinks and then a blunt message: "Kirk wants you out. It's over."[5]

There would be no severance package. Their contract was a handshake, and it didn't come with a golden parachute or any other post-employment promises. Aubrey would be allowed to resign, letting him write his own MGM epitaph. "The job which I agreed to undertake has been accomplished and I have other plans for the future which will be announced shortly," he said in a prepared statement. Privately, he joked to friends he feared ending up a desk clerk at a Vegas hotel.[6]

His rocky four-year tenure was marked by thirty-five hundred layoffs, slashed expenses, canceled projects, and bruised egos. He was pretty much unchallenged as "the most hated man in Hollywood." He had brought the studio back into the black after years of heavy losses, but he also left a box office legacy of cheap and forgettable films—such cringe-worthy offerings as *My Lover My Son*, *Nightmare Honeymoon*, and *Lolly Madonna XXX*. One noteworthy exception was *Westworld*, earning more than $7 million worldwide over two years and launching a franchise that would endure decades later.

Among Aubrey's most expensive decisions was a veto with implications not yet apparent on his last day at MGM. Earlier in 1973 he had rejected a film project based on a popular novel by Peter Benchley. Too expensive and not much of a story, Aubrey had said then. Besides, he asked dismissively, "How do you get a shark to do all those tricks?"[7]

And that's how the big one got away—the future box office monster *Jaws* slipped away from Kerkorian's MGM to enrich Universal Studios instead.

As the MGM Grand neared completion in Las Vegas, the looting of MGM's past continued in Culver City. Benninger dispatched a team of shoppers—what former studio executive Peter Bart called "Benninger's marauders"—to scour what remained of the MGM back lots for artifacts to sell or display at the new hotel.

They found original scripts, cartoon cels, old promotional posters, sketches of costumes and set designs, historic photographs, and more. Souvenirs for the gift shop or, as Benninger described them, "trinkets for the tourists." One of those "trinkets" ending up in an MGM Grand gift shop would turn out to be legendary director William Wyler's personally annotated shooting script of the Academy Award–winning movie *Mrs. Miniver.* The price tag on that priceless piece of history: $12.[8]

A few days before the MGM Grand Hotel was scheduled to open, the board of directors agreed to the special dividend first imagined by Kirk's inner circle. It was late November. Aubrey's replacement as president, MGM attorney Frank E. Rosenfelt, presided over the vote and then met the media.

He said the dividend was made possible by sales of "no longer necessary" assets and that the company was now "revitalized, compact (and) commercially viable." He also defended MGM against claims that cutbacks and corporate reorganization may have muffled the roar of MGM's lion. "Leo the Lion will not be reduced to a weak meow," he insisted.

News coverage focused primarily on the hefty dividend. The *Wall Street Journal* called it "an early Christmas present" for Kerkorian.[9] The *Los Angeles Times* called it "a whopping" amount at $1.75 per share.[10]

Within ten days of the dividend announcement, the first share-

holder complaint was filed in a Delaware court. By the end of December five lawsuits were pending, each asserting in some form—as
in the case of *Harff v. Kerkorian*—that the dividend was "declared
improvidently and for the financial benefit" of Kirk. No fraud or
wrongdoing was alleged, simply unnecessarily risky action. An early
chancery court ruling sided with Kerkorian, dropping some claim-
ants and treating allegations of potential harm to shareholders as de-
batable. The ruling guaranteed the legal squabble that Christensen
anticipated would go on for years.

With Kirk's German bank debt settled thanks to a timely MGM
dividend, he had once again stepped back from a precipice unscathed.
Now, freshly invigorated and feeling flush, the gambler was heading
back to Las Vegas for his biggest wager yet.

EXTRA RISK FACTOR

DECEMBER 5, 1973
LAS VEGAS, NEVADA

Opening night at the glittering MGM Grand Hotel brought celebrities and VIPs to the main entrance in fleets of limousines and vintage cars, greeted by flashing strobes and paparazzi under an eight-lane porte cochere. It seemed ablaze with light. No place on the Strip was brighter. A two-month-old Arab oil embargo had dimmed the rest of Las Vegas, but on this special night the Grand had official dispensation from the State of Nevada to amp up to maximum wattage.

There was star power, too. Cary Grant was there again to support his friend Kirk and to introduce Dean Martin, the night's opening act in the twelve-hundred-seat Celebrity Room. The singer-actor's drunken comic bit spoofed Grant's role as a consultant for Fabergé, the makers of colognes and aftershaves. "I like mine on the rocks," he quipped.

Former tough-guy actor George Raft, who attended the 1946 grand opening of Bugsy Siegel's Flamingo twenty-seven Decembers earlier, was there and looking more dapper than dangerous. And there were beautiful women—Shirley MacLaine of *Irma la Douce*,

Jane Powell from *Royal Wedding*, and television's genie Barbara Eden from *I Dream of Jeannie*.

But the real star of the evening was the MGM Grand itself. It was big. It was gaudy. It was magnificent—the "most spectacular achievement" by MGM in its storied history and "a monument to . . . Hollywood's golden era," proclaimed the *Chicago Tribune*.[1]

It recalled the grand hotels of Europe as portrayed in the MGM classic film. Its fifty-thousand-square-foot casino, longer than a football field, made it the world's biggest gaming floor. There was also a posh penthouse casino for members only and high rollers where the wagers started at $50.

Downstairs was a three-hundred-seat theater for watching old movies. For $2.50 the feature classics came with newsreels and cartoons enjoyed from the comfort of blue leather love seats. The Ziegfeld Room could seat about nine hundred and stage lavish revues big enough for a Busby Berkeley production. Even the gourmet restaurants came with movie themes. Gigi's offered French cuisine amid scenes from the 1957 romantic musical, and Barrymore's served steak and lobsters beneath portraits of Ethel, John, and Lionel.

Shops in the lower level offered fine jewelry, trinkets, and memorabilia from the MGM back lots. Sandals worn by Charlton Heston in *Ben-Hur* were on sale for under a thousand dollars. Jack Benny's first violin required a good night in the casino. It was priced at $20,000.

Everywhere throughout its twenty-six floors under its eleven-acre roof were touches of class and elegance, mixed with excess—six hundred crystal chandeliers, plush carpets, polished mahogany, brass stars on the doors of all twenty-one hundred rooms and suites, and marble, marble, and more marble.

It was, of course, over budget. And not all the voices cheered.

Gossip columnist Joyce Haber seemed to be in a particularly disparaging mood. It was as if she disliked the very idea of the MGM Grand Hotel. She was a friend and fan of Jim Aubrey, the recently booted president of MGM. Since his "resignation," she had devoted hundreds of words to predictions of the film studio's pending ruin. She regarded Kirk as a scavenger picking the bones of a dying movie company. And on that grand opening night, she was picking at . . . everything.

She didn't like Dean Martin's opening act. She was unimpressed by the VIP list of Hollywood stars arriving in their minks and vintage cars. Where were the big names from the past? The hallways were hot; the rooms were cold. There was plaster dust everywhere. Oh, and on the life-sized photos of Cyd Charisse and Lena Horne displayed in the lobby—their names were misspelled.

Haber repeated rumors that Kirk was trying to sell the hotel even before it opened. She exaggerated the cost overrun by more than $50 million. But she offered a backhanded compliment to Kirk. He "may have ruined . . . MGM," she wrote for the *Los Angeles Times*, "but he certainly knows how to go all the way when he builds a hotel." She said it looked like the most lavish of MGM movie sets, suitable for *The Great Ziegfeld*.[2]

Kirk never paid much attention to gossip columnists. But these were difficult times. The embargo-caused oil shortage was driving up gas prices, shutting down gas stations, and discouraging tourist travel. A national recession was looming. He needed nice words. Lots of them.

So much more was riding on the MGM Grand's success than on the performance four years earlier of the International Hotel. That roll of the dice was a straight money bet. This would test Kirk's fundamental belief in the future of a leisure industry. It would settle his big bet that a diversified MGM could thrive, that MGM's Grand Hotel could actually bolster the studio's profitability.

It was that extra element of risk that made this the biggest chip Kirk had ever played.

The suspense didn't last long. As the International Hotel did in 1969—but without a Streisand or Elvis on its marquee—

the MGM Grand rocketed to unprecedented numbers in its show-rooms, the casino, and the hotel. The big returns persisted all through 1974, which happened to be MGM's golden anniversary year.

Never in those fifty years, not once since 1924—when a seven-year-old Kirk Kerkorian was still learning English on the streets of Los Angeles and a trained lion named Slats represented the newly merged film company of Samuel Goldwyn and Louis B. Mayer—did MGM earnings ever show such excellent numbers.

For the fiscal year that ended only nine months after the hotel opening, MGM reported net earnings of $26.8 million, nearly triple its profits the previous year. It blew away the studio's old record of $18 million set in 1946. The hotel and casino produced $22 million in nine months, doubling the film side's $11 million accumulated over the full year.

A headline in the *Los Angeles Times* business section delivered the verdict in 48-point type: "Grand Hotel Gamble Pays Off—MGM Has Best Year Ever."[3]

It started with the showrooms. Performers including Mac Davis, Engelbert Humperdinck, Rich Little, Johnny Mathis, and Donna Summer filled the Celebrity Room every night. And "Hallelujah Hollywood," a $3 million musical stage extravaganza that opened in the Ziegfeld Room in April, managed to average just over one thou-sand patrons per show in a nine-hundred-seat venue—a standing-room-only miracle.

Siegfried and Roy, then–rising star illusionists with a big cat act, were vaulted to fame in the "Hallelujah Hollywood" show. One night Kirk visited the boys after a show and said they were backed by "three magical letters . . . M-G-M. You just keep polish-ing them."

Especially impressive was the massive hotel's occupancy rate. The twenty-one-hundred-room "world's biggest resort hotel" hovered throughout the nine months at or above 90 percent full.

Though overshadowed by the hotel, MGM's film studio had one

of its better years—thanks to its golden past. The release in May of *That's Entertainment*, a collection of footage from the studio's classic musicals, met with instant success and suggested that nostalgia still had commercial value, too. Box office for that film alone doubled the studio's pretax earnings for the previous year.

To be fair to history, the 1946 profits adjusted for inflation would have been a record-holding $46 million in 1974. Nonetheless, Kirk was on a roll. Again. He doubled down—boosting his personal investment in MGM to 50.1 percent.

He also made the decision to finally let go of airline ownership, selling back to the company his 17 percent controlling interest in Western Air Lines. The block sale would be $30.3 million in cash and bonds. He explained that he wanted to devote more time to MGM "in which I have a substantially greater investment."[4] And by selling back to the company, he allowed Western to avoid the potential disruption of taking on a new controlling stockholder. Rather than setting off a more lucrative bidding war, Kirk departed something of a hero to Western management and a majority of its stockholders. His seven-year investment in the airline had benefited from stock splits, dividends, and improved economic conditions throughout the aviation industry.

Kirk used the Western proceeds to pay down what remained of his Bank of America loan—the credit line that had leveraged him into control of MGM in the first place. That, in turn, released his MGM shares from liens securing that loan. And Kirk's net worth resumed its climb, heading again for realms around $200 million. So, of course, he had another gamble in mind.

The "grand old lady of the lake" was a long shot, a 1923-vintage lodge and casino that had seen better days. Shuttered and padlocked, the Cal-Neva Lodge on pristine Lake Tahoe's north shore was in the care of a court-appointed receiver when Kirk offered $2 million and a plan to renovate the seedy beauty.

The resort was a throwback to the days of Prohibition and then illegal gambling, and it came with a history of ownership failures. It was built straddling both sides of the state line—coffee shop in California, casino on the legal gambling side of Nevada. It had once been the state's biggest casino, but that was long before Kirk came to Vegas.

Judy Garland performed at the Cal-Neva in the 1930s as part of the Gumm Sisters' vaudeville act. The lodge was destroyed by fire in 1937 and hastily rebuilt. Frank Sinatra owned it in the early 1960s but lost his state gaming license over a friendship with former Chicago mob boss Sam Giancana.

When Kirk bought the place in the mid-1970s, he was planning ahead, as usual. His motives mirrored strategies behind his purchase of the Flamingo a decade earlier. He needed a training school for managers and staff of another massive hotel project—this one about forty miles away in Reno, Nevada's second city, touting itself as "the Biggest Little City in the World." The future MGM Grand Reno was to start construction on the site of an old gravel pit near the new interstate as soon as Kirk could arrange a $115 million financing package.

Renovations began along the Lake Tahoe shore as Kirk steeled himself for another round of meetings with bankers and a new line of financial campaigning—reminding Wall Street that he had delivered on his promises, "that what we've said in the last few years happened just the way we said they would."

Some of Kirk's advisers believed that investor confidence in MGM was undermined by perceptions that he was aloof, even reclusive. Investors wanted to hear from him, "see him in the flesh," as MGM president Rosenfelt urged. Kirk hated such perceptions, chafed at how false and superficial they were, but at the same time he recoiled from anything smacking of self-promotion.

He didn't like publicity events any better, even those benefiting his hotels, and looked for excuses to be otherwise occupied. Kirk sent his brother Nish to formally open the refurbished Cal-Neva

Lodge on April 1, 1977. Nish was happy to cut the ceremonial ribbon at a craps table, restoring the casino to full and immediate operation. The *Reno Evening Gazette* reported that Kirk was in London on "pressing business." No further details were provided. But he was at the time engaged in his second-least-favorite activity—getting dressed to meet bankers. At the end of the month he flew into the Lake Tahoe resort for an official grand opening with Dean Martin performing and Cary Grant introducing.

By that summer, the MGM Grand Reno was off the drawing boards and under construction. Kirk and Cary Grant returned together for the groundbreaking "Hard Hat Party" in July. With a thousand rooms, it would be half the size of its Las Vegas sister Grand—but the biggest hotel and casino in Reno.

The MGM special dividend of 1973, the $5.25 million that rescued Kirk from default on a German loan and saved his kingdom, remained a legal point of contention into 1977. Sporadic settlement talks had come down to one issue: How much was Kirk going to pay to end the lingering litigation? Lawyers for the plaintiff shareholders suggested that Kirk pay back some of the corporate fees he received as MGM vice chairman, director, and executive committee member.

One big problem with that: Kirk always refused such compensation. He felt that as a major stockholder he should benefit only from his investment, that taking a fee for helping to manage his own investment was, well, inappropriate—and unfair to stockholders. He didn't accept "comped" rooms or free meals at his hotels, either. He had always insisted on paying his own way with personal funds out of his Tracinda accounts.

But the suggestion that Kirk should give up compensation that he didn't even receive gave one of his advisers an idea. Terry Christensen took Kirk aside and proposed that the MGM board authorize both onetime and continuing compensation, funds that would legally bind the corporation but that would not be paid. "But they can be surrendered," the lawyer said, considering the notion a brilliant tactical ruse.[5]

"Absolutely not," Kirk said. "I don't want to be paid."

"But you won't get any of it," Christensen explained. "It's authorized, not paid."

"I don't like it. I don't like how it looks." Kirk was adamant.

"But it will help the company," argued Christensen.

Kirk's lawyer was confident that creating some sort of settlement bait could end the very real risk of a costly court battle with an uncertain outcome. Asserting that the stockholders would benefit finally made the difference. Kirk reluctantly agreed to the ploy.

"Just get it over with," he insisted.

Months later, after shareholder lawyers formally demanded that Kirk give up his compensation, a settlement deal was reached. In December 1977, Kirk agreed to decline a board-approved $125,000-per-year "raise" retroactive to 1974, drop a $50,000-per-year salary, and forgo stock options until 1981.

On paper it appeared that Kirk was surrendering about $1.5 million in past and future compensation. It was all a mirage. Kirk still didn't like it, but the ruse took MGM off the hook for any kind of corporate penalty. He went along for the good of MGM.

25

PUNCH,
COUNTERPUNCH

NOVEMBER 21, 1980
NEW YORK CITY

Like a gunslinger with a reputation, Kirk Kerkorian, sixty-three, was known throughout the corporate business world by now as a dangerous man. It was a reputation reinforced by every success, by each high-profile investment, by appearing always to get what he wanted. He had a mystique about him since riding into public prominence seemingly out of nowhere. Suddenly he controlled a major airline and then deftly reshuffled entrenched management. He outplayed the legendary Howard Hughes to become the big man in Las Vegas. And in a Wall Street showdown, he easily dispatched the billionaire Bronfman family to take over MGM. Then he parlayed that great old movie company's name into the symbol of a modern gaming resort giant.

Already a movie mogul worth more than $200 million, Kirk was now targeting a second movie studio. This time he wanted Manhattan-based MGM rival Columbia Picture Industries—makers of such classics as *It Happened One Night* and *Mr. Smith*

Goes to Washington. Kirk's interest coincided with the studio's recent comeback from financial troubles and scandal. Its deposed and disgraced ex-president David Begelman was at the center of both circumstances.

Begelman had shepherded such big hits as *Close Encounters of the Third Kind* and Warren Beatty's *Shampoo.* But he was also indicted on felony embezzlement charges for forging checks to cover gambling losses. An attorney from the Bautzer firm negotiated those charges down to misdemeanors and Begelman walked away with probation instead of a prison sentence.

The Columbia board of directors tried to keep Begelman and his indiscretions out of the press. He was suspended with pay, then reinstated, and, finally, fired. The *Wall Street Journal* broke the scandal open.[1] But to Hollywood's surprise, MGM plucked Begelman off the discard pile.

MGM president Frank Rosenfelt was looking for some box office magic when he proposed making Begelman his production chief. Greg Bautzer advised Kirk that it was a terrible idea for a publicly held corporation to hire a known thief and liar.[2] It was only through the brilliant work by one of his lawyers, he argued, that Begelman wasn't sitting in a prison cell at that very moment.

Kirk predictably deferred, telling his MGM exec, "If you feel that strongly about it, Frank, then I think we should go with Begelman." Bautzer stormed out in protest. The disgraced architect of Columbia's recent successes would remain part of Team Kerkorian for a couple of years—until he was fired on Kirk's orders for the ultimate sin. He got too comfortable while at the same time failing to improve the company's bottom line.

By late in 1980, Kirk's steel-eyed focus was on Columbia, the studio he didn't control. The wary objects of his interest wanted nothing to do with romance. The antitrust division of the U.S. Department of Justice warned against a marriage of the filmmakers. All of Hollywood was anxious to see what Kirk had in mind.

Would Kirk unleash another version of Jim Aubrey with pink

slips and a budget machete? And what about gambling? Would the new studio also diversify into hotels and casinos? And about Columbia's recently acquired pinball-manufacturing subsidiary, would it be transformed into a slot machine maker? Such fears hardened opposition inside Columbia, despite Kirk's acknowledged golden touch as an investor.

Management insisted that it was doing just fine without Kirk, that the company wasn't in the market for a partner—especially one owning about 50 percent of MGM—and that it would fight a Kerkorian takeover. Two years after Kirk's initial investment in the studio, all pretense of politeness between them was gone.

On this clear, crisp autumn morning in Midtown Manhattan, Kirk and Columbia management were locked in a war of lawsuits and insults. With his legal team, he had flown in for a last confrontation with Columbia's board of directors—one last round of threats and ultimatums before resorting to judges and juries.

To that end, the conference doors were closed. No phone calls. No visitors. No interruptions. Aides and secretaries standing by outside the meeting were ordered to observe one edict without exception: "Do . . . Not . . . Disturb."

Out west, dawn was just breaking over the Pacific Coast. Somewhere beyond sight of shore Fred Benninger was beginning a daylong deep sea fishing excursion with MGM Grand executives Alvin Benedict and Bernard Rothkopf. They could not be disturbed, either. The three bosses were sharing a rare day away from Las Vegas, far from hotel and business responsibilities, and well beyond the reach of telephones.[3]

At the MGM Grand Hotel it was a typically slow early Friday morning. There were a few stubborn gamblers left over in the casino from the night before. The first room service breakfast carts were heading for the elevators. And so far the checkout lines were short at the registration desk. Jac and Blanche Keller had packed and left their bags near the door, ready for a quick departure to the airport. The couple was flying home to Indianapolis. They had just enough time for a quick breakfast in the coffee shop.

Shortly after 7 A.M., assistant chef Kenny Oborn spotted a small fire in the not-yet-open MGM Grand Deli. He quickly alerted the hotel switchboard on a house phone, and then he went back to find the flames had grown.

Back in New York, an urgent call for Kirk came in sometime after 10:30 A.M. Eastern time. It was jotted down on a message slip. More followed, the callers increasingly agitated and insistent on reaching Kerkorian. He was needed immediately. More voices relayed more ominous messages: ". . . an emergency! . . . a fire! . . . on television! . . . call ASAP!" The paper slips piled up.

Jac and Blanche were already dead. Dozens more were dying.

The conference room door remained closed. Kirk remained unaware. And the contentious meeting continued uninterrupted.

The business dispute that so occupied Kirk that November morning started two years earlier in the summer of 1978 with a secret Kerkorian shopping spree in the New York stock market. Tracinda Investment was buying up shares of Columbia Pictures. Anyone paying attention to volume and price fluctuations in July might have noticed both figures hitting fifty-two-month records.

Shortly before Thanksgiving, Kirk stepped out of the shadows to disclose that he had been behind that market activity and that his Tracinda Investment had acquired nearly a half-million shares of the moviemaker's stock—about 5.5 percent. At the same time, he declared his intention to seek an additional 20 percent in a January tender offer. It amounted to a $42 million bid for 25.5 percent of an MGM rival company.

Kirk also moved quickly to reassure everyone at Columbia. He was an investor, he said—not a raider. But the board of directors wanted something more tangible. They wanted a contract—and, no, not simply a handshake. In what seemed a cordial negotiation, Kirk agreed and pledged in writing not to buy any more shares of Columbia Pictures beyond the planned 25.5 percent total for at least three years. He also agreed to resign as a director and vice chairman of MGM. Everyone seemed happy—except for the Department of Justice.

The fact undermining any antitrust case against some sort of MGM-Columbia alliance—real or potential—was MGM's rather anemic slate of films. Lawyers for Kirk called MGM primarily "a hotel company," arguing in court papers that it was "a competitively insignificant producer" of four to six films per year. They acknowledged that retrenchment had been so severe that MGM could "no longer be considered a major factor in the industry."

A request for the court to block Kirk from buying more Columbia Pictures stock was rejected. But once he had purchased 25 percent of the company, the federal antitrust lawyers returned, slapping Kirk with a lawsuit that demanded he divest immediately. It was a galling reminder to Kirk of his earlier days sparring with regulators at the SEC. He had few options then. Now he had time and money on his side. He decided to fight.

A weeklong trial that summer in Los Angeles opened with U.S. District Court Judge A. Andrew Hauk very nearly tossing out the case on day one—before federal prosecutors could even make their opening remarks. But the case went forward. It featured ninety minutes of testimony from Kirk himself. Judge Hauk later called him the best witness in the trial, "sound . . . soft-spoken . . . restrained . . . not given to wild exaggeration."

Columbia director and member of the board Herbert Allen, an East Coast investment banker who opposed a Kerkorian takeover, testified to Kirk's integrity and to trusting Kerkorian when he said his stock purchase was for investment only.

For federal antitrust prosecutors, the case was a debacle. Kirk was still bound by his earlier agreement to hold his ownership stake at 25 percent, but he was more certain than ever in the wisdom of his

Columbia investment. And there were alternate ways to boost the value of his holdings without buying more stock.

He began pressing Columbia management to use cash reserves to buy back stock. Not only would the tactic increase stock values generally but in reducing the total number of shares outstanding it would have the notable side effect of increasing the percentage that Kirk owned as well.

Meanwhile, he also found potential outside buyers for his share, including Kirk's friend Jerry Perenchio, a television producer-partner with Norman Lear. His Tandem Productions offered $163 million for Kirk's 25 percent share. Columbia's board wouldn't approve, however, and management was starting to complain about what it considered backdoor takeover threats.

In May 1980 the rift between Kirk and Columbia blew up in the business section of the *Los Angeles Times*.[4] Columbia president Francis T. Vincent Jr. had said something critical of Kerkorian in front of a group of entertainment security analysts and, taking umbrage, the famously private Kirk had actually gone to the press. He let his lawyers do the insulting, but the animosity now was playing out in public.

Vincent accused Kirk of using the press to further his own interests and of selfishly taking up the time of Colombia management in pursuit of his own personal "interests and ambitions, not . . . Columbia's nor its shareholders."

Kirk's lawyers fired back at Vincent for protecting the status quo: " 'Preserve management and keep Kerkorian away' has been a fundamental philosophy of you and your colleagues."

And so it went—punch, counterpunch.

More than ever Kirk considered Columbia a good fit with MGM. A merger offered the best shortcut available to restoring some of MGM's lost filmmaking luster, plus an instant replacement for its lost distribution operations. He still had more than a year to wait before his obligation to stand pat on 25 percent ownership was scheduled to expire. But with the end of decorum between Kirk and Vincent came new and serious threats to end that agreement prematurely.

Finally, Kirk announced in late September that he was going after controlling interest in Columbia . . . now. Regarding the still valid agreement, Kirk said: "Events have transpired which warrant termination." Those unspecified "events" amounted to what Kirk saw as broken promises by the company.

That summer, MGM had split into two separate companies, spinning off its resort and casino business under the banner of MGM Grand Hotels, Inc. The movie business took on the corporate name Metro-Goldwyn-Mayer Film Co. Kirk retained 47 percent ownership of each. The film company was launching the Columbia takeover bid.

Vincent told the *Wall Street Journal* that Kirk "sounds like a guy trying to commit an invasion who has just torn up the peace treaty." He compared the surprise announcement to a surprise attack: "an early morning bombing and strafing raid."[5]

Kirk landed the first legal blow, a breach of contract suit. It contained dark allegations of insider dealing and "a shadow government" of investment banker Herb Allen and old-time Hollywood producer Ray Stark that secretly ran the company. Stark's long affiliation with Columbia Pictures included such major hits as *Funny Girl* and *The Way We Were*.

Two days after Kirk's suit was filed, Columbia sued Kerkorian. Its suit contained dark allegations of conspiracies, hostile intentions, and "a fraudulent scheme to gain control" of the company.

Both sides found federal judges willing to order their opposing sides to suspend scheduled stockholders' meetings. Both sides responded with outraged public statements.

Punch. Counterpunch.

They were like two fighters trading body blows up against the ropes—with not much to show for all the legal pummeling so far but a lot of bruises. Reputations of integrity took the greatest beatings all around. The prickly Ray Stark fired off a "Dear Kirk" letter that he then shared with the *Los Angeles Times*—a low blow, but it was that kind of a fight.[6]

"Obviously I was naïve in liking you, trusting you and believing what you and your associates advised me you stood for," Stark said in his six-page harrumph against the one corner of Kerkorian's reputation that Kirk himself most guarded: personal trust. It was no trivial insult. It wasn't intended to be.

It was in the immediate aftermath of such disrespect and personal invective that Kirk and the Columbia Pictures leadership convened in the company's Manhattan boardroom on Friday morning, November 21, 1980.

A late-morning break finally gave the embattled negotiators a chance to step away from the table and retrieve messages. Kirk had a fistful of little slips with scrawled notes. As he stood absorbing their contents, his low baritone sounded more like a soft moan: "Oh, my God."

MGM SPELLS DISASTER

NOVEMBER 21, 1980
LAS VEGAS, NEVADA

Jason Rohde, the overnight busboy at the MGM Grand Hotel's coffee shop, noticed an odd odor—a hot smell, maybe something electrical or, more likely, the scorched bottom of a coffeepot. He checked the wait stations and found no suspicious sources. It was the second time in the same shift that he'd circled the Orleans Coffee House on a sniffing and detecting mission. Nothing. No one else seemed to notice. He tried to shrug it off.[1]

At 7 A.M. Jason punched out promptly. He didn't want to be late for school. But halfway to employee parking, he realized that he'd left his hairbrush back at one of the wait stations. He rushed back to retrieve it. The brush was there. So was that "hot" smell. He didn't have time for another futile search. He had to get ready for school.

It wasn't much of a breakfast rush yet, but waitress Velma Turner realized the coffee shop was short of the folding stands she and her colleagues needed for tableside serving. The Deli next door would have some. It would be closed until 8 A.M. Velma went through the kitchen shared by both restaurants. In the empty and darkened Deli the main light source was a three-by-four-foot Keno monitor mounted on a wall. At 7:05 A.M. no one was playing.

But something over by the Keno monitor caught Velma's eye. She turned to face it and a spray of blue sparks spewed out from the electrical connection behind it. She waited to see if that was the end of it. But blue sparks burst out again, this time chased by a puff of black smoke.

She hurried back to the kitchen where assistant chef Kenny Oborn had bacon on the broiler. He immediately retraced her steps and encountered red-orange flames now bursting through the wall. He rushed out to find a phone and inform the hotel switchboard: "There's a bad fire in the Deli."

Out by the coffee shop entrance, three vacationing firemen from Illinois waited to be seated. As they followed their hostess another seated patron interrupted the group to ask, "Do you have the time?"

"It's 7:15," replied the hostess.

"Yeah," added the wisecracking Dave Beshoar, one of the out-of-towners, already familiar with how days and nights can get confusing in a windowless casino. "That's A-M, by the way."

Tim Connor, a tile maintenance man, was entering the closed Deli from its front door, opposite the kitchen side where the assistant chef just exited to report the fire. They didn't see each other. Connor heard the menace before he saw it: "A crackling sound, like a roaring fire going like a big bonfire or something." Then he saw the shadows of flames, "flickering, as a candle flickers." Finally, he was deep enough into the crescent-shaped floor space to see "a wall of flames" from countertop to ceiling.

The maintenance man ran back to the vacant cashier's station, grabbed the house phone, and called hotel security. Speaking with urgency he reported, "We've got a fire in the Deli."

"Is it bad enough to alert the fire department?"

"Hell, yes!" Connor shouted. "Roll 'em!"

The MGM Grand Hotel was more than a big, beautiful building, more than a model of good business, more than a monument to entrepreneurial daring or awesome financial success. It was also the fight in Rifle Right Kerkorian's comeback from near disaster. It was the bold statement of a shy kid from Weedpatch that he belonged with the world's elite captains of commerce. It was the gambler's biggest score.

And it was Kirk's baby.

As the Grand's morning shift of dealers, desk clerks, cooks, security aides, and housekeepers arrived with the sunrise, his baby was waking to a typically quiet Friday morning. A handful of late-night stragglers in the casino occupied a single craps table, a couple of blackjack tables, and scattered slot machines. It wasn't much action, but Louis Miranti was monitoring, as usual, from the casino's "Eye in the Sky"—a remote office on the floor above with a live camera link to the casino floor. Miranti was the house referee, the casino's integrity cop.

There were no lines yet at the front desk. Friday was notorious for late sleeping and late checkouts. And at this early hour, the Orleans Coffee House was always more popular than dice or the slots. The all-night coffee shop was at the easternmost end of the casino—the 140-yard gambling floor once proudly christened the "world's biggest casino." That was until Kirk's Reno MGM Grand added ten yards to the record.

The Orleans anchored Restaurant Row made up of Barrymore's, Gigi's, Caruso's, and the Deli. They were clustered just opposite a central bank of sixteen elevators serving all twenty-one hundred rooms on twenty-six floors.

The hotel was finishing the week at 99 percent occupancy. The stats were gratifying on many levels, especially supporting the notion that Kirk's baby was, in fact, everybody's favorite. His hotels certainly made Kirk proud. And more. Previous year pretax profits for the Vegas and Reno MGM hotels combined had been $33.9 million.

Harvey Ginsberg had a 7:15 business breakfast scheduled in the coffee shop, and he was running a bit late, wheeling into the MGM Grand's magnificent porte cochere at precisely 7:15. He still faced more than a football field's walk from the west entrance to the Orleans's hostess station on the other end of the casino. He couldn't wait for a parking slip. He was sixth in line for the swamped valet. Ginsberg left his keys in the car and hurried through the glass doors.

He was walking fast and wishing he could move even faster without resorting to an unseemly sprint. He couldn't help noticing something unusual about the atmosphere around him. There was a thin haze hanging over the high-ceilinged casino. The air-conditioning system must have failed, he figured. Not that the 38-degree temperatures outside put much of a strain on the machinery, but air filtration was part of its function, too. It didn't seem to be bothering anyone. Ginsberg kept his pace.

Tim Connor, the tile maintenance man who found flames in the Deli and called for a fire department response, had gone to find a fire hose in one of those glass cabinets marked with big letters: "In Case of Emergency Break Glass." It was supposedly in a hall between the Deli and the also closed Barrymore's. Connor headed that way, across the empty Deli seating area just as a sudden explosive burst of smoke and heat knocked him to the floor near the vinyl-covered luncheon booths. He gathered himself and kept going.

The flames were still confined to the walls and interior of the Deli. The adjacent coffee shop remained unaffected and its patrons unaware—until a hotel security man entered and got everyone's immediate attention: "There's a fire in the Deli." He asked everyone to evacuate the restaurant as a precaution. The vacationing firemen from Illinois offered to assist and tried to find an extinguisher—until heat building rapidly around the Deli area drove them back.

Ginsberg's fast-paced walk got him to the far end of the casino by 7:20. He faced a low set of steps up to the restaurant area and the main elevator lobby. But he froze. He could see the flickering reflections of flames coming from the Deli entrance on his right. Beyond that he saw people running from the coffee shop. He knew panic when he saw it. He also felt it. He broke into a jog back toward the center of the casino, away from the flames and the panic, until he felt safe enough to stop and watch.

Louis Miranti, the Eye in the Sky monitor in his office over the casino, was taking a break from watching to writing. He had another hourly report to prepare. In the quiet of an early Friday morning he was distracted by a sound. It was different. Not a noise exactly. Not loud. Not the maintenance crews, either—but something completely out of place. It was, he thought, more like the "crackling of a very intense fire."

Betty Gillihan on the hotel switchboard had received the first fire alert from Kenny, the assistant chef, and in turn called the Clark County Fire Department. Station 11 was located across the street from the hotel. "This is the MGM. We have a fire in the Deli," she said, her voice so calm and unperturbed that fellow switchboard operators thought it was just another routine call, like so many that rarely rated notice in the local news.

The first rescue unit to cross the street brought a four-man crew that included Bert Sweeny, a six-foot-six firefighter known in the station as Godzilla. He was confused upon arrival just a minute or two later. There was no visible smoke, no rush of people trying to get out of the hotel, and, therefore, no obvious point of entry. They pulled up in front of the Flamingo Road entrance. A woman in a dark velvet dress was just outside the doors wiping her eyes and coughing. Still, no signs of panic. No general alarm.

The firefighters pushed through the glass doors and advanced about forty feet into the casino's eastern end nearest the restaurant area. Sweeny noticed the smoke, a stratified layer about eight feet thick and clinging to the ceiling. They had paused only for a moment to consider their first move when a monstrous presence intervened.

From out of the Deli burst a rolling fireball of dense black smoke and red-orange flame, hugging the ceiling as it swooshed out toward the casino, sucking up oxygen and new energy and growing into something suddenly gigantic. Entering the high-ceilinged casino it took the shape of a fiery tidal wave, reaching from floor to ceiling, mixing with a deadly black smoke that Godzilla and his rescue crew couldn't hope even to slow. They ran for their lives.

Betty Gillihan at her switchboard station in the lower level of the hotel was already broadcasting a notice to immediately evacuate the casino. The mass exodus on the casino floor above them sounded like "an elephant stampede" to the crew of phone operators.

Harvey Ginsberg was part of that stampede. He was running from the same fireball that already had firefighters in desperate retreat. The smoke had suddenly descended, too, obstructing vision and burning lungs. Ginsberg couldn't see chairs from abandoned blackjack tables left overturned in this path. He went sprawling on the plush maroon carpet, scrambled to his feet, and kept running.

That fireball apparently caught the Kellers from Indiana waiting together near the elevators just outside the Deli and only steps from their breakfast table at the coffee shop. The elevators themselves were traps for another half-dozen guests, the lifts effectively turned into little gas chambers by the smoke and toxic fumes.

The crackling sound that first alarmed Louis Miranti was, in fact, the fire as it consumed its way through the walls and ceiling of the Deli a floor below his Eye in the Sky. It was spreading fast with an advance column of deadly smoke. Miranti fled, but the smoke pursued. His only hope was to reach a back exit he knew. Cutting through the executive office wing, Miranti used his shoulder to break through glass doors to offices of the bosses fortunate to be fishing off the California coast at that moment, then through the executive washroom, grabbing a Turkish towel for use as a crude breathing device, and down into a labyrinth of dark and increasingly smoky hallways. He collapsed just as the hand of an unseen security guard reached out to drag him out of the building.

Ginsberg managed to escape the casino into the adjacent porte cochere just ahead of the fireball. His car was now first in line for the valet, the keys still in the ignition. He drove off as flames ignited the roof over the valet station.

It was nearly 7:30 on a glorious Las Vegas morning. A raging monster now possessed Kirk's baby. Dozens of guests were already dead and more were dying. All available ambulance and paramedic units were on call. The ominous black clouds of smoke that suddenly fouled the air above the MGM Grand Hotel now loomed as well over Kirk's long and uninterrupted lucky streak.

M ike Agassi at his home noticed the plume of dense smoke in the distance. The smell of smoke was in the air. Kirk's friend and onetime tennis instructor was now a showroom captain, a sort of maître d' or majordomo. His realm was the Ziegfeld Room. He immediately clicked on his television set.[2]

His fears were confirmed with the first news report from the scene. It was the MGM Grand. Mike watched live shots of desperate hotel guests waving from window ledges and balconies, gasping for air through broken windows amid swirling smoke. There were endless street scenes and fire ladder trucks making dramatic rescues from the lower floors. Helicopters kept circling the rooftop crowded with refugees from the toxic smoke and fumes.

Inside the hotel towers, beyond the view of TV cameras, rescue workers were climbing smoke-filled stairwells, crawling over fallen bodies, searching for people with a pulse, people who might still be saved. In one upper-level elevator lobby, rescuers found five couples dead from smoke and toxic gases. The firefighters had determined that the ten victims were couples because each pair had died in each other's arms. Of the eighty-seven guests and employees who died, all but a handful succumbed to smoke and noxious fumes. Some victims died in their sleep.

The fifteen-hundred-degree fire had raced through the casino and lower levels of the hotel in a matter of minutes, leaving utter devastation in its path. The flames were over quickly, spent more than extinguished, with the heaviest damage confined to those lowest floors. The formal investigation and recovery of bodies began once the flames were out and the smoke was dissipating—within two hours of the first emergency call. But in that brief period of compressed terror those eighty-five deaths made it the second-most-deadly hotel fire in U.S. history. Another seven hundred were injured. The casino was in shambles. And the MGM name was now permanently affixed to a heartrending disaster.

Mike Agassi had to see for himself just how bad it was. Up close and in person. He headed for the hotel sometime around 9:30 A.M. His prominent role for years at the MGM Grand made him a familiar face in small-town Las Vegas. He had friends among police and fire officials, and his personal friendship with Kirk was widely known. He was waved through police and fire lines and entered the casino where Godzilla and his first responders had encountered the fireball.

It was a charred and melted mess. Without the glittering casino it was as if the heart of the MGM Grand had been ripped out. Slot machines were still recognizable, but the intense heat had fused whole rows of them into solid blocks of plastic and metal, ghastly remnants frozen in time. The whole place reeked with the essence of smoke and garbage and death. Mike tried to breathe through his mouth.

He roamed through the showrooms. They had escaped the worst of the fire, but smoke and water damage seemed to be everywhere the fire missed. All around him, the business of removing bodies and starting the hunt for clues was proceeding. Mike stayed out of the way.

He had returned to the devastated casino in the early afternoon when a small crowd stepped in through the Flamingo Road entrance. There were uniformed fire officials, a gaggle of photographers, and a group that looked like businessmen.

One of the visitors held a handkerchief over his nose and mouth, clearly bothered by the pervasive odor. But even with his face half covered, Mike knew it was Kirk Kerkorian. His team of top managers surrounded him. Mike also recognized Fred Benninger and accounting boss Jim Aljian.

Earlier that day, after checking his messages in New York, Kirk had walked out of his meeting with the Columbia Pictures board of directors. His private jet was waiting at Teterboro Airport across the Hudson in New Jersey where he pressed his crew to get him back to Las Vegas as fast as possible. He was standing in the doorway absorbing the incredible loss and human suffering about four hours later, a time when the last of the victims' bodies were still being removed from his building.

Mike approached Kirk and his party of VIPs searching for the right words, uncertain what to say. He finally stammered something plain but heartfelt: "I'm so sorry about what's happened."

Kirk's sad eyes showed from behind the handkerchief. He was clearly upset. He responded softly, his voice further muffled by his makeshift air filter, "Thanks, Mike. I'll call you later." And the man who built the place was led off on a somber tour of what remained of his prized possession.

At his home about two weeks later, Mike answered a knock at the door. It was Jim Aljian—the hotel's senior vice president, a member of the corporate board of directors, and a financial adviser to Kirk. Mike knew him as "Kirk's treasury man." Aljian wanted a look at Mike's last couple of tax returns.

"What?!"

Aljian explained that Kirk wanted to be certain that Mike was not harmed by the hotel's shutdown. It would reopen in a few months, he assured the idled showroom captain, but in the meantime Kirk would pay him his monthly take-home. Personally.

"No. No, that's not necessary," Mike protested. "I've saved some money. You don't need to do this."

Aljian had a pleasant round face, very little hair, and a patient smile. He looked around the room filled with the telltale signs of a family with three children. Little Andre Kirk Agassi was nine.

"Of course I have to do this," he said. "It's what Kirk wants."

Later that month Aljian returned in what would be a monthly ritual to deliver Mike and his family an envelope with precisely $9,089 in cash from his friend Kirk.

VILLAIN OF
THE ACTUARIES

EARLY 1981
LAS VEGAS, NEVADA

Kirk and his management team had determined within hours of the fire that they would begin immediately rebuilding the MGM Grand—"bigger and better than ever," he insisted. And in consultations with attorney Terry Christensen regarding damage claims by victims and their families, Kirk underscored his priorities in the difficult negotiations ahead: "The victims were our guests. We aren't fighting them. We're on their side."[1]

But such promises and priorities posed a considerable financial challenge. The hotel's insurance coverage with liability limits in the vicinity of $30 million appeared pathetically inadequate for a tragedy of this scale. The company started the new year facing dozens of unresolved personal injury lawsuits seeking nearly a billion dollars in actual and punitive damages.

Those uncertain and potentially massive liability costs complicated just about everything on Kirk's agenda, including cleanup and hotel reconstruction costs anticipated to exceed $50 million. He had been hoping to break ground in Atlantic City early in 1981 on a new casino project, but that was now on indefinite hold. He also had wanted to complete his takeover of Columbia Pictures, but that fight was looking more costly, and nastier, than ever. The Columbia board of directors had just filed another nuisance suit, acting as aggrieved MGM stockholders. The New York–based film company held a mere ten shares of MGM Grand Hotel stock, but its court filing attracted plenty of press coverage. It claimed those ten shares lost value after the deadly fire that it blamed in part on unsafe and substandard hotel construction.[2]

With so many major issues pending and critical options to consider, Kirk decided to get away for a few days, flying down to Mexico City on his private jet. Kirk's personal life at the time was also facing change and uncertainty. He and Jean were no longer living together, though they continued to make appearances as a couple at social events. Kirk flew to Mexico with his friend Yvette Mimieux.

The actress, then estranged from her film director husband, Stanley Donen, shared Kirk's home on Bedford Drive. She was an active conservationist and naturalist with avid interests in history and art. Her friendship with Kirk would span years.

While Kirk was traveling, Fred Benninger and his staff came up with a plan that could put a lid on the hotel company's liability exposure. It would also set up a high-stakes gamble pitting Kirk against big insurance interests that would ultimately make him the villain of actuaries everywhere.

The Prussian had discovered an insurance product called a "retroactive policy." For the price of a very high premium payment of $38.3 million, a collection of insurance companies guaranteed to cover an additional $120 million or more in liability costs. It was, of course, a rarely used financial instrument, violating one of the basic rules of the insurance business: "Never write a policy on a burning building."

The policy's economic logic lay in expectations that damage and injury payouts were likely to take years of hard negotiations to resolve. Meanwhile, as the years dragged on, that hefty premium payment earned interest or investment returns. What the insurers didn't count on was a policyholder like Kerkorian who considered customer goodwill and social responsibility good for business. He was hardly the stone-cold capitalist assumed in the actuarial formulas for retroactive insurance.

Kirk wanted the disaster forgotten as soon as possible. He pressed the insurance companies to speed negotiations and settle faster. Instead, they dragged their feet trying to prolong the process. Kirk took matters into his own hands, dispatching his own team of insurance adjusters with the same message he gave Christensen: the victims had been guests of the hotel and were not to be treated as adversaries. He put his own money where his priorities were, paying cash settlements out of his own pocket.[3]

The insurance companies were stunned. Kirk had paid $69 million to settle all pending death and personal injury claims against the MGM Grand. He did it in less than two years. But when he billed the insurance companies for reimbursement, they paid about $11 million, then stopped and refused to pay more. They accused Kirk's side of not playing fair, of settling too fast for too much.

The MGM Grand sued its insurance broker and more than twenty carriers that shared various percentages of the risk. The insurance companies countersued the hotel and named a number of building contractors. One of the biggest and most complex legal cases in the history of insurance was launched.

But Kirk, ever the gambler, liked his odds. He would have a Las Vegas jury of ordinary people. And for all its complexity, the case would come down to one thing: the insurance companies' principal gripe against Kirk would be his generosity and prompt response to fire victims and their families. Yes, he had settled too fast for too much. But what jury of ordinary citizens anywhere in the country would side with a greedy insurance company and find fault with Kirk's generosity?

While Kirk had been pressing his insurance adjusters to settle the hotel fire claims, he also was trying to negotiate away the Columbia Pictures stalemate that had him blocked from buying outright control. His 25 percent ownership, if dumped on the market, could have depressed stock prices. Sold as a block it could have posed a threat to management—the same people who united to block his takeover.

Kirk figured he could get his best deal by offering to sell his shares back to the company. It would not only boost stock prices but also consolidate the power of the existing board and its management team. The Columbia team that had fought him so strenuously quickly agreed.

The sale of Kirk's Columbia Pictures stock marked a rare capitulation at that stage in his investing history. But it was by no financial measure a failure. Kirk had purchased the stock at an average price per share of $17.50. Columbia Pictures bought it back at a $20 markup for $37.50. Kirk's failure to take over the Columbia studio had resulted in a nifty net *profit* of $75.6 million.

With all that cash in his pocket, he went shopping again for another movie studio. It happened that United Artists—then owned by Transamerica, the financial services giant that made Kirk wealthy by buying his Trans International Airlines—was suffering through the bad press and internal recriminations of an artistic and box office disaster.

Its $44 million western epic *Heaven's Gate* had been released the same weekend as the MGM Grand Hotel fire to near-empty theaters and sweeping critical rejection. Director Michael Cimino had become the poster boy for artistic excess and self-indulgence. The film's paltry $3.5 million box office return made UA and "fiasco" companions in headlines across the country. So profound was the *Heaven's Gate* flop it prompted existential fears that Hollywood itself might collapse.

By the spring of 1981, Transamerica wanted out—out of a relentless public relations debacle and out of the movie business. Kirk wanted a distribution arm and access to UA's continuing franchise productions of James Bond, Pink Panther, and Rocky films. But he was also keenly interested in regaining rights to MGM productions distributed by UA, including *Gone With the Wind, Doctor Zhivago, Ben-Hur,* and *2001: A Space Odyssey.*

The Kerkorian deal to bring UA and its classic movies library into the MGM family would cost $380 million in cash and a debenture offering. While awaiting antitrust clearance from the government, Kirk and Yvette took another vacation trip on his private jet—this time to Hawaii. The idyllic getaway was to Spanish-American singer-celebrity Charo's seaside residence on the "garden island" of Kauai.

That's where Scoshie bounded into Kirk's life.[4]

Friends described Scoshie as a precocious, affectionate, and plain little dog with big droopy ears and soulful eyes. She was black and of indistinguishable pedigree. But she had one standout quality—she made Kirk laugh. And something about the pup reminded Kirk of a childhood pet.

This puppy belonged to the leasing agent who made daily stops to resupply the Charo rental, and he always brought along Scoshie. Kirk laid in his own secret stash of doggy treats for those occasions. After a week, the dog was leaping from the Jeep the moment it stopped and racing to Kirk's side.

When it was time to fly back and deal with pressing business matters, Kirk opened negotiations with the leasing agent. He wanted to take Scoshie home to Beverly Hills. The leasing agent held out for an undisclosed amount of cash and an expenses-paid trip to Southern California, delivering Scoshie in person after a health department quarantine.

The puppy-love-smitten Kirk returned home to prepare his residence on Bedford Avenue for Scoshie's pending arrival. To replicate a grassy expanse where they played at Charo's place on the island, Kirk had his backyard swimming pool filled in and rolled with fresh sod. A month later Scoshie arrived to assume her new dog's life as the cherished companion to one of America's richest men.

In the weeks that followed, the renovated MGM Grand Hotel moved swiftly toward a summer reopening date. Like the original grand opening, it would again feature Dean Martin in the Celebrity Showroom introduced by Cary Grant. Local journalists knew it was coming, but there was virtually no advance publicity. No national media were invited.

The morning before its doors would open to guests and gamblers for the first time in eight months, Kirk joined the management team for a mass meeting with the entire hotel staff. They gathered in the jai alai fronton, a space big enough to accommodate nearly a thousand employees. Many of them wouldn't have recognized Kirk if they were stuck in an elevator together.

According to one story, a young MGM Grand desk clerk once kept Kirk waiting to check in while she had a brief row over the phone with her boyfriend. She was very apologetic and then asked him for the name on his reservation. "Kirk Kerkorian," he said. She gasped in horror, but he smiled and reassured her. "We all have our days."

At the already unusual all-staff meeting, Kirk did something no one in the room had ever seen before. He got up and made a little speech.

"I told you we'd open the hotel again," he said. "And we'd be bigger and better than ever. And now I just want you to know that there's plenty of money in the bank to take care of this place. Nobody needs to worry."

The next night, on Wednesday, July 29, 1981, the MGM Grand Hotel was back in business with state-of-the-art fire prevention and protection features everywhere. The reopening, however, was without fanfare. No klieg lights. No banners. No red carpet arrivals. A single sign over the reception desk in the lobby said WELCOME TO THE GRAND EVENT, the only reference in the entire hotel to the grand reopening.

Advance local news coverage had characterized the new and improved MGM Grand as the safest hotel in the world, with built-in fire sprinklers everywhere and computerized smoke and fire monitors throughout all twenty-six floors. All of Las Vegas was undergoing upgrades and retrofitting to meet tough new standards for fire prevention and protection.

Cary Grant played official host for the evening, making a point of telling guests and reporters that he was staying on the twentieth floor "and happily so." He was not at all afraid for his personal safety even on the highest of floors. And as a member of the MGM Grand board of directors, he said he doubted that the fire would do any lasting damage to the hotel's reputation. "MGM has been a tremendous name. I don't think it's lost any aura," he told the *Reno Gazette-Journal*.

Grant's confident newspaper quote nicely summed up his friend Kirk's most ardent prayer for the future of his brand. Kirk still regarded it with almost mythic respect, calling MGM the "three magic letters." And in the months following the MGM Grand's understated reopening, the hotel's return to profit seemed to answer those prayers.

Kirk and Jean filed for legal separation in June 1982 and started uncontested divorce proceedings in Los Angeles Superior Court at the end of the year. As the estranged couple opened divorce settlement negotiations, Kirk was named one of the richest men in America. A snapshot of his relative wealth was revealed in a new *Forbes* magazine feature called the Forbes 400 List. Kirk was number 224 out of 400 with an individual net worth in the fall of 1982 estimated to be $133 million.

Other names on that first list were Donald Trump, the New York real estate developer, and Ted Turner, the fortysomething owner of Atlanta-based television superstation WTBS and Turner Broadcasting System. He had introduced the world to the twenty-four-hour news cycle by launching CNN, the all-news cable channel.

Kirk already had an eye on Turner, considering his cable entertainment operation a potential market for the MGM/UA film library. In early 1983 Kirk flew out to Atlanta just to meet the brash entrepreneur who was twenty-one years his junior.

Ted was excited about the prospect, at least in his mind, of a 50–50 partnership with the film studio. He put together an enthusiastic pitch. He emphasized the benefits of joining forces—WTBS could promote new MGM releases and the studio could provide a guaranteed supply of entertainment programming for the station. He talked about big plans and grand schemes, accentuating the positive—ignoring the fact that his CNN newsroom was having some trouble keeping its lights on.

Kirk came away impressed with Turner's ideas and forceful personality, but also uncomfortable with his youth and unpredictability. He decided not to rush into any sort of business relationship with Turner. But he liked the kid. He next noticed Turner a couple of years later when press reports disclosed that the Atlanta cable developer was making a hostile takeover run at television giant CBS. Now, that was brash.

Turner's very public battle for CBS captured Kirk's renewed attention in 1984–85. At the same time, Kirk's legal battles were coming to a head in Las Vegas. At the urging of Greg Bautzer, the MGM Grand retained a Southern California lawyer specializing in bad-faith insurance cases, a hired gun famed for winning large jury verdicts.

Kirk's preference from day one was a quick settlement. He hated depositions. He hated testifying. He would gladly leave dollars on the table—possibly millions of dollars—to avoid the personal stress and lost time of litigation. Bringing in hired gun William M. Shernoff was almost certainly Kirk's way of adding pressure on the insurance companies to cut their losses and settle.

The trial itself was expected to cost millions—at least $350,000 a day, including the lawyer fees—and last eight to ten months. The complex litigation wrapped together a conglomeration of suits and countersuits involving scores of litigants and forty-nine separate legal teams. No courtroom in Las Vegas could hold that many lawyers and interested parties. Court officials assessed fees against all sides to finance construction of a temporary courtroom on the campus of University of Nevada, Las Vegas. It was built and furnished near the school's new basketball arena. Monthly rent was assessed against all parties. On the eve of jury selection, before a single witness had testified, the cost to build and operate the campus courtroom had already reached $500,000.

It was Shernoff's position that the recalcitrant insurance companies were disgruntled gamblers. "They guessed wrong," he said, about everything.[5] For about six weeks before the trial was to begin, he occupied a seventeenth-floor suite that included a "war room" for the legal team. It housed more than a million pages of documents. His co-counsel was hard-charging young Bautzer partner Patricia Glaser.

Kirk never went anywhere near the special courtroom, but he occasionally took the legal team to lunch. "He never asked about details. If he brought up the case, it was only to ask: 'Are we gonna win?'"[6]

Behind the scenes, efforts to head off the costly trial and avoid an uncertain jury verdict had prompted various settlement offers from the insurance company side, each one stubbornly stuck in the vicinity of $20 million. Kirk's team never even bothered to check with the boss. Kirk had a settlement price in mind. He spelled it out to his management team and confidants, like his favorite ex-Marine, Terry Christensen.

Kirk wanted at least another $50 million from the insurance companies. Not a dime less. Kirk wasn't bluffing.[7]

In the special courtroom presided over by Las Vegas judge Paul Goldman—who packed a handgun under his robe—jury selection began in early March 1985. Settlement offers started to edge up. Shernoff wasn't part of those talks. He was focused on trial preparation. He was confident of a jury verdict that could come in well over $100 million. The publicity would be good for his practice.

But lawyers for the insurance companies were still insisting that Kirk's payments to the victims were "astronomical" and disguised to hide the fact that taxable punitive damages had been figured into the payments. They weren't. And the insurers' defense was looking weaker by the hour.

The insurance companies were going to be hammered in front of a jury of ordinary citizens for trying to underpay and delay what was due to a host of sympathetic fire victims. Shernoff couldn't wait to start the trial. He polished his opening arguments.

The weekend before trial was to begin, Kirk called co-counsel Patty Glaser. "Do you have a minute?" He never assumed that his lawyers had time to speak with him, even if it was the fifth call of the hour. In this instance, the gambler wanted one last check on the odds for a favorable verdict.

"Patty, are we gonna win or are we gonna lose?" he asked as she saw her life flash before her eyes. Glaser knew that any judgment short of $50 million meant failure. "We're gonna win," she said, trying not to leave any hint of doubt.[8]

Privately, the legal team was equally certain. From Shernoff to the clerks at the Bautzer office, they bet their chances of winning at 70–30. Apparently the insurance companies saw it the same way.

When Shernoff strode into court rested, ready, and eager for opening arguments, Glaser broke the news that they had an overnight settlement.[9] The insurance companies would reimburse a total of $87.5 million—including the $11.5 million they had repaid earlier. Kirk's hardline negotiating position had added a full $76 million to the settlement.

Attorneys for all sides partied with Judge Goldman in the special courtroom the next day accompanied by free-flowing champagne and rock music. Some wore commemorative T-shirts bearing the Latin phrase NUSQUAM TIBI NIMIUM INSURANCE—"You can never have too much insurance." Shernoff was wistful. A jury verdict could have been worth millions of dollars more.[10] Kirk was delighted. His date with a witness stand had been canceled.

Despite the postsettlement camaraderie, Kirk certainly hadn't made any friends in the insurance business. But he had just won another very big bet—and nothing gave the gambler a bigger charge than that.

ONE ROLL OF THE DICE

Kirk was in Cannes for the annual International Film Festival. It was the year Martin Scorsese's *The King of Comedy* starring Robert De Niro and Jerry Lewis was the featured new release, and Bette Davis was among the honored legends of the screen. Kirk was traveling with his wealthy TV producer friend Jerry Perenchio, the pair of former California farm boys living large. Both had come a long way from the San Joaquin Valley. They liked to call themselves "the Fresno Kids."[1]

The film festival coincided with the grand opening of a casino at the new Loews Hotel in nearby La Napoule, touted as a major addition to gambling on the Côte d'Azur. The owners were Jerry's American friends Preston and Laurence Tisch. He knew them as Bob and Larry.

Kirk wanted to see the new casino and offer the Tisch brothers what amounted to the casino owners' secret handshake. "Why don't we go down there?" he suggested.

The ritual widely observed within the exclusive league of casino owners involved making a visit to the other guy's establishment on opening night and wishing him good luck by losing a load of cash at his gaming tables. It was a polite thing to do, an expression of goodwill, like a housewarming gift.

At the casino that night, Perenchio introduced his friend Kirk and let him explain to his friend Larry Tisch what he had in mind.

"I want to make a bet," Kirk said. "I want to bet a million at the craps table on one roll of the dice."

Tisch, a naturally courteous man and eager to please, wasn't sure what to say. Kirk continued, "I'll either win or lose. I hope I lose, because I want to do this as a goodwill gesture for the hotel."

Of course, everyone knew how the odds favored the House. But the proposed million-dollar risk for Kirk was also a million-dollar risk for the casino. That's why the ever-polite Kerkorian asked permission. Tisch and his casino manager excused themselves to speak privately.

The House decision to accept the bet seemed less than enthusiastic.

"We're willing to do this, Kirk—but only for you," Tisch said. "And because Jerry is a friend of ours."

The casino manager handed Kirk a small orange chip. It bore no numerical markings. But for the next half hour or so, it would be worth exactly $1 million.

The casino floor had a cluster of four craps tables. Kirk accepted a lowball of scotch and stepped up to the first table accompanied by Perenchio, Tisch, and the very attentive casino manager. Kirk wanted to observe the table action before picking his spot for *The Bet*.

Perenchio had known Kirk for years. The Fresno Kids shared many common interests. Both were aviators who loved boxing and tennis. Perenchio had been a U.S. Air Force jet pilot in the 1950s. As a sports promoter he had arranged the "Fight of the Century" at Madison Square Garden in 1971 pitting the undefeated heavyweights Muhammad Ali and George Frazier against each other. And Perenchio was the promoter behind the 1973 "Battle of the Sexes" at Houston's Astrodome where Billie Jean King beat Bobby Riggs in what was then the most watched TV tennis match in history. One thing Jerry Perenchio had never seen was Kirk the casino owner on the gambler's side of the table.

Kirk took his time—watching for several minutes at each table—before moving on. He seemed to study not only how the dice were rolling but also who was in each crowd and how they were betting. After nearly thirty minutes, he went back to Table Three, its green felt playing field surrounded by the most boisterous crowd. The shooter was a woman "rolling numbers like crazy," Perenchio noticed. Everyone was yelling, the excitement building. This was where Kirk chose to stage his own dramatic moment.

With a nod to his entourage, Kirk signaled he was ready. The casino manager stepped in to whisper to the croupier and pit boss that Kirk's special little orange disk was a million-dollar chip. Perenchio stood there transfixed, simply amazed to be watching his two friends on opposite sides of a million-dollar roll of the dice.

Kirk put down his orange chip on the Don't Pass bar.

If the red-hot shooter continued to score, most of the betting crowd around the table would be delighted winners. And Kirk at least theoretically would be the delighted loser. If she rolled a seven and crapped out, he would be the unintentional winner.

Kirk's pleasant expression was inscrutable. He gazed impassively at the table. He made no eye contact with anyone.

The shooter rattled the dice in her fist and to whoops of enthusiasm from the crowd hurled them out across the table. The ivory squares bounced off the green felt and slammed into the honeycombed bumper strip lining the table's low walls and caromed back. When the last die stopped spinning, the verdict was in.

Seven! Craps!

The House owed Kirk $1 million. Sometimes he found it hard to lose even when he tried.

Kirk and Jean were divorced later that summer, ending their marriage after nearly twenty-nine years. Children Tracy (twenty-four) and Linda (eighteen) were young adults. He set up a trust fund for Jean who almost immediately remarried. The Los Angeles Superior Court sealed the record, concealing from public view the terms of their trust agreement. She continued to reside in the posh neighborhoods surrounding Beverly Hills.

For Kirk, now in his midsixties and worth hundreds of millions of dollars, his playboy instincts seemed decidedly tame. He continued to see Yvette Mimieux into the mid-1980s, making the gossip columns simply by dining at Chasen's or Morton's or Ma Maison. They became neighbors in the Hollywood Hills where she grew trees. She shared some of her personally nurtured fruiting Persian mulberry saplings with Kirk.[2]

Their relationship cooled when he was unwilling to marry again. Yvette later married Howard Ruby, founder of Oakwood corporate housing, and an internationally noted photographer and conservationist. Yvette and her new husband remained good friends with Kirk.

In the early 1980s Kirk had hired a valet and fitness guru who served, as well, as his personal chef and traveling bodyguard, alternating as a steward on his yacht and flight attendant on his private jet. Ron Falahi, about forty, had earlier worked on the flight crew of the Fabergé corporate jet where he befriended Cary Grant.

Ron's first assignment aboard the Kerkorian jet was flying Dean Martin and other friends of Frank Sinatra to Washington, D.C., for the inauguration of President Ronald Reagan. Sinatra was handling the entertainment. Kirk hired Ron based on one question: "So, you know Cary Grant?" And although he started exclusively as a flight attendant, Ron's portfolio of responsibilities quickly expanded.[3]

Kirk had always been health-conscious and disciplined about regular exercise. He jogged daily and played tennis religiously. He ate small portions, drank in moderation, and despite bouts of insomnia tried to keep an early-to-bed and early-to-rise schedule.

Falahi was personable and energetic, a would-be actor who held jobs as a waiter, bartender, and vacuum cleaner salesman. The immigrant from Tehran was also a bodybuilder. He guided Kirk into a weight-lifting regimen that focused on improving upper-body strength. The keys to those workouts were two solid iron hand weights welded to Falahi's specifications at seventeen and a half pounds each. Kirk used them in workouts at home but then started taking them on the road when he traveled as well.

Kirk's "go bags"—travel luggage he wanted in addition to his wardrobe and personal items—contained several unusual things: his two weights and a Farberware electric coffee percolator with a full can of ground Folgers coffee. As Ron discovered early in his employ, Kirk expected precision in his morning brew—just the right temperature, not too strong, not too weak, always Folgers.

As Kirk's valet, Falahi also kept track of the time. Despite Kirk's near-phobic insistence on punctuality, he had stopped wearing his gold Rolex years earlier. He abhorred ostentatious displays of wealth—starting with jewelry. He wore no bracelets, no gold chains, no pinkie rings. He kept a simple Timex watch without a band in his pants pocket—or he asked Ron or others for the time.

Kirk drove his own cars, retained no staff chauffeurs, and kept basic American models in his garage—a Ford Taurus and a Jeep Cherokee were typical. He would routinely walk to lunch appointments around Beverly Hills, arriving with neither an entourage nor a bodyguard.

And although he was the controlling stockholder of MGM with ready access to private screenings of the latest films, Kirk preferred to get behind the wheel of his Taurus and take a friend out to one of the movie houses in neighboring Westwood Village. He loved his personal anonymity, the freedom to be able to wait in line and not be recognized—that, and the freedom to make a million-dollar bet on one roll of the dice.

TED TURNER'S
TICKING TIME BOMB

SUMMER 1985
ATLANTA, GEORGIA

Ted Turner was contemplating something he consistently tried to avoid. Lawyers. But his bid to take control of the $5 billion media giant CBS was looking especially hopeless after management ordered up a round of poison pills to run him off. Sometimes litigation was the only option. But then his phone rang with an unexpected alternative.

Kirk Kerkorian was on the line. Did Ted have time to talk? Kirk was thinking of reducing his role in moviemaking. Would Ted be interested in buying MGM studios? Kirk might consider splitting off and keeping the United Artists portion of MGM/UA. He had teamed up with Drexel Burnham Lambert bond genius Michael Milken to test the market, open MGM to the highest bidder. But here was the deal . . . If Ted acted now he could have a free shot—that is, he could bid without competition if he moved quickly and made a strong offer.[1]

For Turner, the MGM studio and its vast film library represented almost instant and total dominance of the nation's fledgling cable television industry. It represented escape from the potential stranglehold of content producers—TV networks and movie studios—that could freeze out cable operators and deny them access to affordable shows.

MGM/UA's cartoon library alone, with Tom and Jerry and Looney Tunes stars Bugs Bunny and Porky Pig and the TV seasonal regular the Grinch, was sufficient to support a twenty-four-hour cartoon network. Acquiring MGM came with much more than back-lot real estate. It was buying the Land of Oz, Tara, and *The Good Earth*. For Turner, it was more like buying the stars and the moon.

Kirk suggested that he wanted something around $1.5 billion, but at whatever price it had to be all cash, no contingencies, a "no outs" commitment, and the deal had to be closed in two weeks. Start the clock.

Moving fast in pursuit of a big prize appealed to Turner's sense of adventure. The yachtsman who seized the winds to win the America's Cup race a few years earlier was a self-proclaimed "bulldog" for a challenge. At the same time, prospects of owning *Gone With the Wind* appealed mightily to his southern pride. But he didn't have a billion dollars' worth of anything, including credit. Nonetheless, after months of trench warfare fighting with CBS, the chance to work a deal with someone like Kerkorian—who actually wanted to make a deal—was exhilarating, maybe even dangerously seductive.

If Turner worried about the danger of taking on too much risk in pursuit of his dream, he must have given it only the briefest of passing thoughts. His gambling nature already had him imagining a life-altering score. Besides, he might have asked himself, what good was a big dream if, when the winds were right, he was too timid to chase it? In fact, Ted didn't bother to hide his enthusiasm.

Back in Beverly Hills, Kirk hung up the phone and sat back, savoring Turner's eager response. He knew at that instant Ted was already making flight arrangements for LAX. It was obvious that

Ted would try to make a deal. Kirk was less confident that the kid from Atlanta could swing it.

The phone call to Turner had been part of a series of major moves Kirk had initiated in recent months putting the MGM studio back in play on Wall Street. After nearly two decades of uneven management and disappointing financial results at MGM/UA, he wanted to take advantage of what he considered its substantial hidden value—its combined film archives. The combined company controlled about 35 percent of all movies ever made, twice to three times as many as any other single studio.

Kirk's price was the catching point. The business side of Hollywood figured Kirk would never find a big enough sucker willing and able to pay at such "cosmic levels," as former MGM exec Peter Bart called Kirk's price tag. But no one had ever really tested the market value of movie archives . . . until now.

When their two-week speed-negotiations began, MGM stock was selling for about $9 a share. Kirk's price amounted to about $28 a share—slightly less than $1.5 billion. Like a new homeowner with an astronomical mortgage, Ted was buying the studio with debt that seemed to exceed his ability to pay even the interest alone.

Kerkorian agreed to buy back United Artists for $480 million, which reduced the necessary borrowing to $1 billion, but in taking on MGM's existing debts Ted was on the hook for another $700 million. Factoring in Turner Broadcasting borrowings was going to put Ted in the red for a whopping $2 billion.

No one, including Ted Turner, knew where he was going to come up with the financing for MGM. A combined Turner-MGM company didn't have the earnings between them to cover interest payments on that size debt. He turned to Michael Milken at Drexel Burnham Lambert, who was already handling Kirk's side of the transaction.

In a highly unusual arrangement—and with Kirk's expressed consent—Milken agreed to help arrange Turner's financing.[2] Drexel investment bankers were assigned to both sides. Arthur Bilger would directly represent Turner's interests; Ken Moelis would work independently with Kerkorian's team. Both reported to Milken, which both Kirk and Ted approved. Drexel issued one of its "highly confident" letters signaling that the investment bank was certain it could raise the funds to finance Turner's purchase.

And then the drama began.

Turner had signed the six-hundred-page agreement in time to meet Kirk's two-week deadline to keep the bid private. But it was after the commitment was made that Ted asked to send a team of forty lawyers and accountants to conduct a belated due diligence review of the MGM books and audited reports. They discovered, for one thing, that the soon-to-be-released slate of MGM movies looked like a lineup of future flops. They were.

Instead of monthly earnings, MGM started out the Ted Turner era delivering losses at the box office averaging $15 million a month. The new owner was looking at another $100 million in debt from pending first-year operating losses. Turner aides, already skeptical that the massive debt could be managed, groused privately that Kirk had led them into a very bad deal. From Hollywood to Wall Street the sniping was a more public tsk-tsking that Turner had overpaid. "That price he's paying is absurd!" an investment analyst told the *Los Angeles Times*.[3]

A month after Turner signed the deal for MGM, Drexel conceded that it was having difficulties finding buyers for its high-yield bonds. Outwardly, Turner kept a positive face. He joked about Milken's persistent aides—Bilger and Moelis—comparing the two average-sized men to a hard-playing, sub-six-footer on his Atlanta Hawks professional basketball team. "You guys are the Spud Webbs of investment banking," he raved.[4] Privately, Turner was taking matters into his own hands, shopping for possible partners in the MGM buy, talking to NBC and Viacom and Allen Neuharth of Gannett/USA Today.

Five months after committing to buy MGM, Turner was still unable to come up with the cash to close the deal. Drexel Burnham Lambert was still unable to sell its promised allotment of high-risk, high-yield bonds—investment instruments more commonly referred to as junk bonds.

At Milken's urging, and after an all-night negotiating session, Kirk eased up on his "no out" rule and agreed to restructure Ted's original deal. To reduce its up-front cash requirement, Turner Broadcasting System would issue preferred stock to Kerkorian. The effect was to convert $200 million of the purchase price into debt. Kirk was effectively helping to finance his own sale.[5]

With renewed vigor and a closing deadline now extended to the end of 1985, Milken's team plunged back into marketing those junk bonds. But continuing MGM losses at the box office were taking a toll on investor confidence. Ted complained that Paramount Studios was hogging all the success: "They have *Top Gun*, and we have 'Bottom Gun!'"

The end of the year arrived with still no closing in sight. Investors weren't cooperating. Drexel had failed for a second time. Ted was half-in and half-out of MGM. Shortly before Christmas 1985, Turner flew to California to meet with Kirk and to barter for more time.

Kirk Kerkorian liked everyone to understand that when a deal was made and sealed with a handshake, the negotiating was over. No do-overs. No altering the conditions. No renegotiating. Some who had been across the table from him over the years might quibble about a notable exception here or there.

Stanley Mallin, for one, complained that after Kirk agreed to a financing deal for Circus Circus, he kept coming back and adding conditions. "We had to hire his brother. Then we had to buy his party boat. It didn't end until we paid off his loan—and then Fred Benninger wanted to charge us extra for paying it off early."[6]

But never in decades of closing tough deals had Kirk ever been asked to restructure a formal agreement so substantially, and so often, as in the case of the Ted Turner deal.[7] Terms of their second revised agreement were announced in a terse written statement issued in January 1986.

Kirk would lower the cash price to $20 a share, making the total value closer to $1.25 billion, reducing Ted's up-front cash by more than $300 million. And Kirk's buyback of United Artists, already anticipated after the sale, would now be made at closing for about $470 million. In exchange for his concessions, Kirk would receive preferred stock in Turner Broadcasting System. That stock came with a hefty 14 percent dividend payable to Kirk in cash or common stock beginning in the second year.

The new terms kept the deal alive. But for Turner it was like agreeing to pocket a ticking time bomb. He would have to pay those dividends when due or start turning over pieces of his company to Kirk. The *Los Angeles Times* headline summed up Ted's dilemma: "MGM Deal Could Cost Turner His Own Firm."[8]

The MGM sale finally closed in late March 1986, eight months and two failed bond sales after the initial agreement. In the end, it was Kirk's unprecedented flexibility and willingness to help finance the sale himself that saved the deal for Turner. "He couldn't have been fairer on the deal," Milken said later. "I always saw him making sure the other guy got a fair deal."[9] And Kirk's patience had the added benefit to Drexel of sparing Milken and his team from a very public pratfall.[10]

On the downside, however, Turner had loaded himself up with massive debt estimated at $1.9 billion. "I owe more money than anyone else in the world," he said. It almost sounded like a boast. For now, Ted was on top of the world. Thanks to Kirk, he was a mogul with his own movie studio. He had the country's biggest archive of classic movies. He owned *Gone With the Wind*. What more could a southern kid wish for.

But that time bomb in his pocket was still ticking.

A BURIAL AT SEA

When their phone rang, Leslie Malone thought it was the middle of the night. It was still dark. She fumbled for the receiver. When she heard the Georgia drawl on the other end of the line, she immediately passed the phone to her husband.

"It's that asshole friend of yours," she said with sarcasm fit for 5:30 in the morning Rocky Mountain time.

"Hello?"

"John! You've got to do something!" blurted an agitated Ted Turner calling from Atlanta. "You've got to do something!"

"What? What have I got to do, Ted?"

"Something!" repeated Turner. "Or else C-N-N will become K-N-N!"

"K-N-N? What the hell is K-N-N?"

Ted bellowed into the phone, "Kerkorian News Network!"[1]

Ted Turner was in trouble and his desperation was showing. Nearly a year after closing the billion-dollar-plus deal with Kerkorian for MGM, he was still suffering from debt hangover. In a few weeks his first dividend interest payment to Kirk would be due. He didn't have it. He might have to start dismantling Turner Broadcasting System to meet his obligations.

On this particularly anxious winter morning Turner was calling one of his most important rivals in the emerging cable TV industry, John C. Malone, the CEO of Tele-Communications Inc. Malone was also among those most concerned about Ted's financial welfare. It was clear throughout the cable world that TBS had come out of the MGM deal dangerously vulnerable. No one in the business wanted a strong, independent operator like Turner to fail.

What was a bleak prospect on the Turner side wasn't particularly popular on the Kerkorian side either. Kirk didn't want CNN. And he liked Ted.

Team Kerkorian had mixed feelings. Picking up some of the prime pieces of Turner Broadcasting looked like a golden opportunity to expand an entertainment empire into cable. Plus, it required so little effort, so little risk—as in none whatsoever. They just had to sit back and let the weight of debt crush Turner.

"You don't have to do anything," Terry Christensen advised Kirk. "We can all go off and play tennis. It's going to happen even if we do nothing."

The problem was Kirk. He, too, was pulling for Ted to make it. "I don't want him squashed," he told his team. "Ted's a good man. He doesn't make excuses. He tries to do the right thing."[2]

Kirk's agreement to buy back United Artists simultaneously with the March 1986 close of their original deal had effectively reduced Turner's cash investment burden by nearly a half-billion dollars. Ted also managed to sell what remained of the MGM back lot to Lorimar-Telepictures for $190 million.

Barely two months after Ted took over MGM, it was clear he still needed substantially more cash to stay afloat. Kirk stepped back into the picture, offering $300 million to reacquire MGM film and TV production units, its home video division, and the MGM logo. So, in a matter of weeks after he sold the studio, Kirk bought it back—lock, stock, and Leo the Lion—for a fraction of the sale price.

Turner controlled MGM so briefly that he joked, "I never even had a chance to use a casting couch."

Some in Hollywood didn't think Kirk did Ted much of a favor, selling high and buying back cheap. But for a billion dollars Turner ended up with what he wanted in the first place—*Gone With the Wind* and a priceless film library.

The preferred TBS stock with a 14 percent dividend that threatened to blow a hole in Ted's dreams also threatened to undermine the best interests of cable operators across the country. Once John Malone was awake and focused on the real threats behind Turner's desperate phone call, he took swift action.

In the weeks that followed, Malone led an aggressive and successful campaign to raise $550 million from cable investors to restructure TBS debt and defuse Ted's ticking time bomb. Turner would lose some clout through diluted shareholdings to Malone and fellow cable guys, but his name stayed on his rapidly expanding company. He would be a billionaire by the end of the decade.

The deals were good for Kirk, too, of course. *US* magazine estimated his net worth at about $600 million and declared him "the richest man in Hollywood." Other headlines, over stories bemoaning the decline and fall of MGM, declared him "The Most Hated Man in Hollywood."

Friends noticed that Kirk seemed to be losing interest in the rebuilt and highly successful MGM Grand Hotel. He skipped executive committee meetings. He stopped offering suggestions. He didn't complain, either, so management didn't take notice.[3] Those who did notice weren't surprised, however, when they woke up to news accounts that Bally's Manufacturing had agreed to acquire both the Las Vegas and Reno hotels for $550 million, including $110 million in assumed debt.

The deal gave Bally's the right to keep and exclusively use the MGM name and logo on its Nevada hotels for three years. And because there were still pending fire claims and court appeals that posed liability risks Bally's refused to assume, Kirk agreed to assume them personally. Public shareholders received about 20 percent more per share than Kirk who, in turn, would make up the difference only if the legal issues ultimately resolved in his favor.

"Who does such a thing," said an incredulous Terry Christensen—who soon after took over as president of Tracinda.[4]

Kirk then turned back to the movie business. With MGM/UA reconstituted, but homeless since Lorimar took over its back lot, Kirk moved the studio's business operations to an office building off Santa Monica Boulevard in Beverly Hills. It posed a very different challenge for Kirk. MGM was barely a shell of its former self. Kirk faced the task of rebuilding MGM/UA, already stripped of its hidden value, pretty much from scratch.

The first thing he did was invoke history, persuading high-level management prospects like Lee Rich—a founder of Lorimar—to take the reins of a company once run by Louis B. Mayer and Irving Thalberg. It was a chaotic and unsatisfying time for Kirk. But sometimes he still got lucky.

A relatively small movie under development for United Artists was slowly edging toward a start date with a budget that might require Kirk's stamp of approval. It was a road story about two brothers, one a greedy, self-absorbed yuppie and the other an autistic savant. Nothing about it suggested a blockbuster—but it already had Dustin Hoffman and it looked good for Tom Cruise as the other important member of the cast. In the turmoil of constant management turnover and Kirk's uncertainties about the movie business, *Rain Man* never got the typical green; it never got killed, either. UA's Lee Rich simply kept Kirk from pulling the plug on its $25 million budget. And it got made.[5]

Rain Man won the Academy Awards for Best Picture and Best Actor. It grossed $355 million worldwide. It put MGM/UA back on the Hollywood map of major players. The management chaos continued. But the Beverly Hills office was an easier commute than Culver City.

Kirk now lived on a hilltop compound at the end of a winding road called Wanda Park. It was really a collection of properties. He had sold one of the parcels, the property with the biggest house, to Sonny and Cher. He bought it back after their 1975 divorce. He sold it again to Sylvester Stallone in the early 1980s and bought it back after Sly completed a major renovation. It had a pool and tennis court and privacy. Kirk had purchased several parcels adjoining the property so that he would have no neighbors—unless, of course, he picked them personally.

The second house was smaller, about eighteen hundred square feet, no bigger than a modest cottage in the Hollywood Hills. But as Kirk said, "It's got a bedroom, a living room, and a kitchen. What more do I need?" It was also especially private and it had the better of the property's two tennis courts. It was perfect as Kirk's bachelor pad. It was also the site for his regular weekend tennis marathons with collections of old friends who engaged in spirited competition and lively luncheons. Valet Ron Falahi became Kirk's regular chef for those occasions.

Kirk's favorite guests for dinner at the Wanda Park house were neighbors from a couple hills away, Cary Grant and his wife, Barbara. It was in honor of the couple's shared British heritage that Chef Ron took his first stab at Yorkshire pudding. Cary proclaimed it good stuff.

The Grants were familiar passengers on Kirk's private jet. They spent a couple of extended summer trips together cruising the coast of Alaska as families, with Cary's daughter, Jennifer, and Kirk's girls, Tracy and Linda.

Cary Grant regarded Kirk as "a brilliant man" who studied things carefully, a self-made man who retained his common touch. Kirk talked about Cary as "a true friend . . . such a humble nice man" and as "a supersmart" businessman whose contributions he especially valued on the boards of MGM Film and MGM Grand Hotel.[6]

So it came as such distressing news when Cary's wife, Barbara, called early one evening in November 1986 with an urgent request:

Could Kirk please send his plane right away to Davenport, Iowa? Cary was ill.

The eighty-two-year-old movie star had been scheduled for a black-tie event, "An Evening with Cary Grant" at the sold-out Adler Theatre in downtown Davenport, part of the Quad Cities' annual Festival of Trees. He had fallen ill during afternoon rehearsals and retired to suite 903 at the Hotel Blackhawk to rest.[7]

He was still feeling sick at showtime and the tuxedoed crowd groaned in disappointment when it was announced that he would be unable to perform.

At the hotel, Cary's condition worsened. Barbara called paramedics at about 9 P.M. A short time later, she called Kirk from St. Luke's Hospital. They discussed getting him back to Los Angeles and to his personal physicians as soon as possible. Kirk started to round up a flight crew.

Less than two hours later, he called off his crew. Cary was dead. He had suffered a massive stroke. The world had lost a movie icon. Kirk had lost a best friend.

Kirk was a man easily moved to tears. He hated funerals. He hated making a spectacle of himself "blubbering and snuffling."[8]

But Cary's wife, Barbara, and daughter, Jennifer, persuaded Kirk to help them with one final tribute. The three of them took a boat out into the Santa Monica Bay carrying along an urn with Cary's ashes.

In a solemn moment, far enough offshore that no one else could see any blubbering and snuffling, Kirk helped scatter Cary Grant's ashes on the gentle blue-green swells of the Pacific.[9]

31

AMONG THE
BILLIONAIRES

DECEMBER 7, 1988
SPITAK, SOVIET ARMENIA

The earthquake struck shortly before noon. It lasted only twenty seconds. Survivors remembered the human screams and the otherworldly shrieking sounds from walls, roofs, and whole buildings being ripped apart by some unseen monstrous force. Towns and villages collapsed into rubble that became instant graves for thousands of people. In twenty seconds fifty thousand lives ended. Hundreds of thousands of victims were left homeless, hungry, and cold. More than a hundred thousand serious injuries overwhelmed emergency medical services. Reports on the devastation and the vast human misery produced an outpouring of public sympathy and aid from around the world.

In Southern California, home of the largest Armenian community outside the Soviet Union, churches and charities of the diaspora scrambled to help. Some worked together. Most worked independently. Old rivalries persisting through the decades made a united Armenian American response appear unlikely.

One thing they all had in common was Kirk Kerkorian's phone number. One by one, the representatives of various groups managed to arrange individual meetings with America's richest Armenian. Each asked for millions—to rebuild schools, to build a hospital, to construct housing, to do good things for Armenia. One clergyman proposed a $50 million gift to do all those things—"something big," he said.

"Build a new town," he said. "It could be Kerkorian City!"[1]

But that sales pitch landed more like a gut punch. The very private Kerkorian wanted his name on nothing. Two things characterized Kirk's charitable giving: generosity and anonymity. Like the old 1950s television show *The Millionaire*, Kirk's gifts came with strict admonitions that he could never be identified as the source—no Kerkorian name on buildings or street signs, no banquets in his honor, not the simplest public expressions of gratitude, not even a public reputation for generosity.

"If you expect something in return for your charity, it isn't charity," he told friends.[2]

Immediately after the quake, Kirk made secret donations of nearly a million dollars each to three different Armenian charities. Absolute anonymity was demanded, as usual. But on this occasion, the secrecy backfired. He was seen as simply indifferent to the plight of Armenia. One Armenian American newspaper, unaware of Kirk's secret gifts, even criticized the world's richest Armenian for doing nothing.[3]

Kerkorian tried not to show his chagrin. But he also decided it was time to create a more transparent philanthropic organization, set up with its own management team and operated under the laws governing California charities.

Thus was born, out of the sting of that uninformed criticism, the Lincy Foundation—a spinoff from Kirk's holding company, Tracinda Corporation. Both companies blended the names of Kirk's daughters, Tracy and Linda. Half of the charity's initial endowment was made up of MGM stock, valued at about $110 million.

Months later in 1989, Kirk was still exploring the best way to deliver meaningful help to victims of the Armenia earthquake when he was contacted by journalist Harut Sassounian, an Aleppo-born Armenian American living in Glendale, California. He was publisher of the *California Courier,* a weekly English-language Armenian newspaper started forty years earlier by Kirk's friend and stockbroker George Mason. Harut was something of a firebrand whose opinion columns typically criticized the Turks, advocated for public recognition of Turkey's role in the Armenian genocide, and crusaded against Armenian government corruption. Kirk read him regularly.

Early in 1989 Kirk had briefly flirted with the notion of taking over the Hearst-owned *Los Angeles Herald Examiner,* the city's scrappy number two daily paper. He called to see if Harut might consider serving as CEO of the newspaper company. But the thirty-nine-year-old was uncertain. He offered to help recruit "a more qualified" publishing executive. Instead, Kirk dropped the matter, and in a few months the *Herald Examiner* closed.

On a morning late in 1989, Harut started his day looking into a story about how earthquake relief supplies were piling up by the ton in closets, garages, and warehouses across the United States. Nearly a year after the disastrous quake, there was still no coordinated transportation system in place to deliver those mounting stores of donated relief material to needy victims in Armenia. He decided to do more than simply write about it. He called Kerkorian's office. Through his friend George Mason, Harut asked for a meeting with Kirk. It was about an earthquake aid proposal, he said without elaboration. Response was swift.

"Mr. K is waiting at his office. Be there by 1 P.M.," Mason said.

Harut was confident of Kirk's generosity. News about creation of the Lincy Foundation and its huge endowment spoke for itself. But unaware of Kirk's prior gifts to Armenian causes, Harut wasn't so sure what to expect from Kirk. The financier seemed aloof to Armenian politics, what Harut and other activists sometimes dismissed as "shish-kabob Armenians." This would be a test. Harut would be proposing costly disaster relief that was already tangled up in politics.

At Kerkorian's Beverly Hills office on Wilshire Boulevard, a receptionist pointed Harut to the conference room door. "He's waiting for you," she said.

Pushing through the door, Harut found four men waiting around a long table—Kirk, Mason, Jim Aljian, and Kirk's newest executive, Alex Yemenidjian. They were all seated. He was still standing, trying to figure out which chair he should take, when Kirk spoke up, "Harut, what's your idea?" There would be no small talk on this afternoon. Harut sat down and proposed launching an airlift to Armenia.

Kirk the aviator and former charter airline operator was immediately receptive. Harut suggested that the Lincy Foundation and six other Armenian charities band together as a pan-Armenian group to charter a cargo jet, split the cost of a $350,000 charter, and then all work together to fill it with donated supplies—keeping in mind that another cruel Caucasus winter was fast approaching. Kirk interrupted.

"You're saying we would split the cost of the plane?"

Harut nodded.

"That's about $50,000 each?"

Harut nodded again.

"And the other groups have agreed to this?"

"I haven't asked them," Harut responded. He thought he detected a slight smile.

"You haven't talked to any of the others?"

"I haven't even talked to my wife!" Harut blurted. "She doesn't know I'm here."

Kirk broke into a full grin, then asked another question: "You know, Harut, Armenians—they don't all dance to the same drummer. How do you know they'll say yes?"

"I don't," he said, shrugging. "I'm here to see if you're interested."

"And you're asking me for $50,000 . . . just like everybody else?"

Harut nodded again.

"Well—" said Kirk, sitting forward with all eyes in the room turned to him. "Here's my counterproposal. I'll pick up the entire expense of the airlift. I'll charter the plane. Your job is to work together with all the other organizations to fill that plane."

Kirk authorized Harut to tell the other charities that he was in, and he would guarantee delivery of all the material and relief supplies that they could assemble. As Harut stood to leave, Kirk added one more thing, "You know, I really like this idea. I like it so much that if those others say no, you come back here—we'll do it together, just you and me."

But Kerkorian's personal role had made unity an easy sale. All the groups signed on to participate as one under the banner of the United Armenian Fund. The UAF, in turn, was launched under the leadership of Kerkorian aide Yemenidjian. And Kirk's wish for Armenians to work together finally seemed a reality. He insisted that all six of the other charities understood from the start: "The only thing that's nonnegotiable is unity."[4]

On December 1, 1989, a chartered Boeing 707 loaded with $5 million in care packages left Los Angeles on a sunny seventy-degree day with Harut Sassounian on board, en route to Yerevan, the capital of Soviet Armenia.

H arut wasn't expecting a brass band and cheerleaders, but he was surprised when no one at all showed up to help off-load the pallets of food, medicine, and warm clothes. The forklift operator was busy. He was in the crew lounge watching a televised soap opera. He was expecting a $100 "facilitation fee," a bribe that Harut refused to pay. If the first thirty tons of desperately needed supplies required a facilitation fee, corruption would almost certainly jeopardize future shipments. The standoff ended when Harut confronted the forklift operator at the TV set and warned him in perfect Armenian, "You have five minutes or you won't have this job tomorrow."

As the first anniversary of the earthquake dawned a few days later, Harut was making his first delivery of food boxes to a homeless camp on a windswept mountainside in northern Armenia. There were three feet of snow on the ground when his convoy of trucks pulled to a stop. Dozens of families lived huddled together for warmth in a village of tattered tents staked to the frozen ground.

Harut guessed it might be minus-ten degrees as he walked to the first tent with an aid worker. He found a family of four, shivering from the raw winds blowing through holes in their tent. Harut held out a box of provisions, but the man made no move to accept it. He seemed suspicious and confused, wary of uninvited strangers who were about as welcome in his tent as the north wind.

Harut spoke in Armenian, "It's food—a gift from America."

The man still didn't move. But he started to weep. So did Harut. Suddenly, everyone in the tent was in tears. The package contained lifesaving cooking oil, powdered milk, canned foods, and winter clothes.

And so it went . . . from encampment to encampment. Upon his return to Los Angeles, Harut prepared an action report for Kirk. He described his encounters, the grateful reception by the people. He declared, "Mission Accomplished," and asked what to do next.

Kirk's one-sentence reply would launch a billion-dollar relief effort spanning two decades: "Keep sending airlifts as long as Armenia needs assistance." His commitment would make the Armenian relief effort the largest to any single country since the historic U.S. government–backed Berlin Airlift of 1948–49.

The sheer size and duration of the Armenian airlift would make it impossible to keep Kerkorian's role a secret. News of his philanthropy spread throughout Armenian American communities in the United States and Europe. The benefactor insisted on only two things: his name would never appear on a monument and Armenians would always work together.

Across their hard-hit homeland, Armenians regarded Kirk as a saint. His name was spoken with a mix of reverence and pride.

Neighboring rival Azerbaijan may have oil, acknowledged some Armenians, "But we have Kerkorian."

Kirk was also getting public attention throughout the international business world from his listing that year in *Forbes* magazine as one of the four hundred richest Americans. Like many moguls on that list, Kirk considered the popular magazine feature of questionable value, questionable accuracy, and an intrusion on his privacy. He saw no benefit to advertising his affluence. Kirk neither cooperated directly with *Forbes* researchers nor confirmed or corrected the magazine's estimates of his wealth.

The 1989 *Forbes* list came with a Kerkorian bonus element. It showed he was now one of sixty-six American billionaires. His estimated net worth: $1.29 billion. Other first-time billionaires on the 1989 list included financier Michael Milken, Microsoft founder Bill Gates, TWA boss Carl Icahn, and the Tisch brothers with their hotel and casino holdings.

Larry Tisch, whose casino on the Riviera suffered the loss of $1 million to Kirk's "one roll of the dice," had been especially brusque and dismissive of the *Forbes* feature. He called the list useless, meaningless, and "completely unnecessary." He acknowledged glancing through it but said he then hurled it aside.[5]

Donald Trump, on the other hand, broke into the upper tier of superrich that year based on a lobbying campaign. He was one of those who very much wanted to be listed as a billionaire, and in 1989 he was included with an estimated net worth of $1.7 billion.

But *Forbes* editors would summarily dump Trump from the billionaires' list midway through the year, explaining in May 1990 that they had been misled by incomplete information provided by Trump. It turned out that the New Yorker's properties were loaded with debt that drastically reduced their net value. And by the time its next list was issued in the fall of 1990, *Forbes* had dropped the New York developer completely from its list of four hundred richest

Americans. The future U.S. president's net worth was then, said the editors, "within hailing distance of zero."

Trump took the *Forbes* demotion very badly. He lashed out at the magazine and accused its late publisher Malcolm Forbes of "finally getting back at me from the grave."[6]

Some of the same economic factors depressing the value of Trump's business interests at that time—notably faltering gaming returns and sagging real estate values—also affected Kerkorian's net worth, but only marginally. Kirk remained solidly ensconced among the billionaires.

For Michael Milken, the billionaire list masked serious personal troubles. He was under indictment for alleged felonies involving securities violations. His company, Drexel Burnham Lambert, was being forced into bankruptcy. He would plead guilty to six lesser charges and pay a fine of about $600 million.

Future billionaire Ted Turner rose to Milken's defense. In public statements he credited Milken with helping to pull off his MGM deal with Kirk and raved about Mike as a financial genius. "If this guy ever goes to jail, then I want to be right there in the cell next to him," Turner said.

Milken served twenty-two months in federal custody, but without Ted's companionship. After prison he resumed luncheons and occasional tennis dates with Kirk.

Throughout the 1990s, Kirk and the Lincy Foundation became major supporters of the American Red Cross with the ascension of Elizabeth Dole as its president. Her husband, U.S. senator Bob Dole (R-Kan.), was a leading congressional advocate of Armenian causes—including official U.S. recognition of the Armenian genocide.

The senator was also very close to a prominent Armenian American surgeon in Chicago. Doctor Hampar Kelikian had saved Dole's mangled arm from amputation after he was wounded in Italy near the end of World War II. The immigrant doctor became like a father to the young soldier. By the time Dole was in the Senate, both Kelikian and Kerkorian had become important figures in the Armenian American community.

"I want you to know each other," Dole said in bringing them together.[7]

Kirk gave only sparingly over the years to politicians, but he made exceptions for his friends. Two of them were Senate rivals—Dole on the GOP side and Harry Reid of Nevada on the Democratic side.

The absence of any direct political agenda made the American Red Cross a favorite target for Kirk's giving. And Elizabeth Dole learned early that he preferred a very straightforward approach to gift solicitations. Her first direct appeal to Kirk came in a phone call. She explained that the American Red Cross was raising an emergency fund to help Rwanda genocide survivors.

"What do you need from me?" Kirk asked. It was his standard response to such calls.

"We need two million dollars," she said.

"You've got it."

That was so easy! The Red Cross president gushed with gratitude. And then she said, "Kirk, you have other wealthy friends that might be willing to help us. Would you mind asking whether—"

"Wait—" he interrupted. "It sounds to me like you need more than two million. How much do you really need?"

"Well, we really need four million," she said.

"You got it."[8]

One thing Kirk would never do: ask a friend to make a contribution to anything.

"Kirk would contribute millions of dollars himself," said his attorney friend Christensen. "But he'd cut off his right arm before he'd ask someone else to give a dime."[9]

III

THE
MAKING
OF
A LEGEND

"TO WIN WITHOUT RISK IS
A TRIUMPH WITHOUT GLORY."

—PIERRE CORNEILLE, FRENCH PLAYWRIGHT

32

BABE RUTH AT BAT

It was a Sunday morning and Kirk had a new investment strategy he wanted to launch as soon as possible. He had asked Alex Yemenidjian to summon his team of financial and legal advisers to the cottage at Wanda Park. It was all very mysterious. But business would be followed by lunch and tennis. Only Alex had a clue what was coming, and he was sworn to secrecy.[1]

Michael Tennenbaum, head of the Bear, Stearns & Co. offices in Century City, would have to drive in from Malibu. He was already Kirk's point man on major Las Vegas projects. Among those, Tennenbaum and Bear Stearns were trying to raise $700 million to fund construction of Kirk's next megaresort in Las Vegas, an all-new, bigger-than-ever MGM Grand Hotel.

Of course, Tennenbaum had time—even on a Sunday morning—for his richest client. He relished any chance to get to know the billionaire better, especially in the casual atmosphere of tennis at the hilltop estate. He brought along his wife and two large dogs.

Tennenbaum was in his early fifties and, like Kirk, an avid tennis player. He was also a skier who commissioned an avant-garde five-story "glass castle" in Vail, Colorado. Unlike his eighth-grade dropout client, he held a master of business administration degree (with honors) from Harvard University.

As usual, Kirk didn't waste time with small talk. With everyone seated around the lunch table he opened the session at one minute past the 11 A.M. start time.

"I suppose you all know why we're here," he said—to universal frowns and a chorus of "No!"

"Hey, you told me not to tell anyone, so I didn't," Yemenidjian quickly interjected.

"Oh, of course," Kirk resumed. "We're here because I'm going to buy nine point nine percent of Chrysler." He planned to start buying the carmaker's stock immediately. His ultimate goal was 22 million shares.

For six months Yemenidjian had been secretly monitoring Chrysler's financial statistics on Kirk's orders. The data gathering was so confidential and Kirk's interest so sensitive that Alex wasn't even to talk generally about the car business with anyone during those six months. "And don't even fly over Michigan," Kirk told him.

Stunned silence greeted Kirk's announcement in the dining room. Kirk waited for reaction. Tennenbaum ventured the first tentative response: "Gee, they're in pretty bad shape."

Chrysler was at the time on no one else's list of recommended stock buys. Not for conservative investors. Not for billionaires. Not for anyone interested in a return on investment. The nation's number three automaker had billions in debt, billions in unfunded pension liabilities, and no apparent prospects for improving its standing.

Tennenbaum thought it was a terrible investment idea, but in deference to Kirk he eagerly offered up "all the resources of Bear Stearns. We will have a huge team comb through the entire country, turn it upside down, and give you our best opinion on Chrysler." They would start first thing the next morning.

Kirk's poker face showed neither pleasure nor impatience. He leaned closer to Tennenbaum and put his hand on the banker's forearm.

"I want you to do me a favor," Kirk said.

"Kirk, whatever you want," Tennenbaum assured him.

"If Bear Stearns does develop an opinion about Chrysler, would you please just . . . keep it?"

Kerkorian's gentle rejection struck Tennenbaum like a slap in the face and a repudiation of prudent counsel. Later, in a phone conversation with his boss—brokerage chairman Alan "Ace" Greenberg—Tennenbaum complained about Kirk's effrontery. Instead of sympathy, Greenberg chided his senior executive. "You don't tell Babe Ruth how to hold the bat."[2]

Kirk's campaign to acquire Chrysler shares began slowly and under the radar in October. It continued through November. When news broke in December that Tracinda Corp. had paid $272 million for 9.8 percent of the automaker, it sent shock waves through Detroit and Wall Street.

Chrysler directors called an emergency meeting to enact safeguards against a takeover. Stock prices jumped 62 cents overnight. Kirk's one-day paper profit was $12.65 million.

Much of the investment world was befuddled. *What was Kerkorian up to, anyway?* The seventy-three-year-old insisted that he was buying as a passive investor with no intention to take over management of the company. He did not, however, rule out buying more stock.

Just as Kirk was moving into automobile manufacturing as a major investor, he was also making arrangements to move out of the movie business. Italian financier Giancarlo Parretti and his Pathé Communications, the oldest film company in France, had agreed to pay $1.3 billion cash for MGM/UA. His source of funds was a mystery and it took Parretti nearly a year to put together his financing package. Even then the news wasn't exactly welcomed.

By that time in the fall of 1990, Hollywood pundits were wringing their hands about foreign intrusions into the American film industry. Already Sony controlled Columbia and Rupert Murdoch's News Corp. owned Fox. Hollywood critics of Kirk's stewardship at MGM/UA now bemoaned the studio's sale to another foreigner.

After rattling Hollywood, Wall Street, and Detroit, Kirk headed back to Las Vegas where he was getting his affairs in order for yet another big move. He was, as usual, sharing little about his long-term goals.

Hints of Kirk's newest megascheme had appeared years earlier with a little-noted side deal appended to his sale of the MGM Grand to Bally. Like a chess master, Kirk had been looking many moves ahead. Bally would retain the MGM name for no more than three years. Then, Kirk wanted it back. He had written a check for $1.4 million to preserve his rights to the hotel name, the logo, and the lion.[3]

After a three-year hiatus, Kirk also moved back into the Vegas hotel and casino business. His first acquisition was a pair of prized properties from the Howard Hughes collection—the Sands and the Desert Inn. He paid $167 million for the two together in 1987, taking over the last remnants of the late billionaire's Las Vegas holdings. There was something personally satisfying to Kirk about owning the penthouse hideaway where his reclusive rival had waged such a bizarre battle to run him out of town two decades earlier.

With the MGM Grand logo and two Hughes properties, Kirk had formed MGM Grand, Inc. He opened investment in the new company to any MGM Grand stockholders of record when the original hotel was sold to Bally. Only a few took advantage of the offer. Once again Kirk saw value in the MGM brand itself—even as most investors continued to miss the lure of his "three magic letters."

He sold the Sands to Sheldon Adelson for $110 million in 1989 and turned to Bear Stearns to shop the Desert Inn with a price tag of $200 million. A Japanese consortium stepped up with a strong offer, and Alex Yemenidjian took over negotiations on Kirk's behalf.

The Argentina-born Armenian and USC-educated accountant had moved quickly since joining Team Kerkorian in mid-1989 to become one of Kirk's frontline negotiators. But he still had a lot to learn. And Alex was new enough to feel at least a little insecure, so he was relieved and pleased to report reaching a deal with those Japanese buyers. Contract formalities would be worked out the next day, he told a delighted Kirk.

First thing in the morning, however, things got complicated. New buyers appeared with a much better deal—an extra $15 million in cash and no contract contingencies. Suddenly, the Japanese deal was looking second rate. Alex called Kirk.

"What should we do?"

"Did you make a promise to the Japanese buyers?" Kirk asked.

"Nothing's been signed, it's still . . ."

"I didn't ask if you'd signed anything," Kirk interrupted. "Did you agree to a deal?"

"Well, I guess I did," said Alex.

"Then why are you calling me?"

The phone call ended abruptly.

The Japanese deal fell apart later that day. In fact, both deals evaporated in the face of an abrupt economic downturn blamed on the First Gulf War. A national recession would further slow business and real estate markets around the country for well over a year.

The Desert Inn sale would languish into 1993 when it was finally sold to ITT for $160 million—nearly the same price Kirk had paid for both hotels in 1986. For a billionaire, it was a modest profit. For Yemenidjian, the real prize was an invaluable lesson. It wasn't the first or the last.

After Alex once negotiated a severance deal with a fired MGM Grand executive, Kirk ordered him to reopen settlement talks. "It's not enough," Kirk said. "You made too good a deal."

To Kirk, Yemenidjian said, "It was never about the money. It was about what was fair." But Alex did acknowledge some personal chagrin at being sent back to ask if they would accept double his hard-fought original terms.

Meanwhile, Kirk was investing elsewhere on the Strip. He bought the Marina Hotel and Casino in 1989, and then he added a hundred acres to the property by acquiring the Tropicana Country Club and golf course. Kirk's grand vision was revealed at a press conference more than a year later. For the third time in twenty-five years he would be building the world's biggest resort hotel.

Kirk attended the press briefing held at the Marina Hotel but let his executive team answer all the questions. When the session ended, however, reporters swarmed around Kirk. "Are you really building the world's largest hotel?" Kirk smiled and tried to wave off the question. "Are you worried about a glut of rooms?" Kirk seemed uncomfortable, even frightened, by the crowd, the microphones, and the cameras. He maneuvered toward a door and finally lunged to push it open and escape. It was locked.

United Press International bureau chief Myram Borders, a veteran gaming reporter, turned to Howard Stutz of the *Las Vegas Review-Journal* and predicted: "He'll never do one of these press events again." She was right.[4]

The first building to go up on the construction site was huge. And it was only the parking garage. Still to come was a very real version of the fictional Emerald City—the green glass-wrapped and all-new MGM Grand Hotel, this one with a *Wizard of Oz* motif and an adjacent Hollywood theme park.

How big was the new MGM Grand? The casino alone was bigger than the playing field in Yankee Stadium. It would open with 5,005 guest rooms, eight restaurants, five bars and cocktail lounges, twenty-three retail shops, and the MGM Garden Arena—a Madison Square Garden West, built specifically to host major concerts and boxing matches. Construction costs averaged $1 million a day and the hotel's final price tag was a cool $1 billion.

Cary Grant was gone, but Streisand was back. Her 1993 opening night New Year's Eve act was the hottest ticket in the desert. It was her first concert in more than twenty years, and she sold out the Grand Garden Arena.

By the time his new MGM Grand opened on the Strip, Kirk had also resumed buying Chrysler shares—what he referred to in a *Fortune* magazine interview as his "chips." He had already added another $400 million in Chrysler stocks. Kirk had started pressing Chrysler to put one of his people on its board of directors. And he was urging the company to be more aggressive in boosting its stock value.

Kirk had also become friends with outgoing Chrysler chairman, Lee Iacocca, and his new wife, Darrien. Once Lee was nudged into retirement by the Chrysler board, Kirk put him on the MGM Grand board of directors. In the summer of 1992, they had spent several days together touring the Italian Riviera aboard Kirk's yacht, the *October Rose*. Kirk's personal companion on that cruise was the slim and athletic Lisa Bonder, a onetime Top Ten ranked women's tennis pro. She would confide to Darrien her secret desire to become the richest woman in the world . . . and Kirk's wife.[5]

Since his separation from Jean in 1982 and eventual divorce, Kirk's love life had made the occasional gossip column, but it was pretty tame reading. After a second extended relationship with Yvette Mimieux, Kirk was mentioned frequently in the company of Cary Grant's widow, Barbara.

Nine months after Cary Grant's fatal stroke, a Liz Smith column said Barbara Grant "may marry one of Cary's best friends, Kirk Kerkorian."[6] And the *Hollywood Reporter* said the couple was shopping for a villa together in the south of France. In fact, they had been living together at Kirk's Wanda Park compound for some time, where she sometimes complained about Kirk's tendency to feed his little dog Scoshie from the dinner table.[7]

Kirk, then in his seventies, was not interested in marriage. And about the worst thing that could happen to any of his romantic relationships was to have public speculation erupt about wedding bells. It marked the end of more than one Kerkorian liaison—though the friendships tended to continue. Kirk would later be among the welcome guests and friends when Barbara Grant did remarry.

He was so jealous of his privacy that he came to require his romantic partners to sign nondisclosure agreements, making both his personal life and business interests confidential. Lisa Bonder, twenty-six, about the same age as Kirk's youngest daughter, reportedly got off to a rocky start over privacy matters.

They were vacationing on the *October Rose* along the French Riviera during the run-up to Wimbledon in London. Lisa had left the women's tennis circuit several months before the birth of her two-year-old son. She was now in the midst of a divorce and contentious child custody dispute.

"Suzy," the grande dame of tabloid gossip columnists, broke news about the Kerkorian-Bonder relationship but also reported that Lisa had been testing Kirk's patience. She was calling her old tennis pals at Wimbledon and bragging about having a wonderful time on the billionaire's yacht.

"This has displeased Kirk, to say the least," wrote the widely syndicated columnist. She went on to tell her readers that Lisa was best remembered for once defeating tennis great Chris Evert "and for having a big mouth."

33

THE IACOCCA
NUISANCE

Chrysler chairman Robert Eaton was in town for the annual New York Auto Show where he was scheduled the next morning to introduce the company's 1996 minivan, almost certain to be the star of this year's Jacob Javits Convention Center event. As he climbed into his limousine the driver handed him a message.

"Call Kerkorian immediately."[1]

Nearly five years after investing his first $272 million in the Chrysler Corporation, Kirk had become something of a nuisance to the board and management of the company. Yes, share prices had improved under Kirk's continuing pressure to increase dividends and to buy back stock. But those stock prices remained low compared to the company's value.

Much to Eaton's delight, Chrysler had been stashing away a billion dollars a quarter in excess cash—rainy day funds, he said. But to Kirk, it was an excess of caution. The billionaire figured he

had a better idea and was whispering about one of the most audacious strategies ever floated over Detroit: a buyout that would
take the nation's number three automaker private. Kirk's people
had been talking to Eaton's people, who thought they had damp-
ened Kerkorian's enthusiasm. Not at all. Their top secret Project
Beta was still very much alive. Kirk's passive investor phase was
ending.

Eaton returned to the nine-room corporate apartment at Waldorf Towers and waited a couple of hours, much of it spent pacing
the floor, before returning Kirk's call. It was 7:30 P.M. in New York
and Eaton was alone when he connected with his single biggest
investor.

"Bob, you know our people have been talking. We're going to
make an offer for the company. We're coming out at fifty dollars a
share," Kirk rumbled in his soft baritone voice.

"Do you have financing?" Eaton asked.

"Yes, we're going to have a press release on it." Everything would
be explained in the morning announcement Kirk said.

History did not record the full exchange that evening. In fact,
the only two parties to the conversation would provide slightly—but
significantly—different versions.

Kirk hung up and told one of his lawyers, "That went very well
with Bob. He is totally on board. They're not going to endorse it, but
it went as well as expected." He thought Eaton was conveying a passive position on the buyout. It might not be friendly, but it wouldn't
be hostile.

According to Eaton's account, however, he told Kirk, "You know,
we can't join you on this." It was intended to convey the message that
the buyout would be vigorously opposed. It didn't.

Next morning at the Javits Center there was panic among the
Chrysler auto show team. Eaton was missing. He was supposed to
present the new minivan, but he wasn't on site. And he wasn't at the
Waldorf. The company's $2.6 billion redesigned minivan was going

onstage without its presenter. "Where the hell is Eaton?" demanded one frazzled public relations staffer.

The boss was heading back to Detroit for emergency consultations.

Word of Kerkorian's $22.8 billion buyout offer would be announced from the podium a short time later by a senior public relations official reading a press release. Lee Iacocca was identified as a member of the MGM Grand board of directors and a leading investor in the Chrysler buyout. BAM! The conference center erupted in shouts and tumult. Reporters rushed for the pay phones. News flew around the world. On Wall Street, Chrysler shares jumped $13 before settling back in heavy trading.

At the Javits Center, shocked Chrysler officials were caught completely by surprise, as uninformed and mystified as everyone else. The confusion would take days to sort out.

At Bear Stearns that morning Ace Greenberg heard the news and immediately grabbed a phone. A deal this size with the Babe Ruth of investing? Ace had to be part of that. He reached Kirk within an hour of the announcement. "I can make a whole team of people available to help you if you need it," he said. In response, Kirk was cordial but noncommittal. "Sit tight," he told Ace.

Alex Yemenidjian, the tax accountant turned Tracinda executive and one of Kirk's front men on the Chrysler deal, met the media, investment analysts, and bankers later that morning on a conference call originating out of Las Vegas. Listening in from Detroit were Bob Eaton and a large cluster of Chrysler execs.

Kirk's man touted his boss as a great champion of Chrysler shareholders, but his audience pressed for answers to the bigger question: Where was Kirk getting $22.8 billion?

The answers were surprisingly vague. Some of it was coming out of Chrysler, from Eaton's rainy day cash reserves. But Yemenidjian acknowledged most of the financial backing was still to be arranged. They rushed the public announcement, he seemed to be saying, to avoid the risk of leaks.

What Chrysler heard, however, was an admission of weakness. Without the apparent backing of any big investment banks or some wealthy foreign interests, the company had more than a fighting chance to repel what it described publicly as "an unsolicited offer." Team Kerkorian didn't like that choice of words. It didn't sound friendly, and it was barely passive. Something wasn't right.

On top of that came a Bloomberg Business News report that Kerkorian had hired Bear Stearns. It was like a cascade of warning bells going off in one of Kirk's cockpits. He turned to his advisers. Who hired Ace? He got only blank stares. Ace must have said too much to a friendly reporter. Yemenidjian tracked him down to re-iterate: "We're not ready to bring you on yet." Stand by, he advised, and please avoid journalists.

When stock markets closed that hectic afternoon, Chrysler shares were up nearly 25 percent for the day. Kirk's one-day paper profit was $342 million. That computed to a rate of return over a twenty-four-hour period of about $14 million an hour. But it didn't buy happiness.

By morning there were more alarming signals. The Chrysler board had unanimously approved a statement declaring: "The company is not for sale." In the company's press release, Eaton had gone a step further, making "absolutely clear that Chrysler management is in no way involved" in the Kerkorian deal.

That scent in the air was trouble. Big trouble. Team Kerkorian detected betrayal.

Chrysler was portraying the deal as unwelcome. The company was going into a fighting crouch. And Kirk was cast as the bad guy—or, as the *New York Times* called him that morning, "one of the country's shrewdest but most ruthless corporate raiders."[2]

It wasn't supposed to be that way. Kirk was outwardly calm, as usual, but deeply frustrated and privately troubled by the harsh characterizations. He did not, however, lash out publicly. But to his team he seemed genuinely puzzled when he said, "It wasn't supposed to be hostile."

Yemenidjian had tried to warn Kirk. After a secret meeting in Detroit with Chrysler's senior management and board members, the Kerkorian aide had flown back to Las Vegas with a message: The otherwise friendly group, as he saw it, seemed disturbed by the presence of former Chrysler boss Lee Iacocca as Kirk's investment partner. Any deal involving Iacocca could be in trouble.

Kirk snapped: "Are you suggesting that I get rid of Lee?"

Yemenidjian had seen it before. Kirk's loyalty instincts had kicked in. He already knew the boss was going to risk the deal rather than dump a friend.

K irk, who was about to turn seventy-eight, and his more famous investment partner, Lee Iacocca, seventy, both sons of immigrants, were considered something of an odd couple—the shy financier and the charismatic salesman. They first met over airplanes back in 1989.

Chrysler had acquired Gulfstream, the Georgia-based maker of popular business jets, and Kirk was shopping. Nothing came of Kirk's interest in Gulfstream—either as an investor or a customer— but in 1990 as the auto industry wallowed into recession, Kirk made a special trip to talk cars with Iacocca. He flew to Detroit.

"He came in a 727 . . . this huge plane and just Kerkorian on it," Iacocca recalled in a *Los Angeles Times* interview.[3]

Chrysler stock prices had been wallowing around $20 per share through the past year but had recently fallen to nearly $10. Was the company in danger of bankruptcy? Kirk asked. What were its prospects?

Iacocca, the salesman who had talked Congress into authorizing $1.5 billion in loan guarantees a decade earlier, was enthusiastic about Chrysler's ability to weather the recession, the great new product line in development, and its profitable future. No, said Iacocca, there was no fear of bankruptcy.

That's why Kirk didn't need Bear Stearns analysts to tell him how to invest—or how to hold his bat. He had heard all he needed to know from his friend in high places. Chrysler was golden. And Kirk's first $272 million Chrysler stock purchase in 1990 had gone a long way to enhancing the company's luster in the investment community.

"That started a wonderful relationship," Iacocca said in the immediate glow of their takeover offer. "He has never sold a share of Chrysler stock. Everyone should have a shareholder like him."

But strains on that friendship began to show almost immediately as their bid ran into stiff resistance. Iacocca had expected to be hailed as some kind of hero for raising Chrysler's value in such a daring and historic privatization move. Instead, the same *New York Times* editorial that called Kirk a ruthless corporate raider had also kicked Iacocca in the teeth. It called his role in the "reckless" takeover bid "a destructive, self-indulgent conclusion to a distinguished career"[4] that would pile debt on the automaker and endanger its future.

From Palm Springs, where Iacocca had adjourned for the Easter weekend, the former Chrysler chief launched a personal PR offensive. Talking to auto and business writers around the country, he defended the creative deal, blamed a couple of unnamed accountants on the Kerkorian team for tactical mistakes, and suggested that an undervalued Chrysler was lucky to have him and Kirk stepping in before anyone else.

But he also told the *Detroit News* that this was "a Kirk Kerkorian deal," that it still needed cash, and—in a quote made all the more inflammatory because it was set in bold 28-point headline type on the front page—that Kerkorian had to "'get cranking on financing. It's not there, yet.'"[5] He even imposed an unnecessary deadline on their loan hunt, saying that Kirk had only "a 10-day window" to arrange financing, or he would fail.

The expletives erupting out of Tracinda headquarters in Las Vegas were never put on the record, but Iacocca was summoned immediately—his Easter afternoon with family canceled. At Kirk's insistence, his partner was heading to New York City "to get cranking," hard feelings notwithstanding, as part of Team Kerkorian to help round up cash for the deal.

In fact, privately negotiating finance arrangements in advance had never been a Kerkorian option. By regulation, the size of Kirk's Chrysler holdings—amounting to nearly ten percent—would have required immediate public disclosure to the Securities and Exchange Commission.

Investment analysts were dazzled by Chrysler's aggressive and effective response to the Kerkorian-Iacocca deal—a collection of strategies that included new poison pill provisions, threats to abandon any bank that dared help finance any part of the deal, and heart-to-hearts with the likes of Bear Stearns.

Ace Greenberg's earlier role raising nearly a billion dollars for Kirk's new MGM Grand Hotel made him a target of concern even before the Bloomberg News story linked them. But Chrysler had its own leverage. Bear Stearns had earned more than $10 million in fees over the previous five years managing $4 billion in Chrysler bonds. The investment banker had a conflict of interest that Chrysler's lawyers would point out. Besides, Bear Stearns could easily be replaced. Ace got that message.

On the Wednesday after Easter, Alex Yemenidjian was getting ready to meet bankers in New York when the phone in his hotel room rang at 7 A.M. It was Greenberg. And it was especially early for a Tracinda executive from the Pacific Time zone. But Ace launched into a description of his dilemma about lawyers and conflicts.

"Do you have any objection if we get back to the Chrysler lawyers and say we haven't done any business with you?" Greenberg asked.

Of course not, Yemenidjian shrugged. "That's the truth."

Two hours later a *Wall Street Journal* reporter reached Yemenidjian and said his newspaper was running a story revealing that Bear Stearns had pulled out of the deal—unless the Kerkorian camp denied it.

"Are you kidding?" Yemenidjian exploded. They couldn't pull out, he tried to explain, because they were never in the deal. Nonetheless, the *Journal* reported that Bear Stearns was out. As Alex saw it, Ace had covered his ass at Kirk's expense.

Yemenidjian called Greenberg for one last angry rant. Bear Stearns was hereby dead to Kerkorian. The Babe Ruth of investing would never again bat for Ace—not if Alex had anything to say about it.

But venting didn't alter the facts. What appeared to the world to be a Bear Stearns retreat was a serious blow to what little momentum the Kerkorian side had going for it. Only Bank of America, Kirk's loyal lender for a half century, was willing to even consider the deal—and it would do so only if at least one other major bank came along.

Time was slipping away. Iacocca's ten-day deadline came and went. Chrysler upped the ante by taking out an $8 billion line of credit spread around sixty-one different banks. Kirk explored foreign alliances. He tried to goad Eaton into putting a sweetened $55 per share offer to a vote of the stockholders. He met with a takeover expert. He hired a public relations consultant. He did not quit. He did not sell any of his Chrysler shares, even though his paper profits approached a billion dollars.

The company floated a secret approach to see if Kirk had a price to walk away. What would it cost to buy out his thirty-six million shares? Offended that he would be cast as a greedy "greenmailer," Kirk could no longer utter Eaton's name without a profanity.

Yemenidjian went public with the secret overture, telling the *Wall Street Journal* that Kerkorian "will not sell at any price unless all other holders are offered similar terms."[6]

Seven weeks after shaking up Chrysler and the investment world, Kirk withdrew his original bid for the company and his $55 per share sweetener. A brief press release from Tracinda ended the takeover drama. Kirk did not, however, sell a single share of his $1.5 billion Chrysler portfolio. Eaton knew what that meant. Kirk wasn't going away.

Fortress Chrysler would be stormed again.

When Kirk returned a couple months later, he announced himself with another $700 million Chrysler stock purchase financed by an $800 million loan from Bank of America. His holdings now reached fifty million shares, slightly more than 14 percent. He was also wooing former Chrysler executive Jerry York away from his financial chief post at IBM. Kirk would propose replacing "that (expletive) guy, Eaton" with York.

Meanwhile, Team Kerkorian had pretty much frozen out Iacocca whose frequent complaining had reached a level of nuisance that was driving "the Perry Como of the craps table" absolutely mad. To be fair, Iacocca had been especially hard hit by vindictive Chrysler officials who rescinded about $45 million in Iacocca's stock options, alleging conduct detrimental to the company.

A woman on Kerkorian's newly retained public relations staff was assigned to take all of Iacocca's calls and to listen intently and sympathetically—regardless of the hours—to his angry tirades about what was happening . . . or not happening. Her broader mission was also to encourage Iacocca to stay away from the press.

While pressure continued to build on the Chrysler takeover front in their business world, the personal lives of both Kirk and Iacocca grew more complicated, too. Darrien Iacocca sued for divorce. She rejected Lee's first $4 million settlement offer.

After four years together Kirk and Lisa Bonder, his tennis and yachting partner, were bickering more and enjoying each other less. But what troubled Kirk most was learning that she talked with friends about using Kirk to become the richest woman in the world. He gave her a five-carat diamond ring for her thirtieth birthday in

October 1995, and two months later told her to move out. Lisa and her now six-year-old son from her previous marriage moved in with Darrien Iacocca.[7]

The estranged romantic partners of the estranged Chrysler takeover partners lived together for about nine months, became close friends, and shared many personal insights. Lisa told Darrien her dream was to be the "'last Mrs. Kerkorian' so that one day 'it' would all be hers."

"It"—Kirk's fortune—happened to be growing by tens of millions of dollars a month as Chrysler stock values steadily climbed.

By the end of 1995 it was clear that while Kirk's campaign to boost share value had been a reasonable success, his takeover attempt was doomed. The gambler knew it was time to fold 'em. Walking away, however, required a bit of delicate choreography.

Kirk and Eaton agreed to meet secretly and alone—against the advice of advisers from both sides—to explore a final compromise. Eaton took a suite at the elegant old Beverly Wilshire Hotel, a short walk from Kirk's Beverly Hills office.

Chrysler would agree to more stock buybacks. It would raise the dividend again. Kerkorian could have a seat on the Chrysler board, just so long as it wasn't Jerry York, who was considered a menace to current management. Kirk had to think about that. York was his top choice.

"You know, Bob, we might be able to do that," Kirk finally agreed. "But it's going to be very expensive."

Eaton agreed to add another billion dollars to the buybacks. And so it went. But Kirk's request that Chrysler restore to Iacocca the $42 million in stock options it had rescinded was adamantly opposed. How about half of it? Eaton shrugged. Maybe.

Formal negotiations moved to Michigan in February 1996. Kirk left York in charge and flew to Florida where he would wait out the final terms aboard his yacht. Key elements of the deal were in place—the expanded stock buybacks, the dividend increases, a five-year moratorium on Kirk buying any more Chrysler stock or attempting a proxy fight, and Tracinda executive Jim Aljian would get a seat on the Chrysler board. Iacocca would get half of the rescinded stock options, but he would have to sign a nondisparagement agreement—essentially a five-year gag order on criticism.

That's when the whole deal suddenly went wobbly. A furious Iacocca wanted $53 million, reflecting the full current value of those contested stock options, and he would refuse to sign any agreement requiring that he shut up.

In a phone call from the *October Rose* with the entire deal hanging on Iacocca's ego, Kirk tried to calm and reassure his partner. Finally, through gritted teeth, Kirk said he would personally make up the $32 million difference himself. You'll get your money, he said. It sounded like the end of a friendship. It wasn't.

One of Kirk's most enduring—and friends found most endearing—traits was his limited capacity for grudges. He didn't collect them. "It's business," he would say, and move on.[8] Kirk and Iacocca were double-dating in the months that followed. And the expletives disappeared from Eaton's name. They dined together as Kirk and Bob on several occasions thereafter.

And Kirk walked away from another failed takeover attempt with an almost unimaginable profit. When all the Chrysler dealing was done, he was up about $2.7 billion over his initial investments. But Kerkorian's financial return could have been twice that, maybe more, had the deal succeeded.

According to Yemenidjian: "His loyalty to Iacocca cost Kirk billions."

SHE PERSISTED

When Kirk's lucrative but failed run at Chrysler ended earlier in the year, it left him at the age of seventy-nine a billionaire bereft of meaningful challenges. He had no pending conquests, no looming takeovers, no underperforming corporations to rescue. He wandered through an uncertain spring. But by summer he was back in the arms of an old flame—his very needy and financially forlorn ex-company—MGM/UA.

The film studio's 1990 merger with Giancarlo Parretti's Pathé Communications had been a disaster for everyone—except Kirk, who had walked away with a majority share of the $1.4 billion sale. Parretti, it turned out, had bribed bankers to finance the deal and then looted the company to support his lavish lifestyle. French banking giant Credit Lyonnais was left with a dysfunctional film company and a bill for well over $2.5 billion. When the bank put MGM/UA back on the market, Kirk was first in line for his third turn at the movie business.

That July Kirk was restless romantically, as well. He kept trying to break off his five-year relationship with former women's tennis professional Lisa Bonder, but she refused to accept "good-bye" as the last word in their affair. They still spent occasional weekends together until she said she was ready to move across the country. She just needed some cash to "start over" in New York City.

At about the same time that Kirk wrote a check for $870 million to buy back MGM, he also withdrew some cash for Lisa—a little something in order to "start over" in New York—$1 million in bank-wrapped stacks of $100 bills.[1]

Kirk always kept plenty of cash on hand for his own use. He hated credit cards. "They leave paper trails wherever you go," he complained. But the first time Kirk ever applied for a credit card, he did so along with financial advisers George Mason and Anthony Mandekic. They were approved. Kirk was rejected. His reliance on cash left him without a consumer credit record.[2]

He was undeterred. Kirk remained a big believer in using his petty cash for daily personal expenses such as lunch or dinner, a cocktail at the Polo Lounge, tips for the parking lot valets, whatever. And $100 tips were common.

He kept rolls of $100 bills in his pants pocket wherever he went. Around town, that meant a wad of $5,000 to $10,000. On foreign trips, he preferred to have at least $50,000 in his pockets. His home safe, whether he was living in Beverly Hills or Las Vegas, was usually stocked with currency, mostly U.S. hundred-dollar bills, that routinely amounted to between $150,000 and $200,000.[3]

Lisa didn't have a home safe. She didn't even have a permanent home. She was still living with Darrien Iacocca. Under the circumstances, $1 million posed an immediate security burden. She asked Wendy Falahi—the twenty-eight-year-old wife of Kirk's valet and fitness guru—for a ride over to Lisa's bank on Sunset Boulevard. The women were friends, both of them outgoing, good-natured, and similar in age. And Wendy often took care of Lisa's seven-year-old son, Taylor.

At the bank, an overly attentive manager escorted the two women into a private room with a table. An armed security guard stood outside. There, alone with a million dollars, the women discovered that a hundred bricks of currency did not fit easily into the space available in her safe deposit box. They had to rearrange, restack, stuff, and jam the last of the wrapped packs, an exercise that left them almost giddy by the time they left the guarded room.

That million-dollar stash never did finance Lisa's new life in New York. She didn't move east, and Kirk didn't seem to mind. In August, about three weeks later, he invited Lisa to join him on the yacht cruising the French Riviera. In October when she turned thirty-one, Kirk took her out for a birthday dinner at Matteo's, one of his favorite restaurants in Westwood. And in November they flew to Maui on his private jet to spend Thanksgiving in a $5,000-a-night luxury suite at the Ritz-Carlton.

Their Hawaiian reconciliation ended abruptly. The bickering had resumed. Lisa was especially persistent about her wish to be married. Kirk didn't even want to talk about it. He walked out, summoned his flight crew, and flew home, leaving Lisa to make her own way back to California.[4]

It was tennis that brought Kirk and Lisa together in 1991—tennis and Lornie Kuhle, a former MGM Grand Hotel and Las Vegas Country Club pro and that year a coach for tennis star Jimmy Connors. Years earlier, Kuhle had managed Bobby Riggs when he lost to women's tennis star Billie Jean King in the nationally televised "Battle of the Sexes" produced by Jerry Perenchio.

Kuhle brought Lisa Bonder along to one of the weekend tennis marathons at Kirk's hilltop house on Wanda Park Drive. The five-foot-ten blonde with a quick wit and a devastating forehand was an instant hit among Kirk's circle of weekend tennis partners.

"She was fun, gracious, charming and she could play tennis like out of this world," recalled Ron Falahi, Kirk's right-hand man and valet who also served as the regular chef for those weekend games. And in March of 1991 she started dating Kirk. He was seventy-three; she was twenty-five. At the time she had been married for three years to Thomas Kreiss, the heir to a furniture fortune. Their baby, Taylor, had just turned two.

Before marriage and pregnancy, Lisa had been ranked in the Top Ten of women's professional tennis. As a teenager she had defeated the legendary Chris Evert in a Tokyo tournament. And in 1984, her best year, Lisa reached the French Open quarterfinals in Paris and later that year in New York made it to the fourth round at the U.S. Open.

Kirk's tennis buddies were impressed with her tennis and camaraderie. Kirk's affection for her was obvious. But his blunt-spoken sister, Rose, was never a fan. Lisa wasn't Armenian, she was still married, and she was so young.

"What do you see in this bimbo?" Rose once scoffed in disapproval.

"She makes me laugh," Kirk replied.[5]

Good humor was a common trait of all Kirk's women, those he dated and those he wed. Wife Jean was among the spunkiest. One evening at a stuffy Beverly Hills dinner party with Kirk, Cary Grant, and Cary's girlfriend at the time, British photographer Maureen Donaldson, the also very British Jean tired of the small talk. The men had retired for scotch and cigars. One of the rich women was complaining about the inadequacies of her household cooks.

"You should have your cook make spotted dick," Jean interrupted in the Cockney accent of her youth.

"What? What did you say?" responded the woman, not quite believing what she'd just heard.

"You. Should. Have. Your. Cook. Make. Spotted. Dick!" Jean repeated more slowly, one heavily accented word at a time.[6]

With a wink and a nudge Maureen chimed in, too. "But without raisins it's not spotted dick," she said, adding suggestively, "if you know what I mean."

The table full of proper Beverly Hills society matrons fell into a moment of seemingly hostile silence—until Jean explained that spotted dick was an English pudding with raisins. Not everyone was amused. But it was precisely the sort of reaction to chitchat that Kirk would have relished. He put a high priority on confident, good-humored women.

Kirk's previous companions, including Yvette Mimieux, Barbara Grant, and Priscilla Presley, were smart, stunning, and discreet. And none of those who came before Lisa Bonder had ever said a word that drew public attention to their ties with Kirk.

As Suzy the gossip columnist suggested early in the Bonder-Kerkorian affair, Lisa talked too much for Kirk's comfort. Worse yet, in conversations with Darrien Iacocca and other friends, Lisa had grumbled that he should be sharing more of his wealth with her. It was a violation of Kirk's jealously guarded privacy, and it cost Lisa his trust.

That Kirk was still lavishing Lisa with gifts and trips and a million dollars in bank-wrapped $100 bills months after their breakup seemed contradictory to friends and family. But Lisa would explain it simply, "He took care of me, and I took care of him."

From the earliest days of their affair, Kirk promised he would provide financially for Lisa and Taylor if she wished to move quickly to divorce. And for his own sense of propriety, Kirk encouraged her to do just that. He did not, however, propose marriage himself. He was very happily unmarried. That never changed through his five years with Lisa. By early 1997, with their relationship chilling into estrangement, her opportunities to woo him into marriage were fast fading.

Nevertheless, she persisted.

E ven as a young man, Kirk had been frustrated by difficulty conceiving children. A childless marriage was one of the great disappointments of his nine years with first wife Peggy. With Jean, they tried for about five years before Tracy was conceived. And after trying for another five years without success, they decided to adopt Linda.

Kirk at first assured Lisa that he long ago had a vasectomy. He later acknowledged that actually he was sterile.

Lisa confided to a friend that she had a solution, a way to get around Kirk's sterility and still convince him to marry her. She told Bonnie Glusman that she had located a clinic in Los Angeles that performed in vitro fertilization. Lisa could get pregnant at the clinic but tell Kirk that the baby was his.

Bonnie, the wife of prominent Las Vegas restaurateur Fred Glusman of Piero's—both of them mutual friends of Kirk—offered no support for that idea whatsoever. She said she called Lisa's plan "deceitful and morally wrong," ending the conversation.

By spring of 1997 it was becoming clear even to Lisa that reconciliation with Kirk was hopeless. She was spending hours a day on the phone fretting with friends and obsessing over how to win back Kirk's affections. But he was adamant. She told friend and socialite Anne DuPont that she would not have much to live for without Kirk in her life. She made similar comments to Kirk that he found especially disturbing.

Lisa also stalked Kirk, keeping track of his travels through inquiries to the aircraft dispatch office at Van Nuys Airport where Kirk based his private jet. She was even familiar with the crew's standard flight routes, and on the phone with friends she would sometimes calculate within a few minutes and a few miles where Kirk was and when he would get wherever he was going.

Kirk finally complained that Lisa seemed to be showing up at odd times and places, as if she were following him.

In April, after another "final" Kirk rejection to her overtures, Lisa was back to considering a sperm bank. She told Anne DuPont that Taylor needed a brother or sister. But Lisa was also ready to party. She started dating Hollywood playboy Steve Bing, the heir to a Southern California real estate fortune. During one double date with Anne at the exclusive Hotel Bel-Air, Lisa and Bing slipped away for a quick lovemaking session.

It was around that time that Lisa decided to try a deal-making ploy on one of the greatest deal makers in American business history. She would agree to move on with her life, but she would need a stake—a nest egg, so to speak. There was a house for sale on Angelo Drive in Beverly Hills. It needed work. If Kirk would give her $4 million, she would use $1.6 million to buy and renovate the place. The rest would be moving-on-with-my-life money.

Kirk agreed. He would give her the full $4 million, but she would have to sign a contract—a legally binding nondisclosure agreement prepared by attorney Terry Christensen—committing her to keep secret everything Lisa knew about Kirk, his business interests, or his personal affairs. She even had to keep secret the secrecy agreement itself. They did more than shake hands on the deal. They spent a week together, in what both of them called "a last fling."

Kirk promptly moved on, inviting another smart, stunning, articulate blonde to join him for dinner at the MGM Grand Hotel's Brown Derby in late June. Una Davis was from La Jolla, an affluent coastal village north of San Diego. She also played tennis, was divorced, financially independent, and very competitive.

Una and Kirk had met two summers earlier when she and some mutual friends of tennis pro Lornie Kuhle drove north to join Kirk's weekend tennis marathon. After a day of tennis, laughs, and one of Ron Falahi's poolside buffet luncheons, Kirk took everyone out for dinner at Mr. Chow. The host was wearing a butterscotch-colored soft corduroy jacket with patches. Una exclaimed, "I love your jacket!" He seemed to keep an eye on her the rest of the evening.[7]

Kirk was in his late seventies at that first meeting, but trim and athletic. He was naturally tanned and had a full head of gray-streaked black hair combed back in a wavy pompadour. In conversations he was humble and self-effacing and had an almost boyish enthusiasm for life. "He was so much fun, so endearing, kind and sweet. You'd never think he was some big deal in business," Una said of those early encounters.

They found the same comfortable rhythm of easy conversation and easy laughs at the Brown Derby, on their first private date. After dinner Kirk escorted Una to the door of her room and bid her good night. "That was that," she says. "He was such a gentleman." One date led to a second—at Spago in Caesars Palace. This time Una noticed the swirl surrounding Kirk's arrival.

"When he walked in, the whole place seemed to shake." She saw people rush from all corners of the restaurant to greet him, seat him, and solicit his every wish. "It was amazing . . . but Kirk, he was almost embarrassed by it. He wanted to be incognito all the time."

To avoid creating such a stir, Kirk liked to park in back, near the MGM Grand service entrance so he could walk down an alley, go through the food court, and get to his favorite restaurant without having to deal with dozens of greetings. One night in an amorous mood, Kirk lingered in his white Taurus with Una making out like a couple of teenagers.

KNOCK. KNOCK. A hotel security officer was pounding on Kirk's window.

"You can't be doing that. You've got to get out of here," ordered the officer. He didn't know he was talking to his boss. And Kirk never told him. In fact, he said nothing at all. But he was furious. Una noticed as Kirk complied with orders to move along that his right fist was clenched and cocked.

"He was ready to clock him!"

Sometimes Kirk seemed almost goofy in love. Another evening he was driving to pick up Una for dinner at her hotel and found himself uncharacteristically running late and in traffic. Abruptly, he wheeled onto the median and roared past the traffic jam, blowing out tires and finally coming to a dead stop.

He peeled off several hundred-dollar bills and paid a bystander to take care of his car, then ran off to keep his date with Una.

Those first dates led to more. It looked like the beginning of another beautiful friendship. Even sister Rose was fond of her.

But suddenly the phone calls stopped. The dates ended. "I figured that was that," Una shrugged. Later in the summer she heard from

Lornie Kuhle. Kirk was in a terrible place, he said. He's depressed. He's sitting alone staring at the walls. Could Una please call to cheer him up?

"My God, what happened?"

"It's his ex," said Lornie. "Lisa Bonder. She's pregnant. She says it's his."

35

RIFLE RIGHT TAKES IRON MIKE

JUNE 28, 1997
LAS VEGAS, NEVADA

Crowds were streaming into the MGM Grand Hotel, people from all over the country and around the world. The biggest event in boxing was taking place that Saturday evening in the sold-out Grand Garden Arena. The biggest gate, the biggest purse, the biggest promotion. It was simply a very big night for Kirk and his hotel. So, of course, Kirk was sneaking into his own party through the kitchen by way of a back door and a labyrinth of back hallways. It was a proven route for avoiding small talk and stray reporters. He just wanted to find his seat and dissolve into the crowd.

The main event would be the much-anticipated rematch of defending heavyweight champion Evander Holyfield and deposed champ "Iron Mike" Tyson in a World Boxing Association title fight. The heavily hyped showdown, billed as "The Sound and the Fury," would rewrite boxing's financial records and funnel 18,187 sports fans through Kirk's casino, making it a very big night for boxing and gambling, too.

Years earlier, Kirk saw nights like this in his imagination, back when he envisioned the Grand Garden Arena. It would be the first permanent indoor boxing venue ever designed and built into a Strip resort hotel. He had insisted on its inclusion in the MGM Grand's original plans despite doubts and resistance from Fred Benninger and his bean counters. "Fred, we're going to have an arena," Kirk insisted.[1] He saw it as his very own Madison Square Garden West.

Finally emerging from his Employees Only sanctuary, Kirk made his way into the packed arena. He settled into his favorite seat. Tennis pal Lornie Kuhle was there, too. They were *not* sitting in the elite ringside seats. Kirk could see the fight better from seats along the first tier of risers where his point of view was just above the top rope. Besides, Kirk told friends, people who sit in the ringside seats "are just looking for attention." He wasn't.[2]

This fight had been scheduled for early May. It was delayed more than seven weeks after Tyson suffered a cut over one eye during a training session in April. It was blamed on a headbutt. There was additional drama leading up to the fight when the Tyson camp demanded that referee Mitch Halpern be replaced. Halpern had worked the previous Holyfield-Tyson bout. Besides stopping the fight to declare a technical knockout in the eleventh round, he had annoyed Team Tyson by ruling that numerous headbutts throughout the match were all accidental. The Nevada State Athletic Commission refused to replace the referee, but Halpern ultimately withdrew voluntarily.

The title bout would be the fifth in a series of six prearranged Tyson fights at the MGM Grand. The agreement was controversial at the time and required Kirk's personal intervention. Terms of the contract were negotiated while Tyson was still serving time on a rape conviction in Indiana.

Rifle Right Kerkorian had been willing to give Tyson another chance that some in his MGM Grand management apparently were reluctant to do. For a publicly owned company that was touting itself as a family-friendly destination, such a prominent business association with a convicted rapist seemed to some executives to be a questionable marketing strategy.

But Kirk was more than a fan and patron of boxing. He knew what it was like to fight for rent money or a meal. He never forgot the beatings his brother took in the ring to bring home a few dollars that fed Kirk and his parents. And he admired the sheer courage of any man risking pain, humiliation, and failure to stand alone and fight to his last ounce of stamina. Kirk saw himself in every scrappy kid fighting to escape poverty, a poor education, and the low expectations of the street. Besides, he knew that there was a lot of money on the business side of boxing.

But contract talks between promoter Don King and MGM Grand executives had finally reached a stalemate in March 1995. King let Kirk know that his "high echelon" executives appeared reluctant to make a deal. They "didn't negotiate fairly and justly," he complained and seemed "disgusted" to be considering such a deal.

One of Tyson's young co-managers, Rory Holloway, described the attitude of MGM executives more crudely: "They're like, 'We ain't giving a fuckin' jailbird this kind'a money. Never been done before.'"[3] Even Kirk's personal involvement had failed to move the MGM Grand management team. Kirk always tried to avoid overruling the officers of his publicly owned companies, and this was no exception. But he wanted the Tyson deal.

The stalemate in fight negotiations came at an extraordinarily busy time for Kirk. He was formulating a buyout plan to take Chrysler public. But as a sign of how important it was to land the Tyson fights for the MGM Grand, Kirk reached out for his key man in the carmaker deal, Alex Yemenidjian.

Alex was in Toronto when he received the summons from Beverly Hills. "How soon can you get back?" Kirk spoke abruptly, without the usual niceties. As Yemenidjian began to recite the various flights scheduled later that afternoon, Kirk cut him off, saying, "No, how soon can you be here?"

Yemenidjian immediately understood. "I'll charter a plane," he said and headed for the airport.[4]

A few hours later and more than halfway across the continent, Yemenidjian walked into a Tracinda conference room where Kirk and Don King sat with MGM Grand chairman Robert R. Maxey and vice president Larry J. Woolf. He barely had time to drop his bags before Kirk stood up and led the MGM Grand contingent toward the door. Everyone was leaving except King and Yemenidjian.

Kirk's final instruction to Alex was brief: "Make it happen." Don King welcomed the change.[5] And somewhere in the wee hours of the morning, Yemenidjian and the fight promoter had a two-page memorandum of understanding that worked for everyone. Tyson would come out of prison a short time later to a six-fight deal that guaranteed him more than $100 million.

The deal made Don King the second-largest stockholder in the MGM Grand Hotel. His six hundred thousand shares worth $15 million came with a Kerkorian guarantee that they would double in value by the sixth fight.

Tyson returned home to Ohio after his prison release, and Kirk sent his private jet. The fighter and his managers joined Don King for lunch and a chat at Kirk's Las Vegas Country Club home. Tyson already was Kirk's favorite fighter.

His brawling, wild-animal style of fighting made him "the guy," Kirk said, "I'd pick in any street fight." But what impressed Kirk when they finally met was the fighter's encyclopedic knowledge of boxing history. He even thumbed through Kirk's personal scrapbook and talked about fighters from the era of Rifle Right Kerkorian. Ron Falahi, who served the luncheon, noticed how "Mr. K was completely charmed."[6]

The failure of executives Maxey and Woolf to make the deal that brought Tyson to the MGM Grand may have been a factor in their departures in the following months. Chairman Maxey would resign without official explanation shortly before the first Tyson fight. Kirk replaced him with Yemenidjian who, in turn, replaced Woolf.

Tyson's handlers were convinced that the shake-up at MGM Grand was tied to what they considered their rude treatment in negotiations. They also felt confident that their man was now on his way to becoming the world's first billion-dollar fighter.[7]

On that night in June 1997 as prefight tensions mounted in the-house-that-Kirk-built, a record crowd had turned the Grand Garden Arena into the noisiest corner of Nevada. Kirk-the-fight-fan savored the moment—the decibels, the heat, the smell of it, the prospects of a great fight.

Others in the MGM Grand entourage might be contemplating the record live gate of $17.3 million, the $100 million return from domestic pay-per-view, the tens of millions from foreign closed-circuit broadcasts, and the who-knows-how-much in a postfight casino drop. But not Kirk. Sixty years after his own stint on the canvas as Rifle Right, his focus was still on the contest. The uncertain outcome. The fight.

Finally, the crowd's long wait was over. The bell to start Round One sent both fighters to center ring and their first harmless jabs and tentative feints. The crowd roared at a hard right from Holyfield and again when Tyson's left hook seemed to slow the more aggressive reigning champ. But Holyfield was winning the crowd as it started to chant his name as the clock ticked down the final six seconds.

A lackluster second round turned suddenly bloody when Holyfield's shaved head came up under Tyson's right eyebrow and opened an inch-long gash over his right eyelid. Referee Mills Lane stopped the fight and the clock. There were about two minutes and twenty seconds left in the round. Tyson's corner man applied medication to stanch the bleeding and wiped a smeared patch of blood from the fighter's right cheek. It was ruled an accidental headbutt. Was this fight going to follow the same course as the last Tyson-Holyfield encounter when Iron Mike was half blinded by bloody wounds incurred from what were ruled as "accidental headbutts"?

An angry Tyson seemed primed to retaliate, poised like a sprinter to burst back out to center ring in the third round, but he was called back to his corner. The fighter had forgotten his mouth guard. Or maybe not.

Like a wild man unleashed, Tyson came out throwing punches that at first hit nothing but air. He recalibrated enough to finally land a series of powerful body blows with left hooks and explosive uppercuts. Holyfield tried to slow things down with one bear hug clinch after another. The crowd was starting to chant "Tyson. Tyson."

With about thirty seconds left in the round Holyfield broke out of his latest clinch, this time spinning and jumping up and down and shrieking, "He bit me!" His right ear was, in fact, a bloody mess. The fight was halted.

Referee Lane consulted a doctor who said the fight could go on, that Holyfield was not unfairly handicapped. The ref docked Tyson two points. Tyson tried to argue that the bloody ear was the result of his left hook. "Bullshit!" Lane shouted and ordered the ring cleared to resume the round where it had been suspended.

The clock was restarted at 00:30. But almost immediately Lane stopped it again, after another clinch, at 00:10. In those twenty seconds Tyson had taken a bite out of Holyfield's other ear. The fight was over. Tyson lost by disqualification. A chorus of boos and epithets rained down from the rafters. MGM security and uniformed Metro Police piled into the ring to keep order as scuffles erupted in and out of the ring.

In the stands, hotel security quickly escorted Kirk and his friends through a side door and out to a secure and private room. Meanwhile, rioting broke out as 18,187 fight fans turned into an outraged mob. The casino had to be closed and cordoned off, but not before gaming tables were looted and overturned and an estimated forty people were sent to area hospitals for cuts and bruises and one broken ankle.

Kirk was disappointed but carried no grudges. Tyson was suspended by Nevada boxing authorities and docked the maximum 10 percent of his $30 million purse. The sixth fight at the MGM Grand had to be canceled. Kirk met with Don King, and they worked out a settlement that, as promised, still doubled the value of King's MGM Grand shares. Kirk bought them all back at a price well over market value—paying a premium above market of about $9 million in order to deliver on his original guarantee.

"He was a man of his word," King said, calling Kirk a great man. "He was bound by his handshake. That's the kind of man he was— a man whose word meant more than money."[8]

36

GENOCIDE
AND
GENEROSITY

Harut Sassounian sat quietly across a low table from Kirk Kerkorian, both men gazing out their windows as Kirk's private Boeing 727 seemed to crawl across the rugged brown landscape below. Neither man had spoken for more than a half hour. Kirk broke the silence.

"We're going over Turkey," he said. "Our historic Armenian lands."[1]

Harut nodded, a bit surprised that Kirk was so aware of their flight path and their relative proximity to old Armenia. Harut had made this flight nearly a hundred times—and as recently as a few days earlier. For Kirk, this flight was his first to Armenia.

"Yes, that's our land down there," Harut fervently agreed. It felt to him as if Kirk might want to talk about Harut's favorite subject— Armenian grievances against Turkey. His weekly *California Courier* columns were filled with unsparing criticisms of the Turks dating back to the early-twentieth-century genocide.

"Harut," Kirk continued, "why don't we go and take back our lands?"

Was Kirk teasing or turning radical? Harut wasn't sure. He stammered something about the impossible dream and then the two men lapsed back into silence. About an hour later they were disembarking at the airport in Yerevan where, despite Kirk's insistence on a low-key reception, he was greeted by the president of Armenia, Robert Kocharyan. Kirk was welcomed warmly to the Armenian capital as a beloved and heroic figure. It made him fidgety.

Kirk and Harut adjourned as quickly as politeness allowed to a once-impressive Soviet-era palace reserved for visiting dignitaries and heads of state. Big industrial fans provided noisy but inadequate air-conditioning against the sweltering summer heat. The rooms had high ceilings, short beds, rusty plumbing, and an eager Armenian-speaking staff.

Dinner that first evening was with the president and his entire cabinet at a Yerevan restaurant that had a view of Mount Ararat. Sassounian was seated near the Armenian defense minister, and in making conversation he mentioned Kirk's comment over Turkey about taking back Armenian lands.

The amused minister laughed. "Tell Kirk if he gives us $50 million, we'll go get them back," he said.

Kirk was sitting next to the president. He asked if there was anything besides humanitarian aid that Armenia needed. Kocharyan talked about infrastructure—more housing, for instance, but especially the need for a highway through the heart of the country, a major thoroughfare linking the country's northern border with Georgia and its southern border with Iran.

"Would $100 million help you?" Kirk asked.

Kocharyan hesitated just a moment, but only to let the reality of the offer sink in. "Of course!" he blurted out.

"We'll do it," Kirk said.

The president asked about issuing a press release first thing in the morning. The usually anonymous donor asked if such publicity would be useful. Kocharyan grinned. "I want our enemies to know that we have a rich and powerful diaspora."

Kirk shrugged. "If it would be helpful," he said, "go ahead."

Harut was surprised. Kirk had agreed to let Armenia tell the world that this son of Armenian immigrants was putting up $100 million to help the homeland of Ahron and Lily Kerkorian. Mr. Anonymous was letting Armenia use him in a way that was unprecedented.

After dinner Harut warned Kirk that U.S. government sanctions against the Tehran government might complicate this $100 million offer. By building a modern highway through Armenia connecting the Georgian and Iranian borders, Tehran would benefit right along with Armenia. It could be a violation of American sanctions. Kirk didn't want to hear that his Lincy Foundation could be legally barred from making such an important and useful investment on Armenia's behalf.

Besides, he said, "If I paid attention to lawyers and accountants, I would've never amounted to anything." Subject closed.

H arut was awakened the next morning by the sounds of people running up and down the hall. He stepped out of his room to see if there was an emergency.

"We have a problem," said an attendant in Armenian.

Kirk had been asked the night before to write on a slip of paper what kind of fresh fruits he would like served with his breakfast. The attendant showed the list to Harut. It said: guava, mango, and pineapple. Members of the hotel staff had consulted an English-Armenian dictionary and were aghast to learn that they had none of Kirk's requests.

"What kind of fruit do you have?" Harut asked

They had apricots, grapes, oranges, and bananas. Harut assured them those would do very nicely. But Kirk was also asking for a cereal bowl. He had brought his own daily supply of cereal in sealed plastic bags. Harut's Armenian vocabulary lacked a word for cereal bowl. He tried describing it as a "deep dish." Later, when he went to Kirk's room to see how his breakfast was going, Kirk nodded toward his "cereal bowl." It was a very large vase resembling some Ming dynasty museum piece.

Kirk summoned Harut back to his room about a half hour later. He led Harut to his shower and turned on the water. It came out chunky, gushing with a thick red-brown gunk. Kirk deadpanned, "Are they trying to poison me?" It was a case of seldom-used and badly rusted plumbing. It was also the last straw.

Harut had a suggestion. They should move into the updated Marriott. It had modern conveniences, fax machines, cable television. "Can I get CNBC?" Kirk asked. That sealed the deal.

News of the move was a blow to the palace staff. The manager was stricken: "If I have offended such an important guest, I could be fired . . . or killed!" But Harut assured him that Kirk was delighted with the staff and would be lavish in his praise. The problem, he explained, was beyond the manager's control. "Unfortunately, the palace doesn't have cable television," he said.

Kirk was missing his access to daily stock market reports, relying instead on updates from spotty telephone connections to business advisers in the States. Even as he was touring Armenia he was trying to arrange major financing deals affecting MGM studios and negotiating long distance to buy out his biggest MGM partner, Seven Network. He needed a Western-style, full-service hotel.

Word of Kerkorian's visit to Armenia had spread overnight like a California brush fire. On their second morning, as Kirk and Harut were leaving the hotel, they encountered a line of people that stretched nearly a block—dozens of Armenians clutching photos and documents. Harut invited them to leave their documentation and he would personally get back to them.

"What is it?" Kirk asked as Harut led him away.

"Well, they all have proof that, one way or another, they're related to the Kerkorians of California," Harut explained. "I guess you're all cousins."

"Oh, my God."

Harut and Kirk continued on to the foreign ministry office where they had a midday meeting to review the government's press release announcing the Lincy Foundation's gift of $100 million for the major highway building project. Harut immediately took out a pen and began scratching out lines and fixing spellings.

"What are you doing?" Kirk asked.

"Editing," said Harut.

"Well, stop. Let them say it however they want."

Harut marveled in silence. What had become of Kirk, the "shishkabob Armenian"?

A visit to the Armenian Genocide Memorial and Museum was arranged for Kirk's last full day in the country.

All modern-day Armenians grow up hearing harrowing tales of forced marches, roadside massacres, and ethnic cleansing campaigns committed or condoned by Ottoman rulers, Turks, and Kurds. Kirk's father, Ahron, and grandfather Kasper were both born and raised in the Harput region of what was then Armenia. It is now east-central Turkey. They both left home before the great onslaught of violence that left 1.5 million dead between 1915 and 1923.

Though Ahron never witnessed such atrocities, he would horrify Kirk and his siblings with disturbing stories of Ottoman soldiers hoisting Armenian babies on their bloody bayonets. If some atrocities from that era were exaggerations or even inventions, plenty of them were all too real. And the human toll was staggering.

Hundreds of Armenian villages became overnight ghost towns, their inhabitants forced to walk hundreds of miles without food, drink, or proper clothing, enduring bands of robbers, rapists, and killers. U.S. diplomats in the region called what they were witnessing appalling. One alerted Washington to "the most awful crime . . . that has ever been committed against any race of people."[2]

The museum visit brought back memories of his father's stories during an emotional tour that ended at a collection of glass jars. The guide knew that Kirk's family came from Harput, an ancient Armenian town east of the Euphrates River. He sorted through containers and pulled out one. It looked very much like the rest, a jar of dirt.

Taking Kirk's hand, the man turned it palm up and filled it with a small mound of brown soil. Maybe a half cup.

"From Harput, land of your father," he said.

Kirk said nothing. He didn't move. He just stared at his hand and the dirt as his eyes filled and flooded over with tears.

Later that day, back in the Marriott Hotel lobby, Kirk and Harut were headed for a bank of elevators when a man rushed to intercept them. He was short and stocky, wearing a T-shirt and toting something heavy in a box.

Please, he said in Armenian, he had been waiting all afternoon for this chance to meet Mr. Kerkorian. His name was Levon Tokmajyan. He was a sculptor. He had something to show and a story to tell. He quickly opened the box.

Inside was the head of Kirk Kerkorian—a chalk-white plaster-cast bust of the financier staring back, blank and lifeless, at a perplexed Kirk. Both heads shared the same telltale pompadour hairstyle.

Harut tried to shield Kirk by stepping between them and giving Kirk the chance to escape on the next elevator. "I'm sorry, we don't have time to—"

"How much?" Kirk interrupted with an Armenian haggling phrase he remembered. But Levon the sculptor launched immediately into the story behind the head in his box.

It had been commissioned by a former mayor of the holy city of Etchmiadzin. Kirk understood the significance. Etchmiadzin is to the Armenian Apostolic faithful what Vatican City is to Roman Catholics. The Armenian pope who resides there had been deeply moved by Kirk's generosity after the great earthquake, and the former mayor had simply intended to honor that generosity. He planned to rename one of the city's boulevards Kerkorian Street and to install Kirk's bust on a stone pedestal in some grassy square at one end of it or the other.

That apparently was before word got back to city hall that the generous Mr. Kerkorian preferred anonymity and would actually be terribly embarrassed by such a public tribute. By then, however, Levon had already made the preliminary plaster cast, relying on photos and videos he tracked down through the American University in Yerevan.

"It's very good," Kirk said with a nod to the bust in the box. At the same time he was reaching into his pocket for a wad of hundred-dollar bills. "I'd like to take it with me when we leave in the morning."

Kirk was peeling off bills as he spoke. After the first four or five, Levon was watching, almost certainly counting. Kirk kept going. Once he reached at least twenty of the hundred-dollar bills, Kirk folded them in half and handed Levon the wad. Harut guessed it was somewhere between $1,700 and $2,200. There was no haggling. The sculptor promised to have the plaster bust back before checkout in the morning, properly boxed and padded for safe travel.

"I tried to run him off," said an apologetic Harut after the transaction. "What will you do with that thing?"

Kirk smiled and shrugged. "If I left it here, who knows where it might have ended up? Now . . . it's safe."

That evening he was in a hurry to get to his room. The markets were about to open in New York. It was early Tuesday morning in Las Vegas where Kirk's management team at MGM Grand was planning to make a major public announcement likely to affect trading—the repurchase of 12 million shares. It was intended as a show of confidence in the company, the gaming business, and Las Vegas itself.

Even halfway around the world, Kirk was busy moving his chess pieces. He couldn't share what was about to happen with Harut. Not yet. Insider stuff, at least for another hour or two. But for now, Kirk was off to tune in CNBC and watch the market drama unfold live.

He was about to make close to a $200 million profit while sitting in a hotel room in Armenia.

For the return on Wednesday morning, Harut was invited to fly along on the private jet as far as Nice. Kirk was stopping there to spend a week or so on his yacht. Harut could have dinner on board and stay the night before catching his commercial flight back to California. They departed Yerevan with Kirk's boxed plaster bust securely stowed with his luggage. It was the last time Harut saw it.

Kirk's yacht was easy to spot in the harbor at Nice. It was by far the biggest thing afloat. At 192 feet it was then the second- or third-largest yacht on any waterfront anywhere on the globe. Like airplanes and the MGM studios, Kirk's yacht was bought and sold numerous times. And even when it was under outside ownership, Kirk leased or chartered the boat when he wanted a week or two in the Mediterranean sun.

The *October Rose*, or whatever the name on its bow at any given time, slept twelve people in six cabins and had separate crew quarters that could accommodate fifteen. It had a fitness gym, BBQ, Jacuzzi, and a disco deck with its own laser light show. But the German-built steel-hulled boat was elegantly simple and unpretentious in design, a nautical reflection of Kirk.

One of its recent buyers and sellers had been Kirk's friend and Oracle chief executive Larry Ellison. He fell in love with the sleek white beauty one evening when he saw it offshore from the steps of a Monaco casino. It was bathed in light. "I felt like I was in a James Bond movie. I didn't know life could be this cool."[3] Ellison offered Kirk $10 million and renamed it *Sakura*. Whatever its name, it was always the *October Rose* to Kirk, and it was always his first choice for cruising between casinos along the French Riviera.

Harut was eager to see the Kerkorian yacht. After they boarded on Wednesday afternoon, Kirk led Harut to a small stateroom and asked if it was adequate for his overnight accommodations. Harut happily accepted. It had a bed and he needed a nap. Dinner would be served on board in two or three hours, once Lisa Bonder arrived from Los Angeles. She and the baby had just cleared Customs in Paris.

Harut had met Lisa before. He knew about the baby, now about three months old. He knew there was widespread skepticism that it was Kirk's baby. But Kirk was not among those openly skeptical, certainly not in front of Harut. He seemed completely at ease with the notion of fatherhood at the age of eighty-one.

Privately, however, Kirk was wrestling with conflicting clues and troubling doubts. Lisa said it had to be him, as she had no other sexual partners at the time. Even before Kira Rose was born in March, Kirk had been to his urologist for an updated sperm test. His sperm count was very low,[4] so low that his odds of fathering a child were about the same as winning a million dollars at craps on a single roll of the dice.

Harut awoke from a light nap to angry voices. It was Kirk and Lisa. They were yelling at each other. Harut couldn't hear the precise words, but the tone was harsh and upsetting. He sat up but made no move for the door. Moments later there was a knock.

Kirk said Lisa was having a fit. She wanted Kira and one of the nannies in this room. Would Harut mind terribly to be moved to a different room?

"Of course not." Harut grabbed his bags and followed Kirk to another cabin farther astern.

Kirk and Lisa were still sniping at each other over dinner—this time she was angry that he had failed to alert her to the MGM Grand stock repurchase announcement.

"I could've made a killing!" she raged. "Why are you keeping secrets?"

Kirk tried to dismiss the question. He was busy. There wasn't time. It was none of her business.

"And it would've been a federal crime if he told you," Harut added softly.

"What?" Lisa said.

"You're talking about insider information. We'd all like some of that," Harut said as if agreeing with her. "But then, Kirk could go to jail. It's a felony."

Lisa went silent. Peace returned to the floating dinner table.

WYNN AND LOSE

MARCH 1999
HOTEL BEL-AIR, LOS ANGELES

Kirk was starting to get used to the idea that at his advanced age he had fathered a child with Lisa Bonder. How many men in their eighties could demonstrate such virility? He wanted to believe it, against all the odds—his low sperm count, the improbably long gap between her pregnancy and their last romantic fling, the gnawing suspicion that this beautiful baby was somehow part of a coercive scheme for more money and marriage.

Lisa was always asking for money, substantial sums of cash and loans. And, if that was all she wanted, no problem. As Kirk liked to say, "Anything that can be solved with money isn't a problem." But for Kirk, marriage was a price too high.

It was also true that little Kira Rose was such a charming bundle of coos and giggles that Kirk had been completely bewitched. She fell asleep in his arms. Her first word was *Papa*. And he was starting to see himself in her features. "Look, she's got a widow's peak just like me," Kirk tried to tell his skeptical sister, Rose.[1]

So it was with mixed emotions that Kirk assumed the twin roles of Lisa's partner and Kira's papa at the toddler's first birthday party. It was on the lush grounds of the Hotel Bel-Air, a three-hour, $70,000 afternoon event described in the formal invitation as "A Victorian Garden Party." Daisies, orchids, and lacey parasols decorated the party venue where adults widely outnumbered children. Iced teas were served in tall crystal glasses. Lisa wore a pale yellow jacket with stiff lace collar and cuffs, a string of pearls, and long French nails. Her wide-brimmed, daisy-covered hat was suitable for an Easter parade. Kirk was color coordinated, wearing a soft gold-and-charcoal windowpane-patterned Italian sports jacket with his trademark open neck white shirt. His good friend Jerry Perenchio and wife, Margie, were there, as was a professional photographer.

Snap! And there was 1/250th of a second frozen on film with Kirk playfully mugging for the camera alongside a bemused Kira. Snap! And there's a shot of Kirk hoisting a stuffed bunny to show off one of Kira's presents. Snap! And there's Kirk and Lisa sharing a happy moment, her right hand resting affectionately on his thigh.[2]

But there was also a darkly audacious irony hanging over the sunny birthday scene that only Lisa could have known that day. This same Hotel Bel-Air was where she and Anne DuPont had partied with playboy Steve Bing and his friend one year and nine months before.

Questions about Kira's paternity had not arisen openly since her birth. Kirk had from the beginning promised to take both financial and personal care of the baby as if she were his biological child, even as he expressed initial doubts that he could be the father. Lisa asked for child support of $20,000 a month. Kirk directed Tracinda treasurer Anthony Mandekic to begin sending those monthly support checks to Lisa immediately after Kira was born.

In the two years between their breakup at the end of 1995 and Lisa's announcement that she was pregnant in the fall of 1997, Kirk had also made gifts and loans to her amounting to nearly $5.5 million—including the million-dollar cash handout to finance her move to New York, the gift that went instead into her safe deposit box. The rest, he said, went to help Lisa buy and renovate homes in

Beverly Hills. He said she kept profits from the sales and the loans were forgiven.

Soon after the birthday party, she came to Kirk for more millions. She wanted to buy a ten-thousand-square-foot Beverly Hills mansion on Greenway Drive with sufficient comfort and safety that it could serve as Kira's childhood home. It appealed to Kirk, too, who liked the idea of his little girl living within a five-minute drive of his residence. He gave Lisa another $3.2 million.

The new acquisition also needed renovation, so Kirk loaned her another $1.7 million and allowed her to move into the big house (formerly the Sonny and Cher house) on his twenty-three-acre Wanda Park estate. They would live for the next several months as neighbors—Lisa receiving rent-free lodging while she spent Kirk's millions on her new home, all while collecting $20,000 a month in child support.

Their daily proximity allowed Kirk to spend more time with Kira. It also allowed Lisa to lobby Kirk. "Let's get married," she pressed him. She told him it was difficult for her to be the "mother to our out-of-wedlock child," that she felt society "looked down upon her," that marriage would "legitimize" Kira and spare her the stigma of being an illegitimate child. Kirk disputed her arguments; after all, Kira Kerkorian already had his name and support. But he became concerned that Lisa seemed increasingly depressed.

Five months after the birthday party, Kirk agreed to a perfunctory marriage—a thirty-day contract marriage with a heavily lawyered prenuptial agreement. The formal understanding was that no legal rights to Kirk's properties, businesses, or personal estate would change in any way. Kirk also agreed that following their prearranged divorce, he would increase child support to $50,000 per month. Also, he would give Lisa another $1.2 million to cover additional remodeling costs on the Greenway Drive house that had surged over budget.

Kirk Kerkorian, the legendary deal maker—perhaps the greatest in capitalist history—was being pushed and shoved to an altar against his wishes. The billionaire was being nickel-and-dimed for nearly $10 million by a girlfriend he'd been trying to dump for four years. And as part of their faux marriage arrangement he was about to accept legal, biological parentage of a baby that he suspected, deep in his heart of hearts, was the child of another man.

It seemed that Kirk had finally met his match in a former tennis star less than half his age who made him laugh . . . and made him pay.

K irk's troubles at home had not dulled the gambler's instincts for opportunity in the business world. Steve Wynn's billion-dollar Bellagio Hotel had recently opened and Kirk considered it one of the finest properties he had ever seen. Roaming the grounds he had been especially impressed by the fact that even in remote areas where visitors rarely wandered, he found thoughtful design touches and careful maintenance. Wynn's Mirage Resorts was a class operation—just the kind of company Kirk would be proud to own.

Kirk and Steve were friends, their relationship dating back to the grand opening of Caesars Palace when the twenty-four-year-old kid he called "Stevie" hitched a ride on Kirk's private jet along with a group of East Coast investors and high rollers. While Kirk still controlled the International Hotel, he threw some of the hotel's beverage business to Stevie who represented a liquor distributor.

By 1999 Steve Wynn had taken the Kerkorian model of building big and going bold and added his own flair of artistry and show-manship to produce the Mirage, Treasure Island, and the Bellagio. When a massive gold nugget was discovered in Australia, Wynn sent his private jet and a load of cash across the Pacific to buy it for permanent display in his Golden Nugget Hotel and Casino. Kirk attended all of Stevie's grand openings. He was like a kid in Disney-land when he first watched the pirates swarm over the British ship at Treasure Island.

Kirk's MGM Grand executives all knew just how much their

boss admired the Wynn operations. They had heard a version of Kirk's hungry alligator story: "The alligator waited motionless as a log near the shore. Though he was hungry, he ignored the minnows. He seemed harmless as a log. Then a big fish swam by. He gulped it down whole."[3]

Mirage Resorts was the biggest fish in gaming.

While Kirk's lawyers in Beverly Hills were negotiating and drafting final terms for a thirty-day marriage to Lisa, Kirk's financial advisers in Las Vegas were keeping him posted about financial troubles in Wynn's world where stock prices were heading steadily downward. Major cost overruns at Wynn's new casino in Biloxi, Mississippi, took a heavy toll on second-quarter earnings. Analysts were caught by surprise. In a two-month span before the Fourth of July, shares of Mirage Resorts plunged 40 percent.

Feuding New Jersey casino rival Donald Trump noticed and piled on, dismissing Wynn's hotel and casino properties as "funeral parlors." He also got personal, mocking Wynn's progressive eye disease—retinitis pigmentosa. "The guy can't see," Trump said.

Kirk said nothing. But he started to buy shares of Mirage Resorts stock.

On the eve of their August wedding, Kirk and Lisa met with a battery of lawyers in his Tracinda office on Rodeo Drive. The prenuptial and confidentiality agreements were signed and notarized. But the center of attention was a five-page stipulation of paternity in which, among other things, Kirk accepted under penalty of perjury that he was the biological father of Kira Rose Kerkorian. He also agreed to pay child support of $35,000 per month until the following February when it would increase to $50,000 and continue until seventeen-month-old Kira reached her eighteenth birthday.[4]

By embracing the paternity issues directly, Kirk was able to accomplish one strategic advantage—everything related to Kira, from child support payments to custody—would be handled confidentially rather than in public hearings or open records. Both Kirk's and Kira's privacy was protected.

They were married the next day, just around the corner from Kirk's office, in the Beverly Wilshire Hotel. It was Friday the thirteenth. There was no rice, no reception, and the couple left in separate cars for their separate homes.

A week into September with the thirty-day deadline for their prearranged divorce approaching, Lisa still was making a case for reconciliation and delay. She told friends she was hoping that Kirk would extend the marriage. Instead, Kirk was losing his patience. But he was also distracted.

At Mirage Resorts, Wynn had just fired his chief financial officer, a Wall Street favorite, and the shock was expected to drive his stock values even lower. When the markets opened on September 8, there was the anticipated trading surge—but without a price plunge. That's because Kirk was buying at about $12 a share. A couple of days later, Tracinda had about $120 million invested in Mirage Resorts, a stake that was still a bit under 5 percent.

Wynn assumed the worst. Takeover. He had visions of Kerkorian at the door to Chrysler or Columbia or MGM. At a fund-raising event being held at the MGM Grand, Wynn tracked down Kirk and confronted him in front of a small group.

"I have no interest in having you take over my company," Wynn said.

Kirk was noncommittal and raved about how little he paid for ten million shares.

"Are you going to do something unfriendly here?" Wynn pressed him.

"Absolutely not," Kirk said.

Wynn left the conversation taking at face value Kirk's assurance that he was attracted by the stock's low price, that he was not seeking control of Mirage Resorts. But news of Kirk's purchase gave a boost to share value as Wynn's stocks jumped three dollars to $15. Kirk's stake had already increased to about $150 million. And he wasn't inclined to go hostile on an old friend.

"Steve isn't interested. I'm just going to sell my stock," Kirk told MGM Grand CEO Terry Lanni. Over the next few days he quietly took his profits and backed away.

The new Lisa Bonder Kerkorian finally surrendered. Kirk was not going to extend their marriage, and many of his financial promises hinged on her keeping their bargain to divorce by mid-September. She filed dissolution papers at the last minute that included the line: "Unhappy differences have arisen . . . which make it impossible for (the couple) to live together as husband and wife."

In a more descriptive complaint, she accused Kirk of treating her "like disposable trash." She said in a letter to Kirk's business manager Anthony Mandekic that the billionaire "alternated between being warm, kind, tender, shy and charming, to the other side of his character, which lent itself to tyrannical screaming and destructive tantrums."[5] Her lawyers would later maintain that Kirk's conduct toward Lisa was "consistent with his reputation as a corporate raider and destroyer."[6]

Immediately after filing for divorce, Lisa flew off to New York with Kira and Taylor to spend a week in a luxury suite at The Pierre hotel. Kirk provided his private jet for her round-trip flight.

If Kirk was expecting Lisa to be transformed, grateful, or even less depressed now that she had legal claim to his name, he was soon disappointed. As he would later attest in a state court filing, Lisa's "animosity toward me increased dramatically" after the divorce. "She hated being my 'ex-wife.'"

More troubling to Kirk were her threats. At times, he said, she threatened to harm him and Kira. Nonetheless, they continued to be seen together at social functions. Lisa was Kirk's guest at a black-tie dinner for the Boxing Hall of Fame. They spent Thanksgiving together. They went to Las Vegas together to see Streisand's millennium New Year's Eve countdown concert at the MGM Grand.

And Kirk kept providing gifts and cash. He bought her a $250,000 sapphire ring for her thirty-fourth birthday. She bought herself eight paintings from Christie's of New York for $1.2 million to hang in her Greenway Drive house. She went on a jewelry-buying spree—$1,075,000 for diamonds, $310,000 for a padparadscha sapphire, and $42,000 for a pair of heart-shaped Chopard watches.

At about the same time, Kirk launched a buying spree of his own.

In the weeks immediately after Kirk quietly took his profits and cashed in ten million Mirage Resort shares, Steve Wynn had been locked in a public relations tiff with investment analysts. He resented their myopic focus on quarterly results to the exclusion of long-term planning and prospects. He wasn't making many friends. And he wasn't helping his stock prices, either. Then came an unusual performance at a Deutsche Bank investors' conference in New York.

Steve Wynn's presentation to a room full of bankers and analysts provided no charts, no graphs, and little comfort about the direction of the company. What Wynn did provide was a Broadway-style musical. Setting up a sound system, he played portions of the soundtrack and talked up a new eighteen-hundred-seat theater he planned to build. Steve sang along. He lip-synched. He danced and swayed and made just about everyone in the room nervous.

The *New York Post* captured some of the reaction with its headline: "Warbling Wynn Shocks Wall St."[7] The assumption that nervous investors tend to be sellers was proven once again.

Alarmed investors started bailing out on Mirage Resorts. A rush to the exits became a stampede when word spread that Kirk was also getting out—even though he'd cashed in his 4.9 percent weeks earlier.

Mirage Resorts stock fell more than $1 to $12.50 a share. And it kept right on dropping. Shares were down to $10 and change by early in 2000, below the asset value of the company.

One evening in late February 2000, the hungry alligator lunged. Kirk dialed Steve Wynn at his Shadow Creek home just north of Las Vegas. He was out to dinner until ten. For Kirk, a notoriously early riser, bedtime usually came early, too. After an early dinner, he liked to retire sometime between 8:30 and 9:00 P.M. Late evening business calls were unusual, but that night Kirk was primed and ready for Wynn when his phone rang at ten.

"I've got a new idea," Kirk said eagerly. "How about I buy Mirage, the whole thing?"

"Are you kidding?" Steve was stunned.

Kirk suggested $17 a share—a $6.35 premium over the stock's current depressed state. Steve laughed. Okay, that was a little low, Kirk conceded. But Wynn didn't have a lot of room to negotiate. Kirk's people would send over a letter in the morning. That would start the clock ticking. The Mirage Resorts board of directors would have to be informed.

There was no avoiding this offer. It could be friendly, or it could be hostile. The two old friends agreed to sit down together for talks. Steve hung up feeling a bit old and weary. It had been a rough stretch leading up to this conversation. A giddy Kirk hung up feeling thirty years younger.

It wasn't a done deal. Not yet. But the game was afoot. Kirk's favorite moment was at hand, the roll of the dice, the chips shoved into the pot, the shares in play. It was time for deal making.

He was in heaven.

They sat down together in Wynn's Bellagio office, just the two old friends. Steve ordered a cup of coconut sorbet for each of them and then they got down to negotiating. He knew to sit to Kirk's right—to be near his best ear.

"We can go as high as $19 dollars," Kirk opened. Steve countered at $21 a share.

Kirk grimaced. Steve was stoic.

And Steve said he had two nonnegotiable terms. Kirk groped for a pen and pad to take notes. First, Wynn would refuse to sign any kind of noncompete agreement. He didn't want to be forced to stay out of the business. Second, Mirage Resorts would make the public announcement. That would underscore that this was a deal by mutual agreement, not a hostile takeover.

Wynn started to rattle off details about the company's financial status, its debts, revenues, and cash flow as Kirk scribbled notes as fast as he could. In between notes, he was spooning down coconut sorbet just as fast.

It took only a matter of minutes. The sorbet was gone. Kirk and Stevie reached out to shake hands, and a $4.4 billion deal was sealed.

Back at MGM Grand headquarters Kirk walked in still high on adrenaline, sugar, and the deal of a lifetime. He slapped tables and made victory noises. He was Rifle Right again—dancing around the ring, feeling the rush from winning a tough fight.

As specific terms of the deal unfolded, however, there was some cringing and muffled howls of regret when Kirk said there would be no noncompete clause for Wynn. Did he mean something less than the standard five-year wait? Wynn was a very dangerous competitor. Surely that was still negotiable. No, Kirk would not bar Steve from rebuilding and returning to the hotel and casino business. Not even for five minutes. They shook hands on it.

"The only reason Steve could get away with saying that was nonnegotiable is because Kirk allowed it," said Kerkorian lawyer and confidant Terry Christensen. "And it caused a huge hang-up on the MGM Grand side. Our guys knew that Wynn would be a serious competitive threat. He was great. He built the Bellagio, for Pete's sake! And Kirk let him off the hook from the get-go."[8]

MGM Grand was in a position to impose whatever terms it wanted. Everyone listening to Kirk's account of his meeting with

Wynn knew it. Kirk liked to say he didn't need to get all the meat off the bone in a deal. He left plenty in this case. But that was Kirk. It may come as a surprise to some corporate executives who desperately fought off Kerkorian takeover advances, but Kirk thought he was making friends, not enemies, in his deals.

"In my experience, Kirk always made sure the other guy got a fair deal," said financier Mike Milken, a mutual friend of both Wynn and Kerkorian. And both men called Milken within hours of their $4.4 billion handshake, each man raving about what a great deal he had just made.[9]

Wynn walked away with $500 million and went on to become the major competitor that MGM Grand executives feared. For Kirk, it was the deal of his lifetime.

Behind closed doors he crowed: "I've got to go pinch myself. I can't believe we pulled this off."

38

===

FATEFUL ATTRACTION

Lisa Bonder was on a mission. Questions about the paternity of her toddler were threatening to expose the mother's deceptions. She was trying to put those doubts to rest and silence the rumors once and for all. Kirk was the father. And Lisa was going to prove it. Let the DNA wars begin.

On this occasion she had invited Kirk's adult daughter Tracy Kerkorian, forty-two, and one of Tracy's friends on an outing to a Southern California amusement park known for its boysenberry pies, an Old West ghost town, characters from the Peanuts comic strips, and roller-coaster thrill rides. She brought along two nannies and the almost-three-year-old Kira. It was a chance for the half sisters to bond.

It was also a very sneaky way to get a DNA sample from one of Kirk's very few blood relatives. The only other close family relation would have been Kirk's nearly ninety-one-year-old sister, Rose. She had never warmed to Lisa and regarded her as a money-grasping "bimbo."

Told that the sample was for Taylor's junior high science project,

Tracy and Katherine Savala readily agreed to spit into jars.[1] Lisa sealed them, tucked them away in her bag, and they all went on to Camp Snoopy and other park attractions.

The guileless little Kira Rose had been doing her part to keep paternity issues at bay. She was by unanimous family agreement "the sweetest little baby." And as she got older and more mobile she delighted in chasing Kirk and squealing "Papa!" all around the putting green at his Wanda Park estate. The sand traps collected her toy shovels and buckets. Fuzzy yellow tennis balls were fun to kick around the tennis court. And she loved Kirk's dogs.[2]

Kirk wanted Kira to be his little girl without caveats or reservation. But as they grew closer, Lisa managed their mutual affection as a financial asset, what Kerkorian lawyers called a strategy of deceit and manipulation that would foster more than a decade of hard feelings and recriminations.

Kira's paternity wasn't an issue to Kirk until a series of events convinced him he had a problem money would never solve.

Early in 2000, at about the same time that he closed his deal of a lifetime with Steve Wynn, his marriage of thirty days to Lisa ended officially with a final decree of divorce. It left him feeling especially free and magnanimous.

Lisa said it left her heartbroken. Kirk sent her, the two children, and a nanny to Palm Beach for a week. They stayed at The Breakers in a $2,600-a-night suite. He chartered a Gulfstream private jet for their round-trip.

It was the beginning of a fresh round of money and support requests, over and above the $50,000 monthly child support Kirk continued to pay. Lisa decided she wanted out of Beverly Hills and wanted to sell the mansion on Greenway Drive. Kirk had provided the funds to buy it and to pay for renovations that continued. Lisa hadn't even moved in yet. Kirk agreed to buy it from her, and he advanced $3.15 million in cash immediately as a down payment.

She would need a place to stay in Southern California before relocating to New York. Kirk leased her a Malibu beach house for the summer at $100,000 a month. She would need more money to live in Manhattan. A suite at the Regency Hotel ran about $1,200 a night. Kirk raised his monthly child support payments—already the highest in California history at $50,000—to a temporary monthly sum of $75,000 until she found a permanent residence.

Kirk certainly never identified with the Michael Douglas "greed is good" *Wall Street* character Gordon Gekko, but he was starting to feel like the Michael Douglas character Dan Gallagher in *Fatal Attraction*. Lisa was starting to show up at awkward times.

One evening at the Polo Lounge a host had barely seated Kirk and his new love and tennis partner, Una Davis. He had his usual scotch on the rocks with a splash of water in his usual booth in the back corner of the bar. And as usual Kirk sat facing the wall. Una had a view of the entry.

She saw Lisa coming.[3] The angry ex had a bewildered Kira by the hand and arrived yelling, "How could you!" She directed her rant at Una. "We have a daughter. He's the love of my life." Kirk sat silently shaking his head as the waitstaff escorted Lisa away.

And there were other incidents that prompted Kirk to accuse her of stalking him. Lisa blamed such conduct and her own "irrational statements" on "the stress, anguish and distress I have endured for years." At the same time, she continued to insist that Kira was Kirk's biological daughter.[4]

Lisa's erratic and embarrassing public conduct emboldened friends and relatives to press Kirk to cut off all contact with her. They also spoke more openly about their suspicions. Hollywood agent Mort Viner, one of Kirk's tennis buddies and a longtime friend, shared information from a good friend that Lisa once had a romantic fling with Steve Bing. That friend was Anne DuPont, Lisa's double-date companion that night at the Hotel Bel-Air when Lisa skipped off for a quickie with the playboy.[5]

Kirk didn't want to believe it. Besides, Kirk's adopted daughter, Linda, had encountered Lisa once at an in vitro clinic, allowing Kirk to imagine that if Lisa were lying, at least the real father wouldn't have a name. But rumors of a Bing connection spread among Kirk's inner circle.

His friend, the retired Las Vegas sheriff Ralph Lamb had a suggestion: "Buy a garbage truck."[6]

"What?"

"Yeah, just drive by Bing's house and pick up his trash. Get some DNA."

Against this backdrop of rumors and growing impatience, Lisa finally overplayed her hand. If Kirk wanted her to give up her suite at the New York Regency and bring Kira back to Los Angeles, she demanded that he first set up a trust fund. Not for Kira, but for Lisa herself. She would be satisfied, she said, with $25 million.

That's when the gravy train careened off its rails. That's when the generous billionaire said "No!" And that's when Kirk decided that he would find out once and for all whether little Kira really was his offspring . . . or not.

Steve Scholl, a former Las Vegas police detective working as chief of security for Kirk, took hair samples from Kira and Kirk and sent them off to a lab in Seattle. A couple of weeks later the lab results came back. Kirk's orders were to call him immediately.

K irk took the call aboard his new private plane, a Boeing 737 business jet. He was flying home after stops to inspect some of his newly acquired Mirage Resorts properties. No one seated around him had any idea who was calling or what the conversation was about. Kirk barely said a word. He listened in silence. He hung up. And he sat in silence. He went directly home after landing at the Van Nuys Airport, went to his room, and called a friend.

In La Jolla, about a hundred miles south, Una Davis was waiting to hear that Kirk was home from his travels. When the phone rang, she picked it up with a cheerful greeting. But Kirk could barely speak. It was Kirk, she was certain of that. But . . . he was sobbing.

Over the next hour, while crying along with the devastated Kirk,

Una was able to piece together what happened. Kirk had been "scientifically excluded" as a possible father of Kira. No business deal, no personal disappointment, had ever seemed to hit him in the gut like this. He was simply undone.

Periodically, Una would appeal to his anger, trying to turn his grieving into outrage. "That goddamned Lisa Bonder!" she'd say over the phone. But Kirk didn't bite. She realized he was too sad to be mad.[7]

It would be a few days before he was ready to confront Lisa with the findings. He said that, regardless of the test results, he wanted to remain close to Kira and he would provide whatever Kira needed. But he was done serving as Lisa's personal ATM.

Lisa immediately challenged the test findings. They were mistaken. Kirk was the only possible father, she insisted. Besides, she said, amateur DNA sampling was notoriously faulty. Hair wasn't as reliable as saliva. She sent him news articles on the subject and said she would order her own tests. She would prove Kirk's conclusions were absolutely wrong.

Lisa first tried to enlist Steve Bing, telling him he was the father of her baby, but that all she needed from him was help faking a DNA test. Bing refused.[8] And so it was that several weeks later Lisa lured Kirk's daughter Tracy to Knott's Berry Farm to spit in a jar.

Unfortunately for Lisa, the ruse would have to be repeated a second time since spit samples were not suitable for testing. So, after months with random and limited contact, Lisa arranged for a second meeting in two days with Tracy and her friend. She took the women to lunch at a Black Angus restaurant, and then strolled around a park. An opportunity arose when friend Katherine went off to buy everyone a treat from an ice cream vendor. Lisa was alone with Tracy.

She quickly explained: the sample in the jar wasn't testable. Could she take a swab? Tracy shrugged and opened wide so that Lisa could swipe a cotton swab inside her cheek. That evening, however, Tracy and Katherine reported what happened in a phone call to Kirk.[9]

When Lisa prepared her DNA sample kit for the lab in Seattle, she labeled the specimens "Kirk Lilly" and "Kira Lilly." The "Kira Lilly" sample, however, was actually Tracy's cotton swab.[10]

A month or so later, the lab results came back positive. "Kirk Lilly" and "Kira Lilly" (a.k.a.: Tracy Kerkorian) were almost certainly father and daughter.

Lisa presented the results to Kirk as though they proved what she had been saying all along. But Kirk shook his head. He wasn't buying it for a moment. Lisa reacted with an emotional outburst that forced Kirk to back off. If it turned out that Kira was not Kirk's daughter, said Lisa, then she would put the girl up for adoption "or kill her!"[11]

In spring 2001 Kirk proposed taking Kira to Maui with him for five days. He would bring along a nanny, but he refused to bring along Lisa. In a telephone exchange that Kirk would report to the Beverly Hills police, he said Lisa told him: "I should just kill Kira . . . or, maybe I should kill you!" Kirk told police he feared for Kira's safety. Lisa later said she was angry and "did not mean it."

She did, however, pack up Kira and Taylor and two nannies and fly to Maui to see for herself, she told Kirk, whether he was alone or with another woman. He often compared Lisa rather benignly to "peanut butter on your finger—you just can't shake it off." But now, in Kirk's favorite paradise on earth, she was more like a nightmare, but he couldn't wake up. She checked into the Grand Wailea hotel, a nine-minute walk from his Four Seasons hotel. He retreated to his private jet and flew home.

No more Mr. Nice Kirk. It had been more than a year since he agreed to buy Lisa's Greenway Drive house. She already had his $3 million down payment, but she refused to close the deal—or return the down payment. After fifteen months, the transaction remained stalled in escrow.

In August 2001 Kirk's lawyers slapped a lien on the Greenway Drive property for more than $3 million. Lisa's lawyers countered that the money was a gift and that Kirk was reneging. They demanded an increase in child support. Terry Christensen confronted one of Lisa's lawyers with the DNA results that showed Kirk was not Kira's biological father.[12]

Suddenly there were hints that Lisa might take her money fight public, this despite six signed nondisclosure agreements under seal in the paternity case. It would mean dragging Kirk the one place he most abhorred: into the public spotlight.

There would be depositions, discovery, sworn statements. Kirk would have to testify. Lisa and her lawyers figured Kirk would pay almost anything to avoid such an unpleasant gauntlet and all that publicity.

While negotiations between lawyers continued, Lisa kept Kira far away, residing in New York City's Essex House overlooking Central Park. But the September 11 terror attack on the World Trade Center abruptly changed that. Kirk sent his private jet to bring Lisa and the children back to Beverly Hills and their Greenway Drive residence. Kirk was happy to have Kira closer, and as Christmas approached he would get to play Santa Claus again.

Kira, now nearly four, had two items high on her Christmas wish list—a Mickey Mouse toy telephone and a pet rabbit. A real live rabbit.

But tensions also were rising. Lisa's lawyers signaled that without a settlement of some kind, they would be going to court for more child support soon. Kirk's lawyers threatened to take "appropriate action" if Lisa's side filed suit in open court rather than under seal.

Christmas morning 2001 Lisa Bonder arrived outside Kirk's residence a few minutes before 9:30. She pulled up to the gate. A security guard would not admit her. Mr. Kerkorian was not available, she was told.

As Rigoberto Tapia, the groundskeeper and live-in landscaper, watched, Lisa got out of her car and hurled a Mickey Mouse toy telephone over the gate. It landed in the parking area and broke into pieces.

She buzzed the guard again. The next thing tossed over the gate, she said, would be the bunny.

Before driving off, Lisa pulled up next to Tapia and shouted through an open window, "Tell Mr. Kerkorian, this time he lost his daughter!"

At Kirk's urgent request, Mort Viner—who had also been a friend to Lisa—called "to calm her down." She said she was angry with Kirk for continuing to see Una Davis.

In the vernacular of professional tennis, Lisa saw Una as "a bad loss"—an upset defeat at the hands of an unranked and unheralded opponent. She made it clear to Mort on the phone that day: Beverly Hills wasn't big enough for Kirk's two lovers.

A GOD AMONG
DEAL MAKERS

EARLY 2002
BEVERLY HILLS, CALIFORNIA

Trash trucks make their morning rounds very early in the exclusive residential neighborhoods of Beverly Hills. That's why Kirk Kerkorian's security chief was out the night before, getting an early peek into the garbage bin of one particular resident. He was looking for a secret that could unmask a fraud and stop a miscarriage of justice.[1]

For Steve Scholl, fifty-four, it was a little bit like being back on the force. He was a retired twenty-four-year veteran of the Las Vegas Metro Police Department. Much of that time he had worked undercover assignments. Steve could handle himself in the toughest, seediest of dive bars. But staking out a garbage can in Beverly Hills? This was something new. Sheriff Lamb, his old boss, had suggested getting a trash truck. Steve preferred the more practical and less conspicuous solo approach.

By late evening black bins lined the street, including the curb in front of Scholl's targeted address. In the stillness of a quiet April night, he lifted the cover and looked inside. The man in the house was a bachelor and lived alone. The playboy didn't generate a lot of trash. The retired cop saw what he was looking for almost immediately— a small trash can liner tied off at the top. It was the size and type of liner typically used in a bathroom wastebasket. Scholl plucked it out and gently shut the bin.

In seconds, he was back in his car, the unopened trash bag beside him, heading for his home over the hill in Sherman Oaks. Later that night he created his own evidence analysis area on a pristine sheet of plastic laid out on the floor of his garage. There, he slowly dumped the contents from the trash bag.

Like a crime scene detective in latex gloves Scholl sorted through the material, careful to avoid contamination.[2] It was the usual bathroom debris—used tissues, used cotton swabs, and used dental floss. Eureka! It was an absolute gold mine. Mission accomplished. Kirk would be pleased.

Scholl could report back with confidence that he had what they were hoping for—testable DNA samples from the unsuspecting Steve Bing.

If the bachelor playboy really was the biological father of Kira Rose Kerkorian, science would soon render that verdict. That same science could undermine Lisa Bonder's aggressive legal actions. Her unsupported claims about Kirk's paternity and that faked DNA test would make her credibility a recurring issue in the courts.

The year had gotten off to a painful start for the Kerkorian side. Lisa Bonder's threatened lawsuit landed like a staggering right hook. It wasn't her stunning financial demands that shook Kirk, though she was trying to get $320,000 a month for her daughter's child support. That was only money. As he told the judge, "I can afford whatever the court deems appropriate."

The blow he could not absorb so easily was personal betrayal. "I took her at her word," Kirk said. And he had come to regret it.

Lisa shredded her nondisclosure contracts with her first court filing, a thirty-three-page sworn declaration detailing the couple's decadelong love affair and falling-out. It was only the first shot in a fusillade of legal filings that would riddle Kirk's privacy protections.

In the following months, every peeping Tom, Dick, and Aram could snoop into Kerkorian's world through press accounts and public records for details about such things as: Kirk's low sperm count (about two million per cc) and history of infertility, the frequency of his haircuts ("every 10 days" at about $150 each) and massages ("frequently" at about $200 each), his personal fashion choices (a closet full of $5,000 Brioni sports jackets), and on which side of the bed he always slept (the left).

Headline writers poked fun at Kirk's dilemma. In his own backyard the cover of *Los Angeles Magazine* trumpeted: "Sex, Lies & Dental Floss—The Tycoon, the Tennis Babe and Their $320,000-a-Month Love Child."[3] Around the world London's *Sunday Express* reported on "Kirk's Costly Canoodle."

Kirk had made Lisa Bonder a multimillionaire with millions in cash as well as gifts of MGM stock, real estate equity, and exotic jewelry. According to an estimate by the court, she had a personal net worth at the time she filed suit in excess of $12 million.

At the time, Kirk was paying monthly child support of $50,000. He paid as much as $75,000 a month when she moved Kira to New York. And he had been paying at least $20,000 a month since the day Kira was born. He had also promised to pay for Kira's education and to set up a trust fund to launch her into adulthood. Still, Lisa wanted more. She justified violating her many secrecy oaths "in order to provide Kira with that to which she is entitled" as the daughter of a billionaire, the same child Lisa knew had been falsely portrayed as Kirk's biological child.

Kirk's most effective palliative against the embarrassment and stress of such a personal battle was to throw himself into what he loved and understood best—business.

Even as early news accounts about Lisa's litigation were beginning to appear, business headlines around the country reported that Kerkorian was selling the MGM studio "again!" He was asking $7 billion.

When it came to setting prices, Kirk was never shy about reaching for the outer limits. In that regard, he may have had an observant companion in Lisa Bonder. She practiced aggressive pricing, too. She would eventually suggest that California courts should impose on Kirk a $1.5 million monthly child support payment. State judges were unmoved and seemed decidedly unamused.

What made Kirk's 2002 version of MGM even more attractive than the first version he sold to Ted Turner and the second version he sold to Giancarlo Parretti was more of the same thing—its film library, still the second largest in Hollywood (after Warner Brothers) despite Turner's purchase of more than three thousand titles in 1986. Kirk had since acquired additional film archives from Orion and other smaller producers. MGM also owned the *Rocky* and James Bond franchises and Woody Allen's films.

Also among the valuable classics in 2002 was MGM's own *Rain Man*, the film project that slipped through a budget squeeze, management changes, and mixed internal support to give Kirk one of his biggest hits as a studio mogul. One of Kirk's biggest disappointments as a mogul was the $115 million box office dud *Windtalkers*. Its 2001 release had been delayed into 2002 to distance the badly timed war movie from still fresh events surrounding the 9/11 terror attacks.

Windtalkers accounted for one of the rare instances when Una Davis witnessed Kirk losing his temper over a business matter. She walked into the kitchen one morning in time to hear Kirk on the phone berating an MGM executive about the cost and bad judgment of backing the war movie. She couldn't help snickering slightly at Kirk's colorful display of profanity. But his scowl set her straight: "This was no laughing matter for Kirk."[4]

The $7 billion price tag for MGM and its library was too steep for a quick sale. But the search for a buyer continued beyond 2002.

S teve Bing didn't appreciate having his trash seized or his DNA tested without his consent. He sued Kirk for invasion of privacy, claiming damages of $1 billion. He ended up dropping the claim. He told the court that he had asked Lisa to introduce him to his daughter, but Lisa instead threatened to call police and get a restraining order.

More conflict was brewing. Kirk's confidant and lawyer Terry Christensen was in trouble and didn't even know it yet. It would arise from his hiring of a colorful—and controversial—private detective named Anthony Pellicano. At the time, Team Kerkorian was gathering everything it could on Lisa Bonder to prove she was lying about Kirk's paternity claim. The private investigator was employed by a number of prominent Hollywood figures over the years. But one of Pellicano's tactics turned out to be illegal wiretaps.

The Kerkorian side launched its own countersuit against Lisa, accusing her of breach of contract. So much litigation—it was a great time to be a lawyer in Los Angeles.

A battle of accountants in the case made for some of the most outrageous public claims. According to Lisa's numbers, her four-year-old now needed $144,500 a month to cover her travel needs, nearly $4,000 a month for clothes, and $6,000 a month for house flowers. Her projected personal food budget of $11,000 a month prompted one outraged letter to the editor of the *Los Angeles Times* by a reader complaining that $11,000 was "enough to feed an entire Afghanistan orphanage for . . . years."

Approaching the end of a nearly yearlong legal battle, those numbers and more were bluntly rejected by an incredulous judge. Superior Court Judge Lee Smalley Edmon cited "grossly inflated" costs and certain expenses that were "not remotely related to the reasonable needs of a four year old." In that category, the judge included a Christmas party for a hundred guests that was budgeted at more than $120,000.

Judge Edmon was unsparing in taking Lisa to task for "her lack of truthfulness" and for "her pursuit of meritless claims" that the jurist said significantly increased court costs. By one estimate, those legal fees alone approached $10 million.[5]

Regarding Lisa's initial petition to raise child support from $50,000 a month to $323,000 . . . and then later to $491,000 . . . and ultimately to $1.5 million a month, the judge responded: all of those sums were "inherently unreasonable." She accused Lisa of using child support as a disguise for spousal support.

The judge agreed to increase Kirk's child support payments by only $316—to $50,316 per month. Case closed. Well, at least for a few years. But like peanut butter on his finger, Kirk wouldn't shake trouble that easily.

B esides staying active in deal making, Kirk remained active on the tennis court. He kept to a religious schedule of daily weight lifting and walking under the guidance of Ron Falahi. Kirk's physique in his eighties was the envy of men thirty years younger. And he continued to train under tennis coach Darryl Goldman.

Kirk wanted one thing that his billions couldn't buy—to be the best eightysomething tennis player in the country. He approached that goal with the same laser focus he brought to all his business deals. Unlike his cool demeanor in business, however, Kirk on the court in his eighties was what friends described as "a tiger," playing with a ferocious intensity that favored plenty of lingering "Rifle Right" power in his forehand. He also trained rigorously, treated every loss as a learning experience, and took on any tournament anywhere to test his game.

Once, in the midst of a complex merger deal between MGM and Metromedia International Group, Kirk faced an inconveniently timed tournament on graffiti-marred public courts in a small town an hour's drive east of Los Angeles.

"It's a sketchy neighborhood. Let's take the van," Kirk told his coach. "I've got a pistol in the glove compartment."[6]

With that, one of the world's richest men headed off without security guards, without an entourage, and without hesitation to focus on tennis while his half-billion-dollar merger deal waited for his return. Kirk took a beating in that early tournament but stuck with it. Under Goldman's tutelage Kirk would win a number of tournaments and doubles matches and was eventually ranked as high as third nationally in senior doubles competition in his mideighties age group.

But his eyesight was giving him problems. Macular degeneration would slowly rob him of his full vision field. Tennis was an early victim.

Kirk fought the creeping disability. He subjected himself to treatments that included painful eyeball injections.[7] And the playfully labeled "grudge matches" on weekends continued with his old pals. Mort Viner was the first to drop out. He did it with a Hollywood flair. He dropped dead of a heart attack on the court while playing doubles with Kirk in the summer of 2003.[8]

A year later in Las Vegas Fred Benninger died at eighty-six. He was Kirk's age. Another year passed and Kirk's old financial team passed on—Walter Sharp, the Bank of America branch manager in Montebello who made those first loans to Kirk the entrepreneurial pilot; and George Mason, one of Kirk's closest friends and the former Fresno stockbroker who was there when Kirk made his first fortune.

These were the relationships that spanned time and station—people who were loyal to Kirk as a struggling businessman, as a used plane trader, as a gambler with a modest stake, and were still close to him on the other side of vast wealth. These were the friends of a lifetime. Their deaths confronted Kirk with his own mortality.

He tried to avoid it. He stopped going to funerals. He wanted nothing to do with celebrations of his birthdays. Terry Christensen said it tested the cleverness of his friends. "We had to come up with all sorts of ways to disguise that we were really trying to say 'happy birthday.'"[9]

It was a charming and amusing trait, but it also had a serious downside. Kirk was eighty and had something approximating a $5 billion estate before he finally drafted his first will. "He didn't want to think about death," said Christensen.

Besides, Kirk was still feeling good and looking for adventures. At the conclusion of a business trip to London he boarded his plane and asked Falahi, his valet and flight attendant and sole companion on the return, "Ron, let's go home the other way." Instead of heading back over the polar route to North America, the flight crew had to recalibrate. They went home by way of China.

One memorable stop was in Kuala Lumpur. Ron was making Kirk his morning coffee in the hotel. As usual, he was using ground Folgers coffee and brewing it in the 1950s percolator he'd brought from home. But when he plugged in the old coffeepot, electrical power went out instantly throughout the entire floor of the hotel.

"That time we blew out the lights in Kuala Lumpur" became one of Kirk's stock travel stories.[10]

F or all the healthy living, regular exercise, and good food, what really kept Kirk young and enthused was the big deal. And by the middle of 2004 he had two of the biggest deals of his big deal–making career in the works in the same summer.

In Las Vegas, Kirk was too busy to think about his birthday. He turned eighty-seven making a $7.6 billion deal to buy Mandalay Resorts—the gold glass towers of Mandalay Bay, the great pyramid of Luxor, the castle turrets of Excalibur—completing his takeover of the south Strip. It made Kirk the undisputed king of Las Vegas. Steve Wynn received news of the transaction by inviting the Justice Department to investigate the deal's antitrust implications. But he also joked that "life will be good in Kirkville."

The transaction put nearly half of all the Strip hotel rooms and casino space under Kirk's control. His MGM Mirage owned and operated the town's biggest, classiest, and most profitable casinos. Almost fifty years after losing $50,000 trying to make his first investment in the Dunes, Kirk was still standing. The Dunes wasn't. It was long ago imploded and replaced by the Bellagio. And Kirk owned it.

James Murren, Kirk's handpicked president and the chief financial officer of MGM Mirage, handled most of the close-quarter negotiating. But it was Kirk who sealed the deal with a handshake.

It was much the same in Hollywood a couple of months later when Kirk's handshake sealed a $5 billion sale of MGM studios to Sony. Kirk's man Alex Yemenidjian was his chief negotiator. Some called it "the deal of the century." Andrew Ross Sorkin, writing the Dealbook column for the *New York Times,* said Kirk Kerkorian "should be anointed the god of all deal makers."

Each of the deals was a blockbuster in its own right. MGM Mirage stock was sent soaring—up more than 55 percent six months after the Mandalay Resorts deal. And in Hollywood, Kirk walked away from the Sony deal for MGM with about $3.5 billion as his share from stocks and dividends.

Sorkin said it was time for Kirk to clone himself, take a vacation, and "write a book."[11]

40

<hr>

BREAKING BAD

MARCH 2009
LAS VEGAS

Media helicopters circled above a cluster of unfinished high-rise buildings just off the Strip, a flock of noisy vultures. They jockeyed for camera position to record the end of Kirk Kerkorian's amazing Las Vegas winning streak. By all accounts, Kirk's ambitious sixty-seven-acre, $8.6 billion CityCenter development was going under—potentially the city's biggest financial fiasco and the costliest construction loan default in U.S. history.

Cost overruns, a cratering economy, and feuding partners had the project and its ninety-one-year-old financier within hours of unprecedented disaster. Security fences were being readied to wall off soon-to-be-idled construction sites.[1] It looked like the town's favorite gambler had just rolled snake eyes.

In recent years, a nostalgic Kirk had told close friends that he sometimes wished he had time to start over—to give up his fortune and enjoy the thrill of making it all over again. It was a fantasy suddenly turning into a nightmare. "Honestly, I never thought I'd see this day," he confessed to companion Una Davis.

As the first default deadline neared, Kirk monitored news from home in Beverly Hills as his MGM Mirage team, headed by chairman James Murren, fought to keep the cranes and crews working. The key was loan restructuring in a time of ultratight money. Kirk had great faith in Murren, the creative force behind CityCenter. They spoke frequently by phone. Kirk's calls rarely touched on business or the crisis at hand. As Murren recalled, the billionaire asked " 'How are you doing? Did you work out today?' There was great empathy there."[2]

"The market could drop a thousand points. He could lose a billion dollars in a day and hardly blink," says Alex Yemenidjian, by then a former Kerkorian executive.

The editors at *Forbes* had most recently estimated Kirk's personal wealth in the realm of $18 billion. Back home he was regarded as the richest man in Los Angeles. But the Great Recession of 2008–09 apparently spared no one, not even billionaires. East Coast billionaire casino owner Donald Trump had already been forced to resign as chairman of Trump Entertainment Resorts after the company filed for bankruptcy protection.[3]

"Timing is everything," Kirk was fond of saying. And making big financial moves into the teeth of an economic storm second only to the Great Depression served to emphasize the point. CityCenter was a visionary project designed as a "city within a city" of residential and commercial developments as well as casinos and hotels. The design emphasis was on architecture more than gaming resorts—less kitsch, more class. But the project Steve Wynn called "as ambitious . . . as this town has ever seen" could also have been a poster child for poor timing. It was conceived in boom times, delivered in a bust. And nowhere was the bust more brutal than in Las Vegas.

Gambling revenues had plunged as much as 25 percent following the 2008 collapse of Lehman Brothers, and those numbers continued to drift downward into 2009. Unemployment in the region soared from a prerecession 3 percent to nearly 15 percent. Home prices fell 50 percent. And Las Vegas claimed the dubious record as

America's foreclosure capital. More than 70 percent of homeowners owed more on mortgages than their houses and condos were worth.

The biggest casinos' operators in town were hurting. Stock in Sheldon Adelson's Las Vegas Sands Corporation, owner of The Venetian hotel, dropped from $144 a share to $1.38. Kerkorian's MGM Mirage wobbled under nearly $14 billion in debt.

But Kirk's steady support, and a lifetime of reliable handshakes and sterling credit, helped pull MGM Mirage through the crisis. A consortium of U.S. and European banks agreed to rework loan terms. Arab investors decided to stick with the project. Even with most of the world gripped by a suffocating lending clampdown, major financial players everywhere still trusted Kirk and his organization.

CityCenter officially opened later that year with a three-day extravaganza in December called "Wow Week." It featured endless bottles of Dom Perignon in the biggest gala grand opening in Vegas history. Jim Murren presided.

Kirk sent his friend Una Davis. He stayed home to avoid cameras, the press, and the embarrassment of public adulation. And no chance for a press conference appearance.

Kirk's interest in automobile manufacturing turned out to be undeterred by his failure to take over Chrysler a decade earlier. In fact, that bid had been such a lucrative failure that it reinforced his confidence that hidden value lurked throughout the industry.

In 2005 Kirk had set his sights on General Motors, ultimately becoming the company's leading stockholder with a 10 percent ownership stake. Again allied with Jerry York, his Chrysler adviser, Kirk warned that GM faced a difficult future unless it partnered with foreign rivals Nissan and Renault. Kirk's team recommended GM sell off its underperforming Saab and Hummer lines.

GM wasn't interested in Kirk's assessment or his recommendations. York quit the GM board of directors and Kirk sold off his shares. Again, though frustrated by his inability to move management, Kirk's investment timing was excellent. He had bought shares when they were trading at a thirteen-year low. He sold out late in 2006 just ahead of the recession—also well before GM filed for bankruptcy in 2009. His estimated profit: about a quarter-billion dollars.

During his run at GM, Kirk also sued German carmaker Daimler-Benz, asserting that Tracinda lost a billion dollars in potential profit in the Chrysler deal. He complained that the Germans lied about what was supposed to be a merger of equals that ended up a takeover, relegating Chrysler to a mere division of Daimler-Benz.

A federal judge in Delaware rejected Kirk's claim. He ruled that Kerkorian had failed to prove significant damages. Attorney Terry Christensen, who argued Kirk's case, acknowledged that "we had a hard time" showing damages with a $2.7 billion profit.[4]

Kirk made one more bid for Chrysler when Daimler decided to dump its North American "division" in 2007, but his $4.6 billion offer lost out to Cerberus Capital Management. It was another lucky loss. A year later, hit by recession, Chrysler would be in Chapter 11 bankruptcy.

His last run at a Detroit blockbuster was especially ill timed. Kirk started buying Ford Motor shares. It was the winter of 2007–08 and the Great Recession was already making its statistical debut— ultimately breaking out into an epidemic of mortgage foreclosures, threatened bank failures, and a nationwide lending freeze.

If Kirk missed some of those early economic warning signs, maybe it was predictable. He was at the time seeing the world through the lenses of a love-struck romantic. The ninety-year-old bachelor had just proposed marriage to Una Davis. The younger woman was fifty-four, a close friend and companion for more than a decade.

In the spring of 2008 Ford shares were priced around eight dollars. In a short time, Kirk was the largest stockholder outside the Ford family. He had fully a billion dollars riding on the company by late September 2008 when the Dow Jones Industrial Average dropped a record 777.68 points in one day.

This time the gambler blinked. Kirk decided he had to stop chasing the carmaker's plunging stock prices. He would fold 'em and walk away somewhere around $2 a share. His losses at the end of 2008: about $800 million.

"I made a mistake," Kirk would later concede to Bloomberg News.[5]

But former MGM and Tracinda executive Yemenidjian blamed "bad timing." Kirk's instincts were right and he was making the right moves, recalled Alex, crediting Kirk with an unerring knack for spotting corporate value missed by others. *Forbes* magazine called Kerkorian "the raider who woke up Detroit."[6]

As history would show, Ford was headed for a strong recovery and double-digit share prices on the other side of the recession. "Timing," repeated Yemenidjian with a shrug.[7]

One reason Kirk couldn't afford to wait out the recession holding on to his Ford shares was the pending critical condition of City-Center. It was already a threat to his MGM Mirage holdings late in 2008. But there were also mounting personal issues that likely affected Kirk's mood and judgment, by some accounts a greater distraction than his business setbacks.

By late summer 2008, Kirk's top lawyer and closest confidant was facing federal felony charges. Years earlier, Terry Christensen had hired celebrity private investigator Anthony Pellicano to help debunk false claims by Lisa Bonder that Kirk was the biological father of her baby.

That was before dental floss finally settled the question. He wasn't.

But when it was discovered that Pellicano had used illegal wiretaps to snoop on Bonder, Christensen and the private eye ended up indicted as co-conspirators. Pellicano would later swear under oath that he had lied and misled Christensen into believing that inside sources, not tapes, were behind salacious tips he passed along to the Kerkorian side.[8] Christensen's defense team, led by Patty Glaser, argued that he neither authorized nor knew about the wiretaps.[9]

Kerkorian volunteered to make a rare court appearance and testify to his friend's character. He attracted a crowd of journalists and paparazzi. The *Hollywood Reporter* described Kirk's "blue sports jacket, red tie and loafers" and said the ninety-one-year-old "stood upright when walking and looked spry and alert" during his twenty-six minutes on the witness stand.[10] *LA Weekly* called Kirk "the unsmiling tycoon" who testified "in measured, sepulchral tones."[11]

He told the court his longtime adviser "has just been excellent—honest, straightforward and a true friend." Kirk also denied knowledge of Pellicano's wiretapping. A week later, Christensen was convicted.

Soon after, U.S. District Judge Dale S. Fischer imposed a three-year term in federal prison on the sixty-seven-year-old lawyer. It turned out to be a major blow to Kirk, too.

Glaser and Kirk's team of advisers told him he would have to avoid all contact with Christensen. Kirk's gaming license in Nevada—the key to his corporate empire and vast wealth—could be in jeopardy if he associated with a convicted felon.[12]

Kirk resisted at first but then, with great sadness, eventually acceded. He also withdrew from social engagements, becoming uncharacteristically reclusive, much like his reaction when his first wife, Peggy, left him a half century earlier. He was moody, had trouble sleeping, and cut back on visits to Las Vegas. Particularly noticeable were abrupt and repeated cancellations of dinners set with friends. He stopped going to movies and spent evenings in seclusion at home.[13]

At the same time, his relationship with Una Davis hit a rough patch. As was Kirk's practice, he tried to mend hurt feelings with a big trip—this one to Maui on his private jet. It was just after Christmas, barely a month after Terry Christensen was sentenced to prison.[14]

About two hours out over the Pacific, Kirk abruptly changed his mind about the trip. He summoned Ron Falahi to advise the flight deck: "Turn around; we're going home."[15]

He had canceled the trip midocean without consulting Una or anyone else on board. A few months later, their wedding engagement was also canceled.

By the end of 2009, it was clear that no other billionaire in the country had suffered so much financial damage from the Great Recession as Kirk Kerkorian. The Forbes 400 list of richest Americans tracked Kirk's fall from twenty-seventh richest person to ninety-seventh. His net worth had fallen from an estimated high of $18 billion to $3 billion. CityCenter's struggles took a heavy toll.

Fellow billionaire Trump was sympathetic in his own way. "I love Kirk and I hope it works out for them," he consoled.[16] But the rival casino developer also called Kirk's CityCenter project "an absolute catastrophe" during an interview on CNN's *Larry King Show*. Later Trump went further.[17] "It will be the biggest bust in the history of real estate . . . too bad."

Murren was optimistic. He predicted that CityCenter would be Kirk's "crowning achievement" in a career that transformed Las Vegas. "By design he gets little recognition for what he's done here," Murren told the newspaper.[18]

Kirk had already moved on. He ended 2009 buying an expensive diamond ring for his latest love, Joan Dangerfield, a glamorous blond businesswoman and the fifty-seven-year-old widow of comic Rodney Dangerfield. She told friends she was Kirk's fiancée.

AFTER "THE FALL"

SPRING 2010
1014 N. ROXBURY DRIVE, BEVERLY HILLS

The hushed house was dark when Kirk roused in the middle of the night, threw back his blankets, and swung his legs out of bed. The soft rustle of sheets and his shuffling feet made enough sound to alert the new night nurse. Kirk was surprised to find her at his side when he reached the open bathroom doorway—surprised and annoyed.

He didn't want her assistance. He didn't want her company. For that matter, he didn't want her sitting awake outside his bedroom all night, either. He thought he had made that clear in discussions with his staff. He was especially annoyed to be ignored. His minders—his doctor, the security team, lawyers, his valet, concerned friends— they all worried about the potential disorienting effects of the pills he took for sleep. And, at nearly ninety-three years old, Kirk wasn't as nimble at any time of the day or night as he used to be. They were concerned he might trip and fall. He was concerned they were treating him like a child, or worse—some old invalid.[1]

He wasn't the least bit fearful, or even tentative, about maintaining his balance. His normal stride was as confident as ever. A few times he'd fallen hard on the tennis court suffering nothing worse than scrapes and bruises, even when he was well into his eighties. He credited his weight-lifting regimen. Sure, his vision continued to deteriorate. And he was slowing down. He was the first to notice.

"Everything started to fall apart when I hit ninety," he told a friend. After a lifetime of healthy eating, regular and rigorous exercise, a conservative schedule of early-to-bed and early-to-rise, faithful visits to the doctor, and timely medical treatments, Kirk seemed surprised to find himself in physical decline.

But, thank God, he still didn't need a nurse to take a pee. Kirk growled orders for her to get out, go away. There may have been a slight push or a shove for emphasis. But as Kirk moved away, he lost his balance.

In the next instant he pitched forward chin-first into a marble countertop. The rock-hard surface caught him like a powerful uppercut. His head snapped back. His legs crumpled. The helpless nurse could only gasp as Kirk's limp body toppled backward. The back of his head slammed against the marble floor. And everything went still.

Kirk lay sprawled at the nurse's feet, motionless.

He had regained consciousness before an emergency medical crew arrived. Kirk insisted he was fine, a little bump on the head and his chin hurt but no need for an ambulance. The rescue team persisted. He showed symptoms of a concussion. Kirk finally relented. He was whisked off to Ronald Reagan UCLA Medical Center and admitted under an assumed name.

When Ron Falahi came to visit later that day, Kirk was in bed and hooked up to an array of tubes and monitors. He looked tired. And old. It was a shocking change from the vital, physically fit Kirk he saw the night before.

Kirk's friend Joan Dangerfield had taken up residence on the deep windowsill of his hospital room. She would sleep there for the next three nights.

The patient, accustomed to almost dictatorial control in his business world, demanded to go home within hours of his hospital admission—to no avail. After a couple of days, Kirk greeted visitors and hospital staff with an angry mantra: "Get me outta here . . . get me outta here . . . get me outta here."

After four days, his medical caretakers reluctantly agreed to discharge Kirk for continued recuperation at home. As a condition, they urged no strenuous physical activities and no climbing stairs. Upon arrival back at the Roxbury residence in an SUV attended by security aides and Joan Dangerfield, Kirk was immediately scooped up into the arms of Falahi, his muscular fitness coach, and then carried to the threshold of his front door.

Kirk entered and immediately marched up the stairs without assistance and without heed to anyone's concerns. In case anyone doubted, the lion was back in his lair. Kirk had resumed control. In truth, he had simply forgotten the no-stairs admonition.

"I took a pretty good hit," he would confess later to friends. "When I came home, my short-term memory was gone. I looked at my house and thought, 'Gee, what a nice house. I wonder who's letting me stay here.'"[2]

The traumatic incident was a turning point. Kirk's life would henceforth be defined as before or after "the fall."

Kirk's impatience was notorious long before the fall. He once left Yvette Mimieux stranded in Paris when she was late to board his private jet. On more than one occasion he considered walking away from one of his own "too boring" seniors' tennis matches—even though he was winning at the time.[3]

And he abandoned slow-paced golf altogether some forty years earlier. Waiting while others dropped flecks of grass "to see which way the wind was blowing" drove him to distraction. "We'd get on the green and it would take us ten minutes to get off . . . My patience just didn't let me stay with it."

Impatience marked his business history as well. When Kirk was buying the Desert Inn and Sands hotels from the Hughes successor firm, Summa Corporation, he grew frustrated by a series of conditions the sellers demanded. Finally, Terry Christensen called the sellers' lawyers to his office on a Saturday and issued an ultimatum: "Mr. Kerkorian is offering cash ($167 million). His cash comes with no strings, no conditions. He wants those properties with no strings, no conditions. Take it, or leave it. End of negotiations." The deal closed shortly thereafter.[4]

Periodically, the steady influx of charity requests coming by mail, phone, and through the front door of Kirk's Rodeo Drive offices also triggered fits of impatience. He once toyed with making a fake announcement closing the Lincy Foundation just to discourage supplicants. Yet, a complete stranger could catch him in the office and walk out with a check for $10,000 to pay for a loved one's cancer surgery.[5]

Several months after the fall, Kirk's impatience flared again. According to Alex Yemenidjian, Kirk felt his generosity was being taken for granted, that the administration of Armenian president Serzh Sargsyan expected more help than it was getting from the Lincy Foundation. Kerkorian-funded projects during Sargsyan's first three years in office amounted to substantially less (a total of about $14 million) than the $160 million Lincy poured into earthquake relief during the ten-year term of predecessor Robert Kocharyan.

Without question, Kirk had a more friendly relationship with the previous Armenian head of state. Kocharyan had traveled to Century City in 1998 to help celebrate the Kerkorian-funded one-hundredth airlift of disaster relief. Kirk received an Armenian passport and honorary citizenship. He had been so moved that he overcame his fear of public speaking long enough to take the microphone and declare in the language of his boyhood: "Long live Armenia."[6]

Whatever set off Kirk's precipitous decision—and it could have been a misperception—Yemenidjian knew that his orders were not subject to appeal. "Close the Lincy Foundation," he demanded. "You have one week. Shut it down."[7]

Harut Sassounian, whose United Armenian Fund was building six schools in the earthquake zone, found out his budget was being suspended when Anthony Mandekic summoned him to the Rodeo Drive office. The checks had to stop immediately, said Kirk's finance chief. There was no explanation—and Harut knew better than to ask why. When Kirk was in a good mood, everyone was in a good mood. When Kirk was in a bad mood, Mandekic routinely alerted everyone to steer clear.[8]

On Valentine's Day 2011 Kirk and UCLA chancellor Gene Block formally announced the transfer of about $200 million in Lincy Foundation assets to the UCLA Foundation and a university-administered Dream Fund.

Kirk continued to support a number of Armenian causes, including Harut's half-finished school construction projects. But the Lincy Foundation, which had dispensed more than $1.1 billion in gifts over the previous twenty-two years, abruptly and without official explanation ceased to exist.

It's likely that Kirk's mood at the time was also burdened by news about his sister, Rose. She was sick and dealing with increasing pain. The billionaire brother who had always taken care of his spunky sister was helpless to ease her suffering. And Rose was in no condition to cheer up Kirk, either.

She had always been good at that. Well into her nineties, the former dancer could turn a fancy restaurant into a lounge act by asking one of Kirk's dinner guests, "Can you touch your nose with your toes?" Rose would push back from the table and demonstrate. She was extraordinarily limber for any age. Next she'd ask, "Can you do the splits?" And she would land a perfect split right there on the restaurant floor.[9]

The shy Kirk loved it—the audacity of it, the show, the awesome big sister.

After the fall, Kirk's home needed safety renovations, including an automated stair lift. Kirk was adamantly opposed. Fitness coach Falahi won him over arguing that the lift would help preserve his energy for daily exercises. Kirk was still working out religiously at an exercise bench in his bedroom, using his custom-made pair of seventeen-and-a-half-pound dumbbells.

Long-neglected changes in Kirk's estate planning also required attention. The man with billions in cash and assets—but also an aversion to considering his mortality—hadn't updated his will in nearly fifteen years. The potential for probate mayhem loomed.

Like his 1997 will, Kirk's 2011 version left the bulk of his estate to charity. The old one named the American Red Cross as primary recipient, a tribute to his friend and then-president of the Red Cross Elizabeth Dole. She had long since left that role. The new Kerkorian document left distribution decisions to a trio of advisers—his doctor, lawyer, and accountant.

Another notable difference in the revised will was the creation of a $7 million trust for Kira Rose Kerkorian, the daughter he didn't father.

Kirk's emotional ties to Las Vegas remained strong, but his visits had declined sharply after the fall. He caught the Manny Pacquiao welterweight championship fight against Shane Mosley at his beloved MGM Grand Garden in 2011. Kirk's party of friends included former sheriff Ralph Lamb, longtime Muhammad Ali business manager Gene Kilroy, and former fiancée Una Davis who came with her college-age son.

Before Pacquiao was declared the winner by unanimous decision, the nearly ninety-four-year-old Kirk turned to the eighty-four-year-old ex-sheriff to say, "Ralph, we must be the only two people here who couldn't see this fight."[10]

Both men suffered deteriorating eyesight. Kirk's macular degeneration made it difficult to focus on anything in front of him. The condition made him increasingly reluctant to go out in public fearing encounters with old friends and acquaintances that he might not see well enough to recognize. His standard reply to anyone calling out his name was a friendly but safe "Hey, buddy!"

"It was easier to hide, to stay home," said Una who always remained friendly with Kirk even when their romantic relationship cooled.[11]

That fear didn't deter him from another black-tie charity event in Las Vegas later in 2011. Kirk bought a couple of tables. The fund-raiser for Andre Agassi College Preparatory Academy would benefit an old friend's famous son. Manny (now Mike) Agassi's boy, retired tennis superstar Andre Kirk Agassi, choked up acknowledging Kerkorian's history of generosity.

If it wasn't for Kirk "and his kindness to my family, I wouldn't be standing in front of you today," Andre told the crowd. "And I mean his kindness long before I ever hit a tennis ball."

That night Kirk didn't stop with simply buying tables. He directed accountant Anthony Mandekic, seated at one of those tables, to write a check for $18 million. That donation put Andre's foundation over the top, completing an endowment that would make it permanently self-sustaining. "We have so much to celebrate," said the grateful tennis celebrity, his face glistening from tears as he singled out Kirk for thanks. Kirk shifted in his ballroom seat.

A few months later, Kirk sent his private jet to pick up Gene Kilroy and fly him to Santa Barbara. Kilroy needed special cancer treatment. Air transport and medical care were all at Kirk's expense. In the vernacular of a casino credit manager, "Kirk used to tell me, 'Gene, you'll always have a marker with me.'"[12]

For Kirk's ninety-fifth birthday in 2012 he got a big surprise. Unfortunately, he didn't like birthdays or surprises. Gifts piled up unopened. One room of his Beverly Hills estate warehoused hundreds of still-wrapped presents accumulated over the years. "He wasn't even curious about them," said one friend.

But on this occasion, companion Joan Dangerfield treated him to a stay in one of the posh bungalows at the Beverly Hills Hotel, one of Kirk's favorite places—not because it was posh, but because it was walking distance to his hangout at the Polo Lounge. As the couple strolled up a garden path toward their bungalow, Kirk didn't notice videographers in the bushes. Cameras captured a series of strangers, young women, who approached Kirk pretending to recognize him. One of them gushed, "I know you! You're Kirk Kerkorian. I love you!"[13]

Then, from out of nowhere, appeared dancing couples and recorded music playing the 1958 hit "To Know Him Is to Love Him."

In a lush green clearing among the palms and giant birds of paradise, about thirty professional dancers broke into a Broadway-style routine as Kirk and Joan looked on.

The well-meaning tribute lasted several minutes. Kerkorian seemed mildly amused on camera, but aides called his response an act of politeness. He hated making a scene. He hated having his privacy violated. And things went from uncomfortable to worse. A video recording of Kirk and the flash mob would turn up on the Internet, becoming an instant hit on YouTube.

Already their relationship had its rocky moments. Months earlier, Kirk had ordered Falahi to help his security team remove Joan's personal belongings from his Roxbury residence.[14] By summer's end, it was over, and he announced his engagement to Lu Beard, the widow of an Oklahoma oilman. Kirk and his new fiancée had been friends since her prior marriage to the late actor Dale Robertson decades earlier.

But summer also brought Rose's death. She was 102. Kirk was bereft. He had lost other siblings. Art, the eldest, had a drinking problem that drove them apart. He died nearly forty years earlier. Nish was close to Kirk until his death twenty years earlier. He and Rose went together to Nish's funeral in 1992. After Kirk's fall, Rose gently chided him for giving her a scare, then turned serious. "Brother, don't you dare leave me," she said. He told her not to worry: "We'll just go together."[15]

When Rose's memorial was scheduled, Kirk recalled the embarrassing spectacle he had made sobbing uncontrollably through Nish's funeral. He advised his family he was unable to attend his sister's tribute. "I'm too sad," he said.[16]

Kirk's ongoing legal battles with ex-companion Lisa Bonder flared up again a few months later, this time over new issues. As his ninety-sixth birthday approached in 2013, she filed conservatorship papers in a Los Angeles Court alleging that Kirk was in declining health and that his Tracinda Corp. managers were "holding him captive." She asked to be named joint conservator with her twenty-four-year-old son, Taylor Kreiss, to help protect Kirk and his assets.

Bonder was "*that* woman" throughout Kirk's inner circle, widely regarded by Kirk loyalists as a villain. She had to be the last person Kirk wanted making any decisions about his life or estate. In court filings, his attorneys accused her of scheming to increase Kira's child support payments to $500,000 a month.[17]

A Page Six item in the *New York Post* further disputed Bonder's conservatorship claims. Crediting Kerkorian inside sources, the newspaper said Kirk was quite "perky for his age" and had recently met with his doctor over drinks at the Polo Lounge. "Yes, he sees his doctor at the Polo Lounge," said the story, quoting an unnamed insider.[18]

Bonder dropped her conservatorship bid two months after it was filed. Yet, its impact lingered like an adrenaline rush after a bad scare. Kirk mulled his future. If someone he so distrusted could actually end up with control over any aspect of Kirk's life, he wanted to be certain that his affairs were in order. He signed a revised and updated "last will" only days after Bonder withdrew her claim.

He also pondered whether there was anyone he could trust with his medical and financial interests. Kirk's world was getting smaller and smaller. His business and social activities were declining. Still, he craved the comfort of trusted friends. That narrowed his search for where to turn next.

He reached for his phone and punched in a familiar number.

O n California Route 52 just outside La Jolla, the cell phone rang in Una's white 300-series BMW. "Private Number," said caller ID. She smiled. It was Kirk. Their conversation began as it almost always began, with Kirk asking, "Is this a good time?"[19]

"It's always a good time," she said, as usual.

His low, rumbling voice was strong that day. Kirk was feeling good, she could tell. He got straight to business.

"Una, I want to marry you. I should've done this a long time ago," Kirk said. "I know you've always had my back. I know I can trust you."

He promised that Una could keep her home in La Jolla where she had family and an active social life. She could live halftime with him in Beverly Hills. He said he wanted to make Una his conservator in case of future medical emergencies.

The cell-phone proposal wasn't quite so romantic as Kirk's 2007 engagement scene—the diamond ring from a jewelry boutique at the Beverly Wilshire Hotel presented from bended knee in a suite at the Beverly Hills Hotel along with vows of eternal love. "He was so romantic, absolutely gooey inside," she recalled.

Kirk's lawyers were aghast. Their new "last will" was barely three weeks old, but it would become instantly obsolete with a new spouse. They advised the couple to "just live together." But he insisted on marriage. So the lawyers insisted on Una signing a waiver of spousal rights. Lawyers took it from there.

In business, Kirk sometimes followed up his handshakes of agreement with a few words of advice, "Don't let the lawyers screw this up."[20] In romance, however, he failed to follow his own advice.

Lawyer-induced delays mounted as prenuptial negotiations dragged on. Una signed some agreements, refused to sign others—including one that denied her consultation rights in case Kirk encountered medical emergencies. A November wedding date came and went. For a couple of months from December into January 2014, Kirk's health and stamina sagged. Una noticed that he sometimes seemed confused and depressed. But by late March he was done waiting for the lawyers.

He finally announced, "Let's get married next weekend."

One final flurry of lawyering failed to deter the inevitable. With a dozen guests gathered around, Kirk Kerkorian and Una Davis were wed late morning on March 30, 2014, at the Roxbury Drive residence. A justice of the peace presided over the brief civil ceremony. Best man was Kirk's UCLA doctor and fellow Armenian, Eric Esrailian.

As the corks popped on bottles of Cristal Champagne, Kirk proudly flashed his new Tiffany silver wedding band and accepted best wishes from his aides, household staff, and tennis partners.

Moments into the celebration, attorney Patty Glaser approached Una. "Congratulations," she said. "I'd like to ask you to keep this private—to not tell anyone" about the marriage.

Barely three weeks later, Kirk ordered Una out of his house. He raged that she had left him alone while she spent several days in Florida with her cancer-stricken sister. Kirk had reacted with similar harshness to his longtime valet, abruptly firing Ron Falahi after he missed a weekend of work to attend a granddaughter's wedding. Both trips had been discussed with Kirk. Both Ron and Una thought they had Kirk's blessing.[21]

"He just kicked us both out," Una said. She wasn't that surprised. "He was getting more difficult in those days. And I was tired of all the people running his life and mine."

Kirk later called to see how Una was doing. He wanted to stay in touch. She told him to call anytime. He said he couldn't call out; she had to call him. It was the last time they spoke.[22]

A year later, Kirk was stricken and bedridden. Alex Yemenidjian came to visit. He had just sold his interest in the Tropicana resort.

"Good! Does that mean you can retire?" Kirk asked.

"No, it just means I'm unemployed for now."

Ten days later, Alex got a phone call that Kirk was slipping. He found his old mentor and friend asleep. He sat on the edge of the bed and took Kirk's hand. He held it for a very long time. And then he left. The call came later that night.[23]

Kirk died June 15, 2015. An invitation-only private funeral was held at Inglewood Park Cemetery under the final approach pattern of big jets landing at LAX. Kirk's parents are buried there, along with sister, Rose. Formal proceedings were slow getting started, prompting a nephew to remind the crowd that Kirk was never late for anything.

"We'd better get this funeral started," he said. "Otherwise, Kirk's gonna get up and leave."[24]

———

KIRK'S LAST DEAL

"My birthplace was California, but I could not forget Armenia."
—WILLIAM SAROYAN, AUTHOR

APRIL 12, 2017
ON HOLLYWOOD BOULEVARD

Traffic barricades funneled a slow-moving line of black limousines toward the TLC Chinese Theatre's famous pagoda entrance. Its marquee announced that evening's American premiere of *The Promise*, a $100 million historical saga set during the Armenian genocide. The independent film was financed entirely by Kirk Kerkorian.

As Hollywood movie premieres go, the opening-night gala was tame. No fireworks. No parachute jumps. No footprints in the cement. When Kirk's friend and rival Howard Hughes premiered his 1930 war picture *Hell's Angels* at the same site, tens of thousands lined Hollywood Boulevard to watch low-flying biplanes engage in mock aerial dogfights—accompanied by fireworks and parachute jumps.

Still days ahead of general public release, the film already was suffering from mixed reviews, distribution delays, and a dirty tricks campaign launched by Turkish partisans. After its world premiere at the Toronto International Film Festival where an audience of a few hundred got a first look at *The Promise,* more than fifty thousand negative online reviews flooded the Internet. The *Wall Street Journal* traced much of the critical commentary to Turkish social media sites.

The film was set to debut in the nation's movie capital on a mild and breezy Southern California evening in the ninety-year-old grande dame of Hollywood movie palaces. The main spectator sport for the well-mannered crowd was watching those limousines deliver film stars—Leonardo DiCaprio with his mother, Cher with a couple of Kardashians, Orlando Bloom, and former Kirk neighbor Sylvester Stallone. The film's Oscar-winning director Terry George strolled the red carpet along with stars from the cast: Christian Bale, Charlotte Le Bon, Angela Sarafyan, and James Cromwell.

Though decidedly low key, it was still the kind of celebrity-studded party with cameras and flashing strobes that Kirk would have hated. The movie project itself was his baby—Kirk's last deal, his last big investment—and a looming financial flop.

But would Kirk have cared about box office numbers? The story was an ode to his Armenian ancestors, a tale with political implications intended to raise awareness about century-old human rights abuses that the Turkish government still fiercely denies. Making the movie had been a Kerkorian dream for years.

"Finally, in the last few years of his life he said, 'I am not waiting for anybody else. I'm going to finance it myself. And I want it to be epic. I want people to come to it,'" Kirk's lawyer Patty Glaser told an Armenian newspaper. She, along with his physician Eric Esrailian and longtime accountant Anthony Mandekic, also served with Kerkorian as film producers.

Kirk envisioned the film as an Armenian-centric wartime romance like one of his favorites, *Dr. Zhivago,* a 1965 classic with an original budget of about $11 million. That would have been about $83 million in 2015 when production started on *The Promise.*

It was never Kirk's goal to profit personally from the movie. He directed that all proceeds flow to charities. But Kirk also never made an investment with the intent of losing money.

"Businessmen like Kirk don't like to make fiascos," observed his widow, Una Davis. "I know he was being assured all along that he might win an Oscar. You can make money with an Academy Award."

She agreed that Kirk was "a proud Armenian" and loved being involved in making the movie. "But he would be extremely upset to spend a hundred million to gross nine."

Two months after its nationwide release, *The Promise* had grossed a disappointing $8,224,288.

The bulk of Kirk's estate was his 100 percent ownership of Tracinda Corp., the holding company through which he held shares in MGM Resorts International, the hotel and casino giant he founded. When he died, the value of Tracinda-held stock was nearly $1.8 billion. An audit of his additional worldly goods showed some of the differences between estates of billionaires and most mortals— with a couple of modest similarities.

The ready cash in Kirk's various personal bank accounts amounted to $1.25 million in a pair of Wells Fargo checking accounts, $7.1 million in a Bank of America money market savings account, and $8.95 million in U.S. Treasury cash reserves held by UBS AG, a Swiss bank. The loose change in his home safe totaled $165,000.

He also owned his Roxbury Drive residence worth an estimated $19 million, maintained a $10,000 membership in the Beverly Hills Tennis Club, refundable upon his death, and was the registered owner of two very ordinary vehicles—a three-year-old Jeep Patriot and an eight-year-old GMC Yukon.

Kirk's last will, drafted and signed in the immediate aftermath of Lisa Bonder's attempt at a court-ordered conservatorship, included a number of personal bequests—cash gifts to Glaser ($6 million) and

Mandekic ($7 million), to Kirk's longtime secretary, Jaclyn Thode ($5 million), and to Terry Christensen's wife ($15 million). About a year after Kirk's death, Christensen lost his final appeal of the 2008 conviction over wiretapping Bonder's phones. And in 2017 the former attorney began serving a three-year term in federal prison. It wasn't quite the last episode in the long-running Kerkorian-Bonder paternity soap opera.

In probate court, Bonder's daughter, Kira Rose Kerkorian—who had just turned eighteen—opened negotiations with the estate to increase the $7 million trust fund Kirk left her. She settled for $8.5 million.

One of Kirk's real estate agents—a Beverly Hills saleswoman who said Kirk asked her to keep him company in his final months—filed a claim against the estate for $20 million. She said that was what Kirk promised for her companionship. Kirk's daughter Linda, who had received a $30 million trust fund as a gift outside the will, took legal action trying to set aside the 2013 document that left the rest to charities selected by Glaser, Esrailian, and Mandekic.

Una Davis also filed a claim against the estate as Kirk's surviving spouse. Although she had filed for divorce after their row, Kirk never signed the divorce papers. He also never signed their prenuptial agreement. He died still wed to Una.

Beyond her claim against the estate, Una also challenged Patty Glaser's dual role as a beneficiary of Kirk's will and as legal counsel to the estate. Underneath it all were lingering hard feelings between Davis and Glaser dating back to prewedding negotiations. Those issues figured to continue playing out in court for years to come.

A lex Yemenidjian says he imagines that Kirk has moved on to new realms of deal making somewhere in the Great Beyond. At Kirk's funeral he told the crowd of invited mourners:

"For those of you who are wondering what Kirk's doing right now—I'd like to think he's just acquired 9.9 percent of heaven. He's meeting with his lawyers about that other 90 percent he doesn't own.

"But if the deal were based on what he did for all of us here on Earth, they should just give him the rest of heaven free."

ACKNOWLEDGMENTS

The late Dial Torgerson's 1974 biography, prominently mentioned in my earlier Note to Readers, covered a broad swath of Kerkorian's youth and his rise to business prominence. But it was published years before Kirk became a billionaire and decades before some of his biggest achievements. For invaluable details that came later and opened up much more of Kirk's wide-ranging business life to this narrative treatment, I am particularly grateful for these extraordinary books and the superb storytellers who wrote them:

Robert J. Serling, *The Only Way to Fly: The Story of Western Airlines, America's Senior Air Carrier* (Doubleday & Company, 1976).

Ted Turner with Bill Burke, *Call Me Ted* (Hachette, 2010).

Christina Binkley, *Winner Takes All: Steve Wynn, Kirk Kerkorian, Gary Loveman and the Race to Own Las Vegas* (Hyperion, 2008).

Bill Vlasic and Bradley A. Stertz, *Taken for a Ride: How Daimler-Benz Drove Off with Chrysler* (William Morrow, 2000).

For access to a treasure trove of Las Vegas history and archives, I am indebted to the UNLV Lied Library staff, most notably the Special Sections crew that included Su Kim Chung, Claytee White, and Delores Brownlee.

I was most fortunate on this book project to be guided from its start by my friend and counselor on all matters literary David Halpern of the Robbins Office in New York. He always brings heart and humor and a generous measure of wisdom to both the business and the mission of storytelling. And he knows all the best steak houses in Manhattan.

My brother Carl Rempel has saved me from computer meltdowns and electronic file disasters of all kinds over the years. He came to my tech rescue again and again to help keep this project on track while also donating untold (and unbilled) hours to website design and repair. Every family needs a genius. He's mine! My friend Roger Smith, a longtime colleague and editor devoted for years to keeping me out of trouble at the *Los Angeles Times*, was an early sounding board and, as always, a valued consultant.

I am especially grateful for my cheerleaders—Jason, Lara, and Emma—for making their Dad richer than any billionaire.

NOTES

PROLOGUE: INTRODUCING KIRK KERKORIAN

1. Unless otherwise noted, the anecdote about groundbreaking ceremonies for the MGM Grand Hotel comes from details in Dial Torgerson's book, *Kerkorian: An American Success Story* (The Dial Press, 1974).
2. Martin Kasindorf, "How Now Dick Daring?" *New York Times,* September 10, 1972.
3. Interviews with Alex Yemenidjian.
4. Patrice Sawyer, "Gaming Panel Oks Resort Deal," *Clarion Ledger,* May 19, 2000.
5. Unreleased family video, "Kerkorian: His Story," by Alan Grossbard, executive producer George Ann Mason (Charliedog Productions in association with Kirk Kerkorian, 2001).
6. Interviews with Una Davis.
7. David Streitfeld, "Born Gambler," *Los Angeles Times,* June 9, 2005.
8. Interviews with Alex Yemenidjian.
9. Interviews with Una Davis.
10. David Colker and David Streitfeld, "Kirk Kerkorian Dies at 98, Shook Up the Car, Movie and Casino Industries," *Los Angeles Times,* June 16, 2015.

CHAPTER 1: GAMBLING ON THE WIND

1. "DeHavilland DH.98 Mosquito Multirole Heavy Fighter/Fighter Bomber (1942)," www.militaryfactory.com.
2. Kirk's experiences as a civilian contract pilot for the Royal Air Force were informed by a variety of detailed sources. Unless otherwise noted, primary source material came from the following: Kirk Kerkorian, Oral History, University of Nevada Las Vegas, Special Collections, #OH-01009, for "The First 100: Portraits of the Men and Women Who Shaped Las Vegas," edited by A. D. Hopkins and K. J. Evans; *Flying the Secret Sky,*

The Story of the Royal Air Force Ferry Command, written, produced, and directed by William VanDerKloot (WGBH Boston and VanDerKloot Film and Television, 2008); Torgerson, *Kerkorian;* and unreleased family video, "Kerkorian: His Story."

3. "Mosquito Creates Atlantic Record," *Flight,* May 18, 1944. Wing Commander Wooldridge would make news again a few months later for his other skill as a classical music composer. The conductor of the New York Philharmonic Orchestra offered to perform the thirty-three-year-old pilot's latest composition every time he shot down five enemy aircraft. "Downs 5 Nazi Planes, Rodzinski to Play Work," *New York Times,* August 18, 1944.

4. Ministry of Information for United Kingdom Air Ministry, *Atlantic Bridge: The Official Account of R.A.F. Transport Command's Ocean Ferry,* reprinted from 1945 edition (University Press of the Pacific, 2005).

5. "Aeroplane Data Base: Lockheed Hudson," www.aeroplanemonthly.com.

CHAPTER 2: THE KID FROM WEEDPATCH

1. Unless otherwise noted, narrative accounts of Kirk's early flying days, his youth, and his family's travails were informed by the following: Torgerson, *Kerkorian;* Kirk Kerkorian, Oral History; and unreleased family video, "Kerkorian: His Story."

2. "Assault Case of Last Year Ended: A. Kerkorian Fined $50 for Attack with Grape Stake Long Ago," *Bakersfield Californian,* May 16, 1924.

3. Interviews with Emmanuel (Mike) Agassi.

4. Interviews with Gene Kilroy.

5. "Kirk Kerkorian Decisions Mendoza Here . . . Boxer Uncorks Savage Attack to Win," *Kern Herald,* Undated, 1938.

6. Poster Advertising Kerkorian-Souza fight on October 23, 1939.

7. Unless otherwise noted, additional background on Pancho Barnes and her flight school came primarily from two detailed sources: Lauren Kessler, *The Happy Bottom Riding Club: The Life and Times of Pancho Barnes* (Random House, 2000); and *The Legend of Pancho Barnes and the Happy Bottom Riding Club,* written by Nick Spark (Nick Spark Productions for KOCE Orange County, 2009).

8. Carl A. Christie with Fred Hatch, *Ocean Bridge: The History of RAF Ferry Command* (University of Toronto Press, 1995)—by far the most comprehensive history of the Ferry Command, its heroic crews, and their wartime mission.

9. VanDerKloot, *Flying the Secret Sky.*

10. Christie with Hatch, *Ocean Bridge.*

11. VanDerKloot, *Flying the Secret Sky.*
12. Ibid.

CHAPTER 3: BET OF A LIFETIME

1. Unless otherwise noted, narrative accounts of Kirk's experiences as a civilian contract pilot for the Royal Air Force were informed by the following: Torgerson, *Kerkorian;* VanDerKloot, *Flying the Secret Sky;* and Kirk Kerkorian, Oral History.
2. Captain Edgar J. Wynn, *Bombers Across: The Story of the Transatlantic Ferry Command* (E. P. Dutton & Co., 1944). This account by one of the early recruits provided wonderful and sometimes harrowing color and detail about ferry pilot routines, camaraderie, and life on the ground in Prestwick, Scotland.
3. Interviews with Una Davis.
4. RMS *Queen Mary* Passenger Manifest, List of United States Citizens, October 2, 1944, accessed via www.libertyellisfoundation.org/passenger.

CHAPTER 4: SCRAPS, CRAPS, AND JOHN WAYNE

1. Unless otherwise noted, narrative accounts of Kirk's return to civilian life and launch of his charter air service were informed by the following: Kirk Kerkorian, Oral History; Torgerson, *Kerkorian;* and unreleased family video.

CHAPTER 5: ON A WING AND A SPARE TANK

1. Unless otherwise noted, the narrative account of this incident was informed by details from various sources, most notably: Torgerson, *Kerkorian;* Kirk Kerkorian, Oral History, UNLV, Special Collections, #OH-01009; and unreleased family video.
2. "How to Fly the C-47, Part 1," www.youtube.com/watch?v=OVXp GYKH0SY.
3. "4 Pacific Fliers Beat Death in Race to Mills Field," *San Mateo Times,* October 12, 1946.

CHAPTER 6: BUGSY SIEGEL'S LAST FLIGHT

1. Unless otherwise noted, the narrative account of "Bugsy Siegel's Last Flight" was informed by: Unreleased family video; B. James Gladstone and Robert Wagner, *The Man Who Seduced Hollywood: The Life and Loves of Greg Bautzer, Tinseltown's Most Powerful Lawyer* (Chicago Review Press, 2013); Torgerson, *Kerkorian;* A. D. Hopkins and K. J. Evans, editors, *The First 100: Portraits of the Men and Women Who Shaped Las Vegas* (Huntington Press, 1999); Su Kim Chung, *Las Vegas Then and Now* (Thunder Bay

Press, 2012); and Deanna DeMatteo's website, www.lvstriphistory.com, an often fascinating and eclectic collection of memorabilia and historical information about all Strip casinos and the pioneers of Las Vegas gaming.

2. Kirk's difficulty fathering children would become a recurring subject of discussion in later years during his conflicts with Lisa Bonder over the paternity of her daughter, Kira Rose Kerkorian. See the voluminous Los Angeles Superior Court case BD-308513, *Lisa Kerkorian v. Kirk Kerkorian*, September 10, 1999.

3. Interviews with Jack Holder.

4. Benny Binion, Oral History, University of Nevada Las Vegas, Special Collections, #OH-00017, transcribed.

5. Interviews with Gene Kilroy.

6. Additional details of Kirk's friendship with Ralph Lamb were developed during interviews with a group of Kirk and Ralph's mutual friends over drinks at the Las Vegas Country Club. They were Nick Behnen, son-in-law of gaming legend Benny Binion and the co-owner with his wife of Binion's Horseshoe Club; Guy Hudson, a senior credit executive for Wynn Resorts and a former credit executive for Kirk's Flamingo and International hotels; and Alda Lanzone, a longtime friend of Sheriff Lamb.

7. "'Bugsy' Siegel Murdered," *Los Angeles Herald-Express*, June 21, 1947.

CHAPTER 7: ART OF THE JUNK DEAL

1. Unless otherwise noted, narrative detail in "Art of the Junk Deal" was informed by: Torgerson, *Kerkorian,* and Kirk Kerkorian, Oral History.

2. Associated Press wire photo of the January 8, 1951, incident was published January 11, 1951.

3. Interviews with Una Davis.

4. Ibid., and a second confidential source.

5. Interviews with Nick Behnen.

6. John F. Lawrence, "Vegas Must Reckon with Another Name as Well as That of Hughes," *Los Angeles Times,* March 2, 1969.

CHAPTER 8: GAMBLING ON GAMBLING

1. David G. Schwartz, "The Long Hot Summer of '55: How a Season of Hubris and Disappointment Helped Reinvent Vegas," *Vegas Seven,* August 4, 2015.

2. Unless otherwise noted, the narrative account in "Gambling on Gambling" was informed by: Kirk Kerkorian, Oral History, and www.lvstrphistory.com.

3. Interviews with Nick Behnen.
4. "Gambling Town Pushes Its Luck," *Life Magazine*, June 20, 1955.
5. Irwin Ross, "Kirk Kerkorian Doesn't Want All the Meat Off the Bone," *Fortune*, November 1969.

CHAPTER 9: JACK MAGIC AND THE BLADE

1. Warren Rogers, "Snow or No, Gala Goes On," *New York Herald-Tribune*, January 20, 1961.
2. Interviews with Una Davis.
3. Ibid.
4. "Floyd Fails to Appear at Show," United Press International, April 30, 1959.
5. "Don Jordan's Scrap Is with Commission," Associated Press, July 28, 1960.
6. "Kirk Kerkorian 95th B-Day Flash Mob—Beverly Hills Hotel," posted June 7, 2012, accessed July 2, 2017. https://www.youtube.com/watch?v=bEL32jBe4MU.
7. William R. Conklin, "Griffith Beaten on Split Decision," *New York Times*, October 1, 1961.
8. Robert Dallos, "Tape Alleges Kerkorian Talk With Mafia," *Los Angeles Times*, January 17, 1970.

CHAPTER 10: A CRAPSHOOTER'S DREAM

1. Unless otherwise noted, narrative accounts of Kirk's search for a jet and its funding in "A Crapshooter's Dream" was informed by: Torgerson, *Kerkorian*, and Kirk Kerkorian, Oral History.
2. Nicholas Gage, "Kerkorian Is Named in Crime Hearing," *New York Times*, September 28, 1971.
3. www.planespotter.net.
4. Interviews with a confidential source.
5. David Anderson, "A $41 Million Lawsuit Charges Plot to Loot Vending Machine Company," *New York Times*, July 3, 1965.
6. "2 Executives Convicted Over Loan to Union Official," *New York Times*, May 22, 1963.

CHAPTER 11: HIS FIRST MILLION

1. Kenneth S. Smith, "Studebaker Seeks to Acquire a West Coast Non-Sked Airline," *New York Times*, September 20, 1962.
2. Torgerson, *Kerkorian*.

3. www.lvstriphistory.com.
4. Kirk Kerkorian, Oral History.
5. David G. Schwartz, *Grandissimo: The First Emperor of Las Vegas—How Jay Sarno Won a Casino Empire, Lost It and Inspired Modern Las Vegas* (Winchester Books, 2013).
6. Ibid.
7. Burton Cohen, videotaped speech, Jewish Leaders of Las Vegas series, 2005, Special Collections, University of Nevada Las Vegas.

CHAPTER 12: THE ARMENIAN CONNECTION

1. Unless otherwise noted, narrative details in "The Armenian Connection" were informed by: Torgerson, *Kerkorian*, and interviews with Emmanuel (Mike) Agassi.
2. Mike Lupica, "Bud Collins: The Best Friend Tennis Ever Had," *New York Times*, September 6, 2015.
3. Unreleased family video.
4. Interviews with Gene Kilroy.
5. Interview with Michael Milken.
6. Kirk Kerkorian, Oral History.

CHAPTER 13: TROUBLE WITH MOBSTERS

1. "Last Good-byes Said to 'Nick the Greek,'" United Press International, December 30, 1966.
2. Ibid.
3. Tricia Hurst, "Nick the Greek Turns Out to Be Jolly Old St. Nick," *Los Angeles Times*, December 16, 1980.
4. Benny Binion, Oral History Special Collections, University of Nevada, Las Vegas.
5. Ibid.
6. Dmitri N. Shalin, "Erving Goffman, Fateful Action, and the Las Vegas Gambling Scene," *University of Nevada Las Vegas Gaming Research & Review Journal*, Volume 20, Issue 1.
7. Unless otherwise noted, the narrative account of Kirk wooing Alex Shoofey to work for him was informed by: Alex Shoofey, Oral History, Special Collection, University of Nevada Las Vegas, OH#-01694, for Jay Sarno Project, March 4, 2007.
8. "How the Mafia Built Las Vegas," (London) *The Independent*, January 11, 2003.
9. Schwartz, *Grandissimo*.
10. John L. Scott, "Caesars Palace Creates Setting Fit for the Gods," *Los Angeles Times*, August 8, 1966, for a colorful account of the extravagant hotel opening.

11. Steve Wynn, Oral History, Special Collections, University of Nevada Las Vegas, OH#-02036, for Gaming Project, interviewed by David G. Schwartz, December 8, 2006.

12. Gene Blake and Bob Jackson, "Grand Jurors Here Probing Gathering of Big Gamblers," *Los Angeles Times*, December 18, 1966.

13. Hank Greenspun column, "Where I Stand," *Las Vegas Sun*, October 16, 1971.

CHAPTER 14: A CLASH OF TYCOONS

1. Norman Sklarewitz, "Enigmatic Howard Hughes' Real-Life Game of Monopoly Uses All Las Vegas as 'Board,'" *Wall Street Journal*, October 6, 1967.

2. Michael Drosnin, *Citizen Hughes* (Random House, 1985).

3. Torgerson, *Kerkorian*. His book provided extensive details informing this narrative account of negotiations behind the Transamerica deal for Kirk's Trans International Airlines.

4. "Plan for $150 Million Sands Addition Told by Hughes," Associated Press, January 25, 1968.

5. Donald L. Barlett and James B. Steele, *Empire: The Life, Legend and Madness of Howard Hughes* (W. W. Norton and Co., 1979).

6. Greenspun, "Where I Stand," October 16, 1971.

7. Barlett and Steele, *Empire*.

8. Ibid.

9. Drosnin, *Citizen Hughes*. His book provided detailed background on the circumstances of Hughes's arrival in Las Vegas.

10. "Gaming Commission Approves Flamingo Sale," *Reno Gazette-Journal*, August 17, 1967.

11. Alex Shoofey, Oral History.

12. "Laxalt: Hughes 'Exists,' Isn't Monopoly Threat," Associated Press, January 27, 1968.

13. Irwin Ross, "Kirk Kerkorian Doesn't Want All the Meat Off the Bone," *Fortune*, November 1969.

14. Drosnin, *Citizen Hughes*.

15. Barlett and Steele, *Empire*.

16. Drosnin, *Citizen Hughes*.

17. Ibid.

CHAPTER 15: A $73 MILLION SIDE BET

1. Unless otherwise noted, the narrative account of Kirk's Western Air Lines bid in "A $73 Million Side Bet" was informed by: Robert J. Serling, *The Only Way to Fly: The Story of Western Airlines, America's Senior Air Carrier* (Doubleday & Company, 1976).

2. Interview with Stanley Mallin.
3. Alex Shoofey, Oral History.
4. Shoofey's troubles with Fred Benninger were colorfully detailed throughout: Alex Shoofey, Oral History.

CHAPTER 16: HELLO, WORLD!

1. Robert E. Bedingfield, "An Armenian with a Flying Carpet," *New York Times,* February 16 1969.
2. Lawrence, "Vegas Must Reckon."
3. Ibid.
4. Serling, *Only Way to Fly.*
5. Ibid.
6. Ibid.

CHAPTER 17: CARY AND KIRK AND BARBRA AND ELVIS

1. Alex Shoofey, Oral History.
2. Interview with Bobby Morris.
3. Torgerson, *Kerkorian.*
4. John L. Scott, "$20 Million Key Opens Hughes' 6th Vegas Hotel: Landmark Opens," *Los Angeles Times,* July 3, 1969.
5. "Half Million Dollars Lost by Hughes," Associated Press, July 9, 1969.
6. Earl Wilson, Syndicated Columnist, "New Hotel Opens in Las Vegas," July 8, 1969.
7. Robert Maheu and Richard Hack, *Next to Hughes: Behind the Power and Tragic Downfall of Howard Hughes by His Closest Advisor* (Harper Collins, 1992).
8. Interviews with Guy Hudson.
9. Kirk Kerkorian, Oral History.
10. Alex Shoofey, Oral History. His recollections inform the narrative account behind the deal that made Elvis an International Hotel regular.

CHAPTER 18: THE SMILING COBRA

1. Unless otherwise noted, the narrative account in "The Smiling Cobra" was informed by: Gladstone, *The Man Who Seduced Hollywood.*
2. The narrative account of Bautzer's run-in with Bugsy Siegel was informed by details in Gladstone, *The Man Who Seduced Hollywood.*
3. Interviews with Terry Christensen.

CHAPTER 19: A KICK IN THE ASS

1. "MGM Head Talks to Mafia," *New York Post,* January 15, 1970.
2. Kirk Kerkorian, Oral History.
3. Torgerson, *Kerkorian.*

4. Thomas F. Brady, "Kerkorian's Name Is Brought in as Crime Inquiry Hears Tapes," *New York Times,* January 17, 1970.
5. Stanley Penn, "Kerkorian Hints That Money Mentioned in Mob Wiretap Involved Sports Wager, Mafia Ties Denied," *Wall Street Journal,* February 4, 1970.
6. Alex Shoofey, Oral History.
7. Torgerson, *Kerkorian.*
8. Bob Wiedrich, "Tower Ticker" Column, *Chicago Tribune,* August 24, 1971.
9. Torgerson, *Kerkorian.*

CHAPTER 20: MAKING DEBBIE REYNOLDS CRY

1. Unless otherwise noted, accounts of the MGM auction in "Making Debbie Reynolds Cry" were drawn from the following sources: the documentary *The Search for the Ruby Slippers,* written and produced by Rhys Thomas, Greystone Communications (A&E Network, 1998); a YouTube collection of auction scenes posted by The Prop King, www.youtube.com /watch?v=YOOtUs1wXUo; Steven Bingen, Stephen X. Sylvester, and Michael Troyan, *MGM: Hollywood's Greatest Backlot* (Santa Monica Press, 2011); and Peter Bart, *Fade Out: The Calamitous Final Days of MGM* (William Morrow, 1990).
2. Fred Zinnemann Papers, archives of the Academy of Motion Picture Arts and Sciences, Margaret Herrick Library.
3. Interviews with Terry Christensen.
4. This account and detailed conversations are based on the book by Robert Evans, *The Kid Stays in the Picture* (Hyperion, 1994).
5. Serling, *Only Way to Fly.*
6. Ibid.
7. Torgerson, *Kerkorian.*

CHAPTER 21: THE RIVAL VANISHES

1. Drosnin, *Citizen Hughes.*
2. Kirk Kerkorian, Oral History.
3. Ibid.
4. Leonard Sloane, "Lawyer Keeps Late Hours," *New York Times,* December 14, 1969.
5. Interviews with Una Davis and Ron Falahi.
6. Kirk Kerkorian, Oral History.
7. "Howard Hughes Acquires Las Vegas' Desert Inn," United Press International, March 15, 1967.
8. A comment Maheu shared with Kirk, according to interviews with Una Davis.

CHAPTER 22: PUTTING ON THE MOVES

1. Walter Scott columns "Personality Parade," *Parade*, July 11 and October 24, 1971.
2. Interviews with Una Davis.
3. One example: Joyce Haber column, "Movie Premiere: Rich and Famous Celebrate the Same," *Los Angeles Times*, October 6, 1980.
4. Another example: Joyce Haber, *Los Angeles Times*, January 5, 1972.
5. Interviews with Terry Christensen.
6. Robert Dallos and Al Delugach, "MGM to Specialize and Diversify, Too," *Los Angeles Times*, October 24, 1971.
7. Joyce Haber, "A Hollywood Farewell to Beloved Metro," *Los Angeles Times*, November 18, 1973.
8. Torgerson, *Kerkorian*.

CHAPTER 23: A VIEW TO THE ABYSS

1. Interviews with Terry Christensen.
2. Joyce Haber, "$20 Million Deal Sealed at Bistro," *Los Angeles Times*, October 29, 1973.
3. Charles Champlin, "Muffling the Lion's Roar," *Los Angeles Times*, September 28, 1973.
4. Vincent Canby, "Leo's Roar Becomes a Whimper," *New York Times*, September 30, 1973.
5. Details leading up to Aubrey's ouster covered by Gladstone, *The Man Who Seduced Hollywood*.
6. Earl Wilson, syndicated column, November 7, 1973.
7. Bart, *Fade Out*.
8. Ibid.
9. "MGM Declares Payout of $1.75 per Share, First Since April '69," *Wall Street Journal*, November 23, 1973.
10. Al Delugach, "MGM Ends Payout Drought with $1.75 Dividend Per Share," *Los Angeles Times*, November 22, 1973.

CHAPTER 24: EXTRA RISK FACTOR

1. Norma Lee Browning, "MGM Opens a Truly Grand Hotel," *Chicago Tribune*, December 10, 1973.
2. Joyce Haber, "Sinatra's Case of 'Vegas Throat,'" *Los Angeles Times*, January 30, 1974.
3. Al Delugach, "Grand Hotel Gamble Pays Off," *Los Angeles Times*, December 10, 1974.
4. "Kerkorian Moves to Sell Holdings in Western Air," *Wall Street Journal*, January 15, 1976.

5. Details of the tactical ruse come exclusively from interviews with Terry Christensen.

CHAPTER 25: PUNCH, COUNTERPUNCH

1. David McClintick broke the Begelman scandal with "Columbia Pictures Begelman Case," *Wall Street Journal*, December 20, 1977.
2. Gladstone, *The Man Who Seduced Hollywood*.
3. Unless otherwise noted, details about the MGM Grand Hotel fire for "Punch, Counterpunch" came primarily from the book by Deirdre Coakley with Hank Greenspun, Gary C. Gerard, and the staff of the *Las Vegas Sun, The Day the MGM Grand Hotel Burned* (Lyle Stuart, 1982); official investigative reports by the Clark County Fire Department, undated, and the National Fire Protection Association, January 15, 1982; and a comprehensive aftermath story by the *Los Angeles Times*, by Bob Secter, Gaylord Shaw, and Ronald Soble, "A Fire Dissected: What Caused the MGM Grand Blaze?" December 21, 1980.
4. Robert Dallos, "Rift Develops Between Columbia, Kerkorian," *Los Angeles Times*, May 14, 1980.
5. Hal Lancaster and Earl C. Gottschalk Jr., "What's Behind Kerkorian Bid for Columbia?" *Wall Street Journal*, September 30, 1980.
6. Charles Schreger, "Stark Denies Kerkorian Charges," *Los Angeles Times*, October 10, 1980.

CHAPTER 26: MGM SPELLS DISASTER

1. Unless otherwise noted, details about the MGM Grand Hotel fire for "MGM Spells Disaster" came primarily from the book by Deirdre Coakley with Hank Greenspun, Gary C. Gerard, and the staff of the *Las Vegas Sun, The Day the MGM Grand Hotel Burned* (Lyle Stuart, 1982); official investigative reports by the Clark County Fire Department, undated, and the National Fire Protection Association, January 15, 1982; and a comprehensive aftermath story by the *Los Angeles Times*, by Bob Secter, Gaylord Shaw, and Ronald Soble, "A Fire Dissected: What Caused the MGM Grand Blaze?" December 21, 1980.
2. All details about the MGM fire aftermath attributed to Mike Agassi come from interviews with the author.

CHAPTER 27: VILLAIN OF THE ACTUARIES

1. Interviews with Terry Christensen.
2. Robert Dallos, "Columbia Sues Kerkorian, Directors at 2 Firms," *Los Angeles Times*, December 11, 1980.
3. Interviews with Terry Christensen.

4. The story of Scoshie from interviews with Ron Falahi.
5. Myrna Oliver, "MGM Grand Set to Battle Its Insurers, Case Expected to Last 8 to 10 Months, Cost $342,000 a Day to Try," *Los Angeles Times,* May 18, 1985.
6. Interview with William M. Shernoff.
7. Interviews with Terry Christensen.
8. Rose Nisker, "Ms. Glaser, I Presume?" Southern California Super Lawyers, 2007 at https://www.superlawyers.com/california-southern/article/ms-glacier-i-presume/eacd4f1f-3159–4a6d-9346-b118638a71ed.html.
9. Interview with William M. Shernoff.
10. Ibid.

CHAPTER 28: ONE ROLL OF THE DICE

1. Unless otherwise noted, details about Kirk's gambling portrayed in "One Roll of the Dice" were provided by Jerry Perenchio in a rare interview with the author. Like Kerkorian, Perenchio avoided the media. His motto: "Stay out of the spotlight; it fades your suit."
2. Interviews with Ron Falahi.
3. Ibid.

CHAPTER 29: TED TURNER'S TICKING TIME BOMB

1. Unless otherwise noted, the narrative account of negotiations between Kerkorian and Turner in "Ted's Ticking Time Bomb" was drawn from the book by Ted Turner, *Call Me Ted* (Hachette, 2010).
2. Interview with Michael Milken.
3. Al Delugach, "Turner Acknowledges MGM Merger Trouble: Firms Renegotiating," *Los Angeles Times,* January 14, 1986.
4. Interview with Arthur Bilger.
5. Interview with Michael Milken.
6. Interview with Stanley Mallin.
7. Interviews with Terry Christensen.
8. Al Delugach, "MGM Deal Could Cost Turner His Own Firm," *Los Angeles Times,* January 23, 1986.
9. Interview with Michael Milken.
10. Interview with Terry Christensen.

CHAPTER 30: A BURIAL AT SEA

1. The telephone exchange and other details about Turner's money troubles in "A Burial at Sea" come from Turner's book, *Call Me Ted,* unless otherwise noted.

2. Interviews with Terry Christensen.

3. Ibid.

4. Ibid.

5. Bart, *Fade Out.*

6. Kirk Kerkorian in videotaped interview with Jennifer Grant, 2006.

7. Bill Wundram, "The night Cary Grant died in our arms," *Quad-City Times,* November 29, 2011.

8. Interviews with Una Davis.

9. Jennifer Grant, *Good Stuff, A Reminiscence of My Father, Cary Grant* (Alfred A. Knopf, 2014).

CHAPTER 31: AMONG THE BILLIONAIRES

1. Unless otherwise noted, details informing the narrative account of Kirk Kerkorian's launch of an earthquake relief airlift were provided in interviews with Harut Sassounian, the leading force behind that project.

2. Interviews with Alex Yemenidjian.

3. Ibid.

4. Ibid.

5. N. R. Kleinfield, "Forbes Hunt For Richest 400," *New York Times,* September 11, 1982.

6. Donald Trump with Charles Leerhsen, "Forbes Carried Out Personal Vendetta in Print," *Los Angeles Times* Syndicate, Part 4 of 5 parts, October 4, 1990.

7. Interview with Bob Dole.

8. Interviews with Harut Sassounian.

9. Interviews with Terry Christensen.

CHAPTER 32: BABE RUTH AT BAT

1. As Kerkorian's lead negotiator, Alex Yemenidjian played a key role from beginning to end in Kirk's Chrysler bid. Unless otherwise noted, the author's interviews with Yemenidjian provide the narrative detail in "Babe Ruth at Bat."

2. Interviews with Alex Yemenidjian.

3. Interviews with Terry Christensen.

4. Howard Stutz, "Kerkorian Negotiated Blockbuster Deals But Shunned Limelight," *Las Vegas Review-Journal,* June 17, 2015.

5. Los Angeles Superior Court case #BD-308513.

6. Liz Smith syndicated column, August 19, 1987.

7. Interviews with Ron Falahi.

CHAPTER 33: THE IACOCCA NUISANCE

1. No journalist in the country did a more thorough job of covering Kerkorian's bid to buy Chrysler than *Detroit News* reporter Bill Vlasic. His work informs much of this narrative. Unless otherwise noted, the primary source for details in "The Iacocca Nuisance" come from the book by Bill Vlasic and Bradley A. Stertz, *Taken for a Ride: How Daimler-Benz Drove Off with Chrysler* (William Morrow, 2000), and from the author's interviews with Alex Yemenidjian.
2. "Mr. Iacocca's New Bottom Line," *New York Times* editorial, April 14, 1995.
3. Mike Hiltzik, "A Bold Play by Mr. Inside and Mr. Outside," *Los Angeles Times*, April 13, 1995.
4. "Mr. Iacocca's New Bottom Line," *New York Times* editorial, April 14, 1995.
5. Bill Vlasic, "Iacocca: Still Need Cash for Deal—Kirk Kerkorian Needs 'to get cranking on financing. It's not there yet,'" *Detroit News*, April 16, 1995.
6. Gabriella Stern, "Chrysler Ends Plan for Holder Meetings to Spur Resistance to Kerkorian Moves," *Wall Street Journal*, May 3, 1995.
7. Los Angeles Superior Court case #BD-308513.
8. Terry Christensen interviews.

CHAPTER 34: SHE PERSISTED

1. This anecdote is based on the late Wendy Falahi's account as told by her husband, Ron Falahi, in interviews with the author.
2. Interviews with Alex Yemenidjian.
3. Los Angeles Superior Court case #BP-164011.
4. The voluminous archival record gathered over the years under Los Angeles Superior Court case #BD-308513 was contained in more than sixty bankers' boxes and kept in storage three floors beneath the Los Angeles County Hall of Records. In those files are tens of thousands of pages of sworn declarations, depositions, financial accounting records, claims, and counterclaims—the bulk of which have been reviewed by the author. Unless otherwise noted, it is from those official documents that the narrative account of Kirk's romantic relationship and long-running legal battles with Lisa was drawn.
5. Interviews with Gene Kilroy.
6. Maureen Donaldson and William Royce, *An Affair to Remember: My Life with Cary Grant* (G. P. Putnam's Sons, 1989).
7. Una Davis described her first impressions of Kirk and their early romance in interviews with the author.

CHAPTER 35: RIFLE RIGHT TAKES IRON MIKE

1. Interview with Daniel M. Wade.
2. Interviews with Gene Kilroy.
3. Rory Holloway with Eric Wilson, *Taming the Beast: The Untold Story of Mike Tyson* (Rough House, 2014).
4. Interviews with Alex Yemenidjian.
5. Interview with Don King.
6. Interviews with Ron Falahi.
7. Holloway with Wilson, *Taming the Beast.*
8. Interview with Don King.

CHAPTER 36: GENOCIDE AND GENEROSITY

1. Harut Sassounian was Kirk's only companion on the billionaire's first trip to Armenia and his account provided in interviews with the author informs the narrative in "Genocide and Generosity" unless otherwise noted.
2. William C. Rempel, "Racing to America," *Los Angeles Times,* July 4, 1998.
3. Tracy Seipel and Camille Mojica, "Ellison Sails Through Testimony: Billionaire Recounts Search for Mega-Yacht," *(San Jose) Mercury News,* July 22, 2000.
4. Los Angeles Superior Court case #BD-308513.

CHAPTER 37: WYNN AND LOSE

1. Interviews with Ron Falahi.
2. Photos from the party are part of the court file in Los Angeles Superior Court case #BD-308513.
3. By far the most impressive coverage of Kerkorian's bid for Wynn's Mirage holdings was under the byline of *Wall Street Journal* reporter Christina Binkley. Unless otherwise noted, narrative details in "Wynn and Lose" rely on her book, *Winner Takes All: Steve Wynn, Kirk Kerkorian, Gary Loveman and the Race to Own Las Vegas* (Hyperion, 2008).
4. Los Angeles Superior Court case #BD-308513.
5. Lisa Kerkorian letter to Kirk's business manager Anthony Mandekic, submitted as an evidentiary exhibit, Los Angeles Superior Court case #BD-308513, dated September 6, 2000.
6. Lisa Kerkorian, Stephen A. Kolodny, and Jeff M. Sturman Reply Declarations, Los Angeles Superior Court case #BD-308513, filed March 14, 2002.
7. "Warbling Wynn Shocks Wall St.," *New York Post,* November 10, 1999.
8. Interviews with Terry Christensen.
9. Interview with Michael Milken.

CHAPTER 38: FATEFUL ATTRACTION

1. Unless otherwise noted, narrative details in "Fateful Attraction" come from litigation files in Los Angeles Superior Court case #BD-308513, including the sworn declarations of Tracy Kerkorian and Katherine Savala, each dated March 7, 2002.
2. Interviews with Ron Falahi.
3. Details of the encounter were provided in interviews with Una Davis.
4. Lisa Bonder Kerkorian letter to Kirk's business manager Anthony Mandekic, submitted as an evidentiary exhibit, Los Angeles Superior Court case #BD-308513, dated September 6, 2000.
5. Anne DuPont sworn declaration, Los Angeles Superior Court case #BD-308513, dated March 7, 2002.
6. From interviews with Nick Behnen, Guy Hudson, and Alda Lanzone at the Las Vegas Country Club.
7. Interviews with Una Davis.
8. Steve Bing sworn declaration, Los Angeles Superior Court case #BD-308513, dated August 14, 2002.
9. Sworn declarations of Tracy Kerkorian, and Katherine Savala, Los Angeles Superior Court case #BD-308513, both signed on March 7, 2002.
10. Ibid.
11. Kirk Kerkorian sworn declaration, Los Angeles Superior Court case #DB-308513, dated March 8, 2002.
12. Interviews with Terry Christensen.

CHAPTER 39: A GOD AMONG DEAL MAKERS

1. Details about the DNA sample collection are from various documents in Los Angeles Superior Court case #BD-308513, including the sworn declaration of Steve Scholl, dated May 10, 2002.
2. Interviews with Ron Falahi.
3. Jesse Katz, "Sex, Lies & Dental Floss," *Los Angeles Magazine*, September 2002.
4. Interviews with Una Davis.
5. The Honorable Lee Smalley Edmon, Los Angeles Superior Court Judge, "Amended Statement of Findings . . . and Statement of Decision," Case #BD-308513, March 12, 2003.
6. Interviews with Darryl Goldman.
7. Interviews with Una Davis.
8. Interviews with Darryl Goldman.
9. Interviews with Terry Christensen.
10. Interviews with Ron Falahi.

11. Andrew Ross Sorkin, "Greatest and Lamest Deals of 2004," *New York Times,* January 2, 2005.

CHAPTER 40: BREAKING BAD

1. Jonathan O'Connell, "The CEO Who Nearly Lost His Shirt in Vegas Tries His Luck in Washington," *Washington Post,* December 9, 2016.
2. Howard Stutz, "CityCenter Opening Is Murren's Moment," *Las Vegas Review-Journal,* December 13, 2009.
3. Lauren Carroll and Clayton Youngman, "Fact-checking claims about Donald Trump's four bankruptcies," PolitiFact, September 21, 2015.
4. Interviews with Terry Christensen.
5. Beth Jinks and Brett Pulley, "MGM Resorts Founder Kirk Kerkorian Will Step Down from Board," Bloomberg News, April 13, 2011.
6. Micheline Maynard, "The Raider Who Woke Up Detroit," *Forbes,* June 16, 2015.
7. Interviews with Alex Yemenidjian.
8. Anthony Pellicano oral deposition (pages 192–211) related to Los Angeles Superior Court case #BC-316318 (*Busch v. Pellicano et al*), conducted in the state of Texas, on February 3, 2015.
9. *United States v. Anthony Pellicano and Terry Christensen,* case #CR-05–1046.
10. "A Rare Kerkorian Sighting," *Hollywood Reporter,* August 20, 2008.
11. "The Billionaire Wore Loafers: Kirk Kerkorian Testifies," *LA Weekly,* August 20, 2008.
12. Interviews with Terry Christensen.
13. Interviews with Una Davis.
14. Ibid.
15. Interviews with Ron Falahi.
16. Norm Clarke column, "The Donald Slams New Mega-Resort," *Las Vegas Review-Journal,* December 16, 2009.
17. Norm Clarke column, "Trump Fires Back About CityCenter," *Las Vegas Review-Journal,* December 19, 2009.
18. Howard Stutz, "Kerkorian Labels CityCenter 'Amazing,'" *Las Vegas Review-Journal,* December 13, 2009.

CHAPTER 41: AFTER "THE FALL"

1. The incident that night in 2010 was described in a series of interviews with various sources. The narrative account in "After 'the Fall'" is based largely on information provided by Ron Falahi and Una Davis. Others with knowledge asked not to be identified.

2. Interviews with Alex Yemenidjian.
3. Kirk Kerkorian, Oral History.
4. Interviews with Terry Christensen.
5. Interviews with Harut Sassounian.
6. Videotape of gala banquet celebrating United Armenian Fund's "100th Humanitarian Airlift," Century Plaza Hotel, September 26, 1998.
7. Interviews with Alex Yemenidjian.
8. Interviews with Harut Sassounian.
9. Interviews with Alex Yemenidjian.
10. Interviews with Gene Kilroy.
11. Interviews with Una Davis.
12. Interviews with Gene Kilroy.
13. "Kirk Kerkorian's 95th B-Day Flash Mob—Beverly Hills Hotel," posted June 7, 2012, accessed January 23, 2016. https://www.youtube.com/watch?v=bEL32jBe4MU. Choreographed by Rob Schultz.
14. Interviews with Ron Falahi.
15. Interviews with Gene Kilroy.
16. Based on recollections of several friends including Terry Christensen, Ron Falali, Gene Kilroy, and Una Davis.
17. Los Angeles Superior Court case #BP-141317.
18. Page Six Staff, "Kirk, Ex, in New Court Clash," *New York Post,* May 19, 2013.
19. Details of Kirk's marriage proposal and negotiations leading to their marriage are based on interviews with Una Davis and related records filed with Los Angeles Superior Court case #BP-164011.
20. "Phil Ruffin Offers Farewell Toast to Fellow Billionaire Kirk Kerkorian," *Forbes,* July 1, 2015.
21. Interviews with Una Davis and Ron Falahi.
22. Interviews with Una Davis.
23. Interviews with Alex Yemenidjian.
24. Alex Yemenidjian's recollection. He was one of the emcees at Kirk's funeral.

SELECTED BIBLIOGRAPHY

BOOKS

Agassi, Andre. *Open: An Autobiography*. Alfred A. Knopf, 2009.

Barlett, Donald L. and James B. Steele. *Empire: The Life, Legend, and Madness of Howard Hughes*. W. W. Norton & Co., 1979.

Bart, Peter. *Fade Out: The Calamitous Final Days of MGM*. William Morrow and Company, 1993.

Bibb, Porter. *Ted Turner: It Ain't as Easy as It Looks*. Crown, 1993.

Bingen, Steven, Stephen X. Sylvester, and Michael Troyan. *M-G-M: Hollywood's Greatest Backlot*. Santa Monica Press, 2011.

Binkley, Christina. *Winner Takes All: Steve Wynn, Kirk Kerkorian, Gary Loveman, and the Race to Own Las Vegas*. Hyperion, 2008.

Breffort, Dominique. *Lockheed Constellation: Legend of the Sky, from Excalibur to Starliner*. Translated from French by Alan McKay. Histoire & Collections, Paris, 2006.

Christie, Carl A. *Ocean Bridge: The History of RAF Ferry Command*. University of Toronto Press, 1995.

Chung, Su Kim. *Las Vegas: Then & Now*. Thunder Bay Press, 2012.

Coakley, Deidre with Hank Greenspun, Gary C. Gerard, and the staff of the *Las Vegas Sun*. *The Day the MGM Grand Hotel Burned*. Lyle Stuart Inc., 1982.

Cobello, Dominic and Mike Agassi. *The Agassi Story*. ECW Press, 2004.

Denton, Sally and Roger Morris. *The Money and the Power: The Making of Las Vegas and Its Hold on America, 1947 to 2000*. A Borzoi Book by Alfred A. Knopf, 2001.

Dole, Bob. *A Soldier's Story*. HarperCollins, 2005.

Donaldson, Maureen and William Royce. *An Affair to Remember: My Life with Cary Grant*. G. P. Putnam's Sons, 1989.

Drosnin, Michael. *Citizen Hughes: In His Own Words, How Howard Hughes Tried to Buy America*. Holt, Rinehart and Winston, 1985.

Evans, Robert. *The Kid Stays in the Picture.* Hyperion, 1994.

Fischel, Daniel. *Payback: The Conspiracy to Destroy Michael Milken and His Financial Revolution.* HarperCollins, 1995.

Gladstone, B. James and Robert Wagner. *The Man Who Seduced Hollywood: The Life and Loves of Greg Bautzer, Tinseltown's Most Powerful Lawyer."* Chicago Review Press, 2013.

Grant, Jennifer. *Good Stuff: A Reminiscence of My Father, Cary Grant.* Alfred A. Knopf, 2011.

Holder, Jack. *Fear, Adrenaline, and Excitement: A WWII Naval Aviation Story.* 2014.

Holloway, Rory and Eric Wilson. *Taming the Beast: The Untold Story of Mike Tyson.* Rough House, 2014.

Hopkins, A. D. and K. J. Evans. *The First 100: Portraits of the Men and Women Who Shaped Las Vegas.* Huntington Press, 1999.

Kessler, Lauren. *The Happy Bottom Riding Club: The Life and Times of Pancho Barnes.* Random House, 2000.

Kornbluth, Jesse. *Highly Confident: The Crime and Punishment of Michael Milken.* William Morrow and Company, 1992.

Maheu, Robert and Richard Hack. *Next to Hughes: Behind the Power and Tragic Downfall of Howard Hughes by His Closest Advisor.* HarperCollins, 1992.

McCann, Graham. *Cary Grant: A Class Apart.* Columbia University Press, 1996.

Ministry of Information for United Kingdom Air Ministry. *Atlantic Bridge: The Official Account of R.A.F. Transport Command's Ocean Ferry.* University Press of the Pacific, 1945.

Nelson, Nancy. *Evenings with Cary Grant.* Applause Theatre & Cinema Books, 2012.

Roberts, Randy and James S. Olson. *John Wayne: American.* Free Press, 1995.

Schwartz, David G. *Grandissimo: The First Emperor of Las Vegas; How Jay Sarno Won a Casino Empire, Lost It, and Inspired Modern Las Vegas.* Winchester Books, 2013.

Serling, Robert J. *The Only Way to Fly: The Story of Western Airlines, America's Senior Air Carrier.* Doubleday & Company, 1976.

Sheehan, Jack. *The Players: The Men Who Made Las Vegas.* University of Nevada Press, 1997.

Shernoff, William M. *Payment Refused: How to Fight Back and Win When Your Insurance Company Turns You Down.* William & Sons, 2004.

Sinatra, Barbara. *Lady Blue Eyes: My Life with Frank.* Three Rivers Press, 2011.

Smith, John L. *Of Rats and Men: Oscar Goodman's Life from Mob Mouthpiece to Mayor of Las Vegas.* Huntington Press, 2003.

———. *Sharks in the Desert: The Founding Fathers and Current Kings of Las Vegas.* Barricade Books, 2005.

Stewart, James B. *Den of Thieves*. Simon and Schuster, 1991.

Torgerson, Dial. *Kerkorian: An American Success Story*. The Dial Press, 1974.

Turner, Ted and Bill Burke. *Call Me Ted*. Hachette, 2008.

Vlasic, Bill. *Once Upon a Car: The Fall and Resurrection of America's Big Three Automakers—GM, Ford, and Chrysler*. William Morrow and Company, 2011.

Vlasic, Bill and Bradley A. Stertz. *Taken for a Ride: How Daimler-Benz Drove Off with Chrysler*. William Morrow and Company, 2000.

Waldman, Allison J., *The Barbara Streisand Scrapbook* (revised and updated). Citadel Press, 2001.

Weiss, Stephen L. *The Billion Dollar Mistake: Learning the Art of Investing Through the Missteps of Legendary Investors*. John Wiley & Sons, 2010.

Wynn, Edgar J. *Bombers Across: The Story of the Transatlantic Ferry Command*. E. P. Dutton & Co., 1944.

VIDEOS

100th Humanitarian Airlift. United Armenian Fund gala banquet, videotaped at the Century Plaza Hotel, September 26, 1998.

Flying the Secret Sky: The Story of the Royal Air Force Ferry Command. Produced by William VanDerKloot Film & Television, Inc., for WGBH Boston, 2008.

Jewish Leaders of Las Vegas Series: Burton Cohen. University of Nevada Las Vegas, Lied Library, Special Collections, 2005.

Kerkorian: His Story. Produced by George Ann Mason and Charliedog Productions in association with Kirk Kerkorian, unreleased, 2001.

The Legend of Pancho Barnes and the Happy Bottom Riding Club. Written and produced by Nick Sparks, Nick Sparks Productions, for KOCE Orange County, 2009.

The Search for the Ruby Slippers. Written and produced by Rhys Thomas, Greystone Communications, for A&E Network, 1998.

MAJOR ARTICLES

Bedingfield, Robert E. "An Armenian with a Flying Carpet." *New York Times*, February 16, 1969.

Cassidy, John. "Kirk's Enterprise: What is Kirk Kerkorian, the Reclusive Las Vegas Billionaire, Up To at Chrysler?" *The New Yorker*, December 11, 1995.

Colker, David and David Streitfeld. "Kirk Kerkorian Dies at 98; Shook Up the Car, Movie and Casino Industries." *Los Angeles Times*, June 16, 2015.

Dallos, Robert E. and John F. Lawrence. "Millionaire in Motion." *Los Angeles Times*, October 26, 1969.

Demick, Barbara. "The 400 Richest: Many Folks Try to Stay Off List." *Philadelphia Inquirer*, October 7, 1990.

Greenspun, Hank. "Where I Stand." *Las Vegas Sun,* October 16, 1971.

Kandell, Jonathan. "Kirk Kerkorian Dies at 98; Made Billions by Remaking Hollywood and Las Vegas." *New York Times,* June 17, 2015.

Katz, Jesse. "The Game of Love: Sex, Lies & Dental Floss." *Los Angeles Magazine,* September 2002.

Pulley, Brett. "The Wizard of MGM." *Forbes,* May 28, 2001.

Ross, Irwin. "Kirk Kerkorian Doesn't Want All the Meat Off the Bones." *Fortune,* November 1969.

Schwartz, David G. "The Long Hot Summer of '55: How a Season of Hubris and Disappointment Helped Reinvent Vegas." *Vegas Seven,* August 4, 2015.

Sklarewitz, Norman. "Enigmatic Howard Hughes' Real-Life Game of Monopoly Uses All Las Vegas as 'Board.'" *Wall Street Journal,* October 6, 1967.

Streitfeld, David. "A Born Gambler Rolls the Dice at 88." *Los Angeles Times,* June 9, 2005.

Stutz, Howard. "Kerkorian Negotiated Blockbuster Deals But Shunned Limelight." *Las Vegas Review-Journal,* June 17, 2015.

ARCHIVES

Academy of Motion Picture Arts and Sciences, Margaret Herrick Library, the Fred Zinneman Papers.

Statue of Liberty–Ellis Island Foundation, Port of New York air and sea passenger records, 1944–1945.

University of Nevada, Las Vegas, Lied Library, Special Collections, oral histories recorded by, among others, Benny Binion, Kirk Kerkorian, Alex Shoofey, and Steve Wynn.

INDEX